Understanding Nonprofit Work

Understanding Nonprofit Work

A Communication Perspective

Matthew A. Koschmann

and

Matthew L. Sanders

WILEY Blackwell

This edition first published 2020

Registered Office
John Wiley & Sons, Inc., 111 River Street, Hoboken, NJ 07030, USA

Editorial Office
111 River Street, Hoboken, NJ 07030, USA

For details of our global editorial offices, customer services, and more information about Wiley products visit us at www.wiley.com.

Wiley also publishes its books in a variety of electronic formats and by print-on-demand. Some content that appears in standard print versions of this book may not be available in other formats.

Library of Congress Cataloging-in-Publication Data
Names: Koschmann, Matthew A., author. | Sanders, Matthew L., author.
Title: Understanding nonprofit work : a communication perspective / Matthew A. Koschmann, University of Colorado Boulder and Matthew L. Sanders, Utah State University.
Description: Hoboken, NJ : Wiley-Blackwell, 2020. | Includes bibliographical references and index.
Identifiers: LCCN 2020008777 (print) | LCCN 2020008778 (ebook) | ISBN 9781119431251 (paperback) | ISBN 9781119431275 (adobe pdf) | ISBN 9781119431329 (epub)
Subjects: LCSH: Nonprofit organizations. | Business communication.
Classification: LCC HD62.6 .K668 2020 (print) | LCC HD62.6 (ebook) | DDC 658.4/5–dc23
LC record available at https://lccn.loc.gov/2020008777
LC ebook record available at https://lccn.loc.gov/2020008778

Cover Design: Wiley
Cover Images: © enjoynz/iStockphoto, © Alexey Blogoodf/Shutterstock

Set in 9.5/12.5pt STIXTwoText by SPi Global, Pondicherry, India
Printed and bound by CPI Group (UK) Ltd, Croydon, CR0 4YY

10 9 8 7 6 5 4 3 2 1

To Laurie Lewis, scholar, mentor, and friend who got us started on this journey and supported us along the way.

To Matthew Isbell, our partner for so much of this journey, valued friend and colleague.

To the countless nonprofit folks we've worked with over the years – managers, volunteers, clients, donors, board members – who are the inspiration and motivation for so much of our work.

And to our families, who give meaning and purpose to everything we do. We love you all.

Contents

Preface

We have two main goals for this book: First, to develop a distinct communication perspective on nonprofit work; and second, to then apply this communication perspective to a number of key issues that are at the heart of organizing to promote the common good – all of which will lead to a better understanding of nonprofit work. Throughout this book, we will often say "the nonprofit" instead of nonprofit organizations or the nonprofit sector to signal something more than just the tax status of a company or a collection of organizations in our economy. Instead, we have in mind a more profound ethos or character, a spirit of civic and political engagement, cooperation and social entrepreneurship, service delivery and welfare provision, and religious faith and ideological expression. This certainly involves specific organizations that can be identified as a particular economic sector of our society – both of which are important manifestations of the nonprofit that we will address as we frame each chapter. But the soul of the nonprofit is much more than this. And for the nonprofit to thrive and flourish, we need to develop a deeper sense of its core values and beliefs, and then see how these play out in our attempts at forming and managing organizations to carry out the critical task of the nonprofit. We also emphasize the notion of nonprofit *work*, as you'll notice in the title. We want to focus more on the *doing* or *practice* of the nonprofit, rather than just the "thing" of an abstract sector or a static organization. This is a big part of what a communication perspective is all about.

The nonprofit is near and dear to our hearts, and we bring a fair amount of experience and expertise to this book. We've worked for nonprofit organizations, we volunteer and donate to nonprofits, we've served on nonprofit boards, we teach classes on communication and the nonprofit sector, and much of our research has been with or in or about nonprofit organizations. Echoing Alexis de Tocqueville, the nineteenth century French diplomat who famously wrote about America democracy, we see the nonprofit as essential to our republic and critical for human flourishing. The nonprofit represents the core of civil society and democratic life. The voluntary association of citizens in free nations to organize and address their own needs and improve their collective wellbeing has been at the heart of all civil, political, and economic progress of the past 300 years.

Yet despite being so central to civil society, the nonprofit is also harder to understand and manage because of its unique relationship with both the market and the state. Being nonprofit means working with significant economic constraints while also trying to tackle difficult, complex, and even intractable problems. Being nonprofit means operating with both private autonomy and public accountability. This isn't easy or straightforward; it's a distinctly challenging organizational environment and thus calls for a more sophisticated understanding of organizational communication. Many people have been working on understanding what it means to be nonprofit for a long time, and we have made great strides in concepts and theories that explain how we can best engage in nonprofit work. Our objective in this book is to add our disciplinary voice of communication to this important conversation and expand our collective knowledge and understanding of nonprofit work.

We represent a burgeoning group of communication scholars doing a substantial amount of theoretical, empirical, and applied research on the nonprofit sector and with nonprofit organizations. Communication scholars have been doing work in and with the nonprofit for decades, but since the early 2000s there has been a more deliberate effort to build a scholarly community and develop a distinct line of research and applied knowledge. More specifically, in our academic subfield of organizational communication, there is a strong and growing interest in the nonprofit. That's because the unique dynamics of the nonprofit magnify several key communication issues, making this a great site to study the complexities of organizing and enhance our understanding of human interaction. Additionally, developments in communication scholarship have given us new intellectual resources to comprehend and explain a variety of organizational phenomena, and there is much about the nonprofit that would benefit from fresh thinking and new perspectives.

As you'll see throughout this book, we offer a different and more complex way of understanding communication. We go beyond the conventional wisdom of communication that it is a simple process of message transmission, that misunderstandings are fairly easy to resolve with just a bit more clarity, and that organizational communication is mainly about sharing information "in" organizations. After all, sometimes the more we communicate the *less* we understand and work well together. So there has to be more to communication than just making sure everyone gets the memo and is on the same page. Instead, we present a more sophisticated approach to communication as the fundamental process that constitutes all social realities and organizational phenomena. This means thinking about communication in a way that is very different from what you might be used to, and giving up easy answers that rarely work well in practice. Instead, we'll use this alternative perspective of communication to tackle some of the most challenging questions and offer a novel way to account for the complexities of human interaction and the nonprofit.

While this book is based on research and scholarship on communication and nonprofit organizations, we put all the references in footnotes so that the narrative we share is not cluttered with citations. This will allow for a smoother read, and those who wish to review the sources can easily find them at the bottom of each page. But our review and application of communication scholarship here is intended to be representative and demonstrative, not exhaustive. We will review and apply research that best helps us illustrate the value of a communication perspective and the explanations it provides to key issues in the nonprofit, and our citations will point readers to further resources that develop these ideas in more depth. And even though this book is a coauthored project, you'll notice that we alternate authorship of Chapters 2–6. Chapter 1 is our collective statement on nonprofit organizational communication and serves as the foundation for the rest of the book. Then Chapters 2–6 are individually authored, which reflects our personal experience and scholarly expertise on these subjects, even though we worked with each other on the final editing. We come back together in our coauthored conclusion to wrap up the book and discuss the broader implications of our contributions.

For the scholars who read this book, we hope to offer you a distinct look at the nonprofit that will expand your view and augment your own perspectives. Our purpose is not to advocate that a communication perspective is necessarily better than others are, but rather to show that this lesser-known field of study offers distinct and useful ways of understanding and enhancing nonprofit work. And with that knowledge, we can together promote more interdisciplinary scholarship. For the nonprofit executives, managers, and other practitioners who read this book, we hope to empower you with new ideas for everyday practices and problems that will enable you to better understand and manage your organizations, build their capacity, and more fully realize your social missions. We want to help you see and address common concerns in a new way that expands the repertoire of skills that makes your work successful. Ultimately, we hope that we can empower you to ask new questions that will provide more solutions to the challenges and opportunities that lay ahead.

There is much to gain from developing a communication perspective on the nonprofit. Rather than just studying communication events or episodes, as important as that may be, we can begin "thinking communicatively" about our organizations and nonprofit work. Thinking this way helps us see that we have influence and responsibility over how we talk and interact in the nonprofit, and that our communication then shapes what our organizations are and do. We're not at the mercy of communication and its challenges, but have the opportunity to engage our work in ways that will create more positive, productive, and impactful outcomes. If you maintain that belief throughout this book, and begin to develop the ideas and practices we explain, then our work will have been a success. Let's get started.

About the Authors

Matthew A. Koschmann is Associate Professor of Communication at the University of Colorado Boulder. His research focuses on organizational communication and collaboration, especially in the civil society sector. His work has been published in numerous scholarly outlets such as *Management Communication Quarterly, Academy of Management Review, Journal of Communication, Journal of Applied Social Science,* and the *International Journal of Disaster Risk Reduction*; plus, his research has been funded by multiple grants from the National Science Foundation. Professor Koschmann teaches classes on organizational communication, leadership communication, group interaction, persuasion, conversation, and research methods. He is also a Fulbright scholar and worked as a visiting research professor at Ateneo de Manila University in the Philippines. Professor Koschmann and his wife Jennifer live near Boulder, Colorado with their sons Søren and Anders.

Matthew L. Sanders is Associate Professor of Communication Studies at Utah State University. His research focuses on communication and nonprofit organizations. He also writes about communication and teaching. His research has been published in scholarly outlets such as *Nonprofit and Voluntary Sector Quarterly, Organization, Management Communication Quarterly,* and *The Review of Communication*. He is also the author of *Becoming a Learner: Realizing the Opportunity of Education*, and *Studying Communication: An Invitation to Purposeful Learning*. Professor Sanders teaches classes on organizational communication, nonprofits and social change, leadership, interpersonal communication, qualitative research methods, and teaching communication. He received the Distinguished Teaching Award in 2018 from the Western States Communication Association. Professor Sanders and his wife Julie live near Logan, Utah with their children Dallin, Spencer, Henry, Clara, and Lucy.

Acknowledgments

We know that a project like this book is always a team effort and we acknowledge the many people who helped make it possible.

We are grateful to our editorial team at Wiley, especially Todd Green, Ajith Kumar, and Sakthivel Kandaswamy who believed in our project and supported us every step of the way.

We are thankful for our colleagues at the University of Colorado Boulder and Utah State University who support our work and provide great scholarly environments. It is a pleasure to work with you each day.

Also, for years we have been involved with a wonderful network of scholars in the field of organizational communication whose research and teaching focus on nonprofit work. This has been a great community for developing ideas, improving our work, and fostering invaluable personal and professional connections. We greatly appreciate the many people in this network including (alphabetically): Yannick Atouba, Katherine Cooper, Sarah Dempsey, Maria Dixon, Beth Eschenfelder, Kirsten Foot, Shiv Ganesh, Renee Heath, Renee Houston, Matthew Isbell, Joel Iverson, Erika Kirby, Laurie Lewis, Kirstie McAllum, Rebecca Meisenbach, Alexandra Murphy, Stephanie Norander, Brittany Peterson, Michelle Shumate, Consuelo Vasquez and many others who have participated in the various professional gatherings and conversations about nonprofit organizational communication. We are especially thankful to Lacy McNamee and Jennifer Mize Smith for reading early versions of our book chapters and offering invaluable feedback that made the final product even better.

And finally, we acknowledge *you*, the reader. You are the reason we wrote this book and we are grateful for your interest in our work. We assume you have some important connection to the nonprofit world – as a nonprofit worker, volunteer, researcher, board member, educator, or something else – and we hope our ideas in this book help you in that endeavor. Thank you for considering what we have to say, and please contact us if you have something to add to the conversation.

1

Developing a Communication Perspective on the Nonprofit

Matthew A. Koschmann and Matthew L. Sanders

Introduction[1]

What exactly is a *communication perspective*, and how could it enhance our understanding of nonprofit work? How is a communication perspective different from other approaches to the nonprofit, and what can we gain from this alternative perspective? These are questions that have guided our research and teaching for years, and provide the foundation of our work in this book. We think there is much to gain by "thinking communicatively" about the nonprofit, but it will require *re*thinking some common assumptions we have about communication, organizing, and the nonprofit sector. Our goal in this chapter is to develop the intellectual foundation and justification for a communication perspective as it relates to the nonprofit, which sets the stage for the ideas we expand upon in subsequent chapters. Overall, we want to enlarge the territory from which we understand nonprofit work by developing an explanatory framework centered on communication as the fundamental process that constitutes all social and organizational phenomena.

***

It should be obvious that communication is central to nonprofit organizations and the activities of the nonprofit sector. Things like fundraising and donor relations, client relationships and service delivery, volunteer management and board

1 Portions of this chapter are adapted with permission from the article: Koschmann, M.A., Isbell, M.G., and Sanders, M.L. (2015). Connecting nonprofit and communication scholarship: a review of key issues and a meta-theoretical framework for future research. *Review of Communication* 15 (3), 200–220.

Understanding Nonprofit Work: A Communication Perspective, First Edition.
Matthew A. Koschmann and Matthew L. Sanders.

governance, collaboration and cross-sector partnerships – just to name a few – all involve dynamic processes of human interaction, language, symbols, and interpretation. There are numerous books and research articles on nonprofit communication, communication consultants are in high demand for nonprofit organizations, and nonprofit professionals consistently cite "effective communication" as a key aspect of organizational success, while also listing "communication problems" as the root of so many struggles and complications. Surely, there is much to gain by studying various messages of the nonprofit sector, and many aspects of nonprofit organizations can be improved through more effective communication.

But we think communication is important for another reason. We believe the prevalence and significance of communication points to a more central, underlying reality: the nonprofit is *fundamentally communicative*, and therefore we should seek to understand the nonprofit "communicationally," from a perspective that is distinctly "communicational." Conversely, we are likely to miss important aspects of the nonprofit if we are not thinking from a communication perspective, and we limit our ability to account for the role of human interaction in creating and sustaining the social realities of nonprofit organizing. Our main goals in this book are to explain what a communication perspective means, why it is important, and how it can enhance our understanding of nonprofit work.

In order to accomplish these goals, we need to do two initial things in this chapter. First, we need to develop an alternative way of thinking about communication, one that goes beyond the conventional wisdom of seeing communication as merely the *transmission of information* between senders and receivers through various channels. Instead, understanding communication as a *process of social construction* improves our ability to account for the complexities of human interaction and better explain a variety of nonprofit phenomena. Therefore, this opening chapter will be the most theoretical and conceptual as we lay the intellectual foundation for a communicative approach to the nonprofit. Second, we need to juxtapose this alternative approach to communication with other perspectives that are commonly employed to explain and understand the nonprofit, especially economic, psychological, and sociological perspectives. Our intent here is not to argue for the intellectual superiority of our communication approach, but rather to expand and take a seat at an already impressive table and offer a contribution that we believe will enrich the overall conversation about the nonprofit.

Rethinking Communication

Certainly most people recognize the importance of communication in all aspects of life, though we don't always think about the *theories* of communication that shape how we understand our world and influence how we interact with other people. Yet we all have a theory of communication; we all have underlying assumptions and explanations about what we think communication is, what people are doing when they communicate, and the role of language, symbols, and interaction – even if we don't always acknowledge these assumptions or cannot articulate them clearly. Much of the time, our taken-for-granted or "native" theories of communication work just fine and help us get along in our daily lives. But there are also times when these theories reach a limit – when they are no longer capable of explaining a particular situation, when they cannot help us fully understand our experiences, when they prevent us from developing appropriate responses, or they restrict our ability to see new possibilities. In this way, theories are sort of like the operating system on your computer, tablet, or smartphone, humming along in the background, enabling you to run various programs and applications, and something you usually don't think much about until you run into a compatibility problem – there's something you want to accomplish or some new possibility you could explore that your current operating system prevents. When this happens you need an update or an upgrade, either a newer version or a completely new operating system. Otherwise you're stuck with the limitations of your current system.

When it comes to communication, we think that many people are running an outdated operating system, so to speak – a system that may have worked well in the past and still has some utility in certain situations, but overall is ill-suited for all the complexities and complications of human interaction. We think it's time for an upgrade, and depending on what "version" of the previous system you're running this may involve a big change or a minor adjustment. Either way, changing how we think about communication affords us many new and exciting possibilities, especially to enhance our understanding of the nonprofit.

Communication as Transmission

Today the dominant theory (i.e. operating system) of communication in our society is the *transmission model of communication*, with a philosophical orientation toward human interaction known as *functionalism*. Here, communication is understood as the transmission or exchange of information between senders and receivers through certain channels, and subject to noise and feedback loops, with the functional purpose of achieving some sort of instrumental goal or outcome. This is also known as the sender–receiver model of communication. Communication-as-transmission is the taken for granted, conventional wisdom about communication in much of our society; the factory-installed operating system, if you will. The transmission model of communication is based on the groundbreaking work of Claude Shannon in the field of information theory in the 1940s, and later published with his colleague Warren Weaver[2] (sometimes referred

2 Shannon, C.E. and Weaver, W. (1998). *The Mathematical Theory of Communication*. University of Illinois Press.

to in textbooks as the Shannon and Weaver model of communication). The transition model is popular and prevalent for several reasons. It certainly has a simple, intuitive feel, as it seems to describe much of our day-to-day communication experiences. Furthermore, it became institutionalized in the field of communication throughout the twentieth century as our academic discipline sought to align with dominant scientific paradigms, and thus the foundation for most communication research, instruction, and consultation (communication scholar Everett Rogers wrote a fascinating book about the history of how communication developed as an academic field in American universities in relation to information theory and the transmission model of communication[3]).

The transmission model of communication works very well when messages are accurate and clearly represent the meanings of the sender, and are interpreted by the receiver in the way they were intended; and when both sender and receiver have compatible perspectives on the underlying norms, values, and beliefs that shape the communication situation – which is the context for much of our communication, like sending quick updates or clarifying various details. The transmission model explains this process well (e.g. people are conceived as senders and receivers and interaction is information exchange), it suggests helpful ways to improve our communication (e.g. clarify the message content or change the communication channel), and it enables us to make fairly accurate predictions about the outcomes of various interactions (e.g. if this kind of message is transmitted via this channel, it will likely have this effect on the receiver). Consequently, "information" became a central concept in the academic study of communication (in communication departments and beyond), and "message effects" the primary outcome of interest. Thus the idea of *functionalism* has emerged as a prevailing intellectual paradigm for much communication research and practice (i.e. What is the *function* of communication in this situation? Or how can we make communication *function* more effectively in this context?). A functionalist approach to communication – based on a model of message transmission and information exchange – offers a straightforward way to comprehend human interaction in ways that adhere to many of our experiences and overall common sense; it's a decent factory-installed operating system that enables us to perform a variety of basic tasks and applications. Certainly much of our communication could be improved if we thought more critically about the messages we send, the channels we use, the noise that interferes, and the feedback loops that develop. And considerable work has been done to improve nonprofit organizations and the broader work of the nonprofit sector by attending to communication from a functionalist approach that is informed by the transmission model.

3 Rogers, E.M. (1997). *History of Communication Study*. New York: Free Press.

Subsequently, this line of thinking leads to a particular conception of *organizational* communication that shapes our understanding of the nonprofit: the *container metaphor.* Organizations are conceived as containers and communication as flows of information within the container. Just as containers exist independently from what flows within them, and the shape of the container dictates how things flow, so do organizations exist separately from communication, while organizational "shapes" or structures determine how information flows. Thus, we often think of communication happening *within* organizations, with the functional purpose of enabling the organization to operate more effectively. And from a certain (though limited) vantage point, this approach to organizational communication rings true. After all, organizations seem so stable and real, with their imposing buildings, organizational charts, bureaucracies, hierarchies, legal charters, and persistence over time. And much of what we observe on the surface certainly looks like information flowing within the organization (i.e. the container) – people sharing emails, having meetings, delivering messages, conversing with colleagues – all within the confines or boundaries of the organization.

As you might expect, this way of thinking about communication is very prevalent in the existing nonprofit research literature and practitioner writings. This material generally presents an instrumental or functional approach to communication that is focused on message transmission and information sharing – communication used as a tool to achieve some notion of organizational effectiveness. For example, studies look at how advocacy organizations use social media as a communication tool to execute various message strategies, or investigate message strategies that affect the likelihood of charitable donations, or examine information sharing as an important management strategy for effective nonprofit mergers and restructuring, just as a few examples.[4] This instrumental approach to communication is also evident in the term *communications* (with an "s"), which is common across this literature and implies a message-centered view of communication (e.g. email communications, nonprofit communications planning, nonprofit organizational communications). Also prevalent is an emphasis on information communication technologies and communication channels, which reinforces assumptions about message transmission and functionality. The clear implication from this nonprofit literature is that communication is primarily about message transmission and information exchange in order to accomplish strategic goals and improve organizational effectiveness.

---

4 Guo, C. and Saxton, G.D. (2014). Tweeting social change: how social media are changing nonprofit advocacy. *Nonprofit and Voluntary Sector Quarterly* 43: 57–79; Bennett, R. (2013). Factors influencing the break even probabilities of agency recruited low value charity donors. *Voluntas* 24: 1091–1112; Campbell, D.A. (2008). Getting to yes ... or no: nonprofit decision making and interorganizational restructuring. *Nonprofit Management & Leadership* 19: 221–241.

But is that really all that's happening? Is communication only about message transmission and information exchange? Is communication only a functional endeavor in service of some vague notion of organizational effectiveness? Is this a sufficient operating system (i.e. theory of communication) to run all the programs and applications we need? As we will see, this simplistic notion of organizational communication doesn't stand up to scrutiny, nor is it well-suited to account for the complexities of human interaction in today's organizational world. Furthermore, it limits our ability to understand and explain key aspects of the nonprofit, and may prevent us from achieving the sort of creativity and innovation needed for nonprofits to thrive in modern society. Yes, the transmission model can explain many of our communication experiences, especially when things are going well and we're getting along with the people around us. This is one reason we're tempted to think that communication is easy and straightforward; there are times when communication seems effortless and works well with reasonable people who are on the same page. But this ignores the fact that we don't get to live and work in situations that are always going smoothly or interact with people who understand us well. In particular, nonprofit work requires significant coalition building and working with diverse people who often see the world differently than us.

In a perfect world, we could create more efficient structures of message transmission so that the right people would always have the right information and miscommunication would be a thing of the past. But a funny thing happened on the way to communication paradise. Turns out different people interpret the exact same message very differently; that people can be deceptive in their communication and their motives are incredibly difficult to figure out; that the meaning of language changes depending on the context; that what you *don't* communicate is often more important that what you *do* communicate; or that *what* you say is often much less important than *how* you say it; and that people often (if not usually) communicate for many other reasons than to just transmit information. And these are not just aberrations; *this is the normal state of affairs for human interaction*. Why is it, after all, that "communication problems" are continually mentioned as one of the main difficulties for most organizations? Is it just that people aren't getting the right information? If so, this is merely a technical problem that should improve as we develop new ways to get better information to more people more efficiently. But it seems like almost the opposite is happening, that the more sophisticated our communication technologies have gotten over the years, the more communication problems we have. Now why is that? Perhaps it's because there is more going on with communication than just transmitting information.

Despite its intuitive appeal, the functionalist approach to organizational communication – based on a transmission model of communication – is rooted in several faulty assumptions about communication that we should examine. First and foremost, information theory (the basis for the transmission model of communication) was never really intended as a theory of *human* interaction. Claude Shannon always claimed that his model did not apply well to human communication. His model was designed for static, technical systems that involved intentional, formal, explicit, and logical transmission of information. Things like nonverbal communication, unintentional messages, and interpretive differences had no place in Shannon's model – these were all considered "noise" that interfered with channel capacity and the efficient transmission of information. Communication scholars responded with adaptations of Shannon's model that transformed engineering concepts in human terms; for example, conceptualizing message receivers as having the capacity for emotion and sense-making. These adaptations worked fine for some communication scholars, but others grew increasingly dissatisfied with adapting a theoretical model that was never intended for human interaction in the first place.

The primary critique of a functionalist approach to communication is that it fails to account for the complexities of human interaction that are essential to many communication practices and situations. People communicate for so many more reasons than to transmit information, and communication is rarely just a linear process that can be assessed solely in terms of message effects. Also, communication is filled with intricacies such as nonverbal behavior, unintended messages, multiple interpretations, conflicting motivations, and changing contexts that cannot be easily explained in terms of a straightforward sender–message–channel–receiver model of communication (even if we include components like noise and feedback).

At a deeper, more philosophical level, the problem with functionalism is that it depicts communication as a relatively neutral conduit that transmits already-formed realities – inner psychological states that merely await expression through communication. Communication from this perspective is seen as separate from social realities themselves and not significantly involved in their production. This renders communication as epiphenomenal, a surface-level manifestation that is driven by other structural mechanisms or the "natural" order of events, a byproduct that does not have any causal influence on the process. Communication is seen as the way we transmit pre-existing meanings between people, but those meanings are formed and reside elsewhere – and thus understood psychologically, sociologically, or even biologically, but not *communicatively*. However, this idea of meaning as a psychological substance located within people and transmitted via communication is misguided because it ignores how meaning is fundamentally a *social* process, created and sustained through our interactions with other people. As communication scholar Timothy Kuhn explains:

> Communication... is not a vehicle for representing, externalizing, transmitting, and reproducing preexisting meanings; it is the dynamic process of meaning production, and meanings are "in" communicative action.[5]

The problem is that meaning and information are not synonymous, and any approach that reduces the complex processes of meaning-making through human interaction (communication) to the mere transmission or exchange of information (functionalism) is troublesome. That's one reason why the eminent philosopher Ludwig Wittgenstein famously said, "Nothing is more wrong-headed than calling meaning a mental activity."[6] The point here is that the social world is mainly about what things *mean*, not simply what they *are*, and we are sorely mistaken if we think that meaning is just something mental we figure out on our own and then straightforwardly transmit to other people through our communication. Instead, the very process of communicating with people is what creates meaning and where meaning resides – meaning is "in" the interaction, not simply in our heads.

By now, we hope you can see the shortcomings of the transmission model theory of communication/operating system and the functionalism it entails. Yes, it does enable us to run a variety of basic programs and applications that involve exchanging information with people where issues of meaning, interpretation, and understanding aren't at stake or are not as problematic. However, most of us want and need to run more advanced programs and applications because many of our communication situations are fraught with issues of meaning, interpretation, and understanding. In that case, we need an upgrade to a more sophisticated operating system; we need a different theory of communication. Instead of viewing communication as merely the transfer of information, an alternative approach goes deeper and sees communication as the fundamental process that creates and maintains our social reality. Communication is not just about transmitting already-formed data between senders and receivers, but rather a complex process of continually producing and negotiating the meanings and interpretations that shape our lives. We (and many others) call this the *social construction model of communication*, and we believe it's the alternative theory or operating system needed to enhance our understanding and practice of nonprofit organizational communication.

---

5 Kuhn, T. (2012). Negotiating the micro–macro divide: thought leadership from organizational communication for theorizing organization. *Management Communication Quarterly* 26 (4): 543–584, p. 548.

6 Wittgenstein, L. (1958). *Philosophical Investigations* (1953), 172 (trans. G.E.M. Anscombe). Oxford: Blackwell.

Communication as Social Construction

Social construction is a broad concept that has developed over several decades in a variety of academic fields and applied contexts. Like any big concept, social construction has no standard definition that everyone agrees with. There are strong, moderate, and weak versions of social construction among scholars and practitioners, and there are ongoing debates about the meaning and application of social construction. But the basic idea that most everyone supports is that our social realities (or social worlds) are constructed through our interactions with other people. And the key point for our purposes here is that pretty much everything that composes the nonprofit are social realities that are constructed by people through our communication with each other. Therefore, if we want to change, improve, create, or maintain any aspect of the nonprofit – like leadership, collaboration, international work, organizational strategies, or labor relations – we need to focus on the communication practices and processes that construct them, and we need to put communication at the center of our understanding of the nonprofit.

Now, this idea of social construction can get quite philosophical and complicated, and we don't want to get bogged down here in academic debates about the nature of reality. But since this book is all about developing a communication-as-social construction perspective for the nonprofit, and since this chapter provides the theoretical foundation for the rest of the book, we do need to say a bit more about social construction, especially how it developed as a concept and how it has been taken up in the field of organizational communication. If you're already on board with the basic idea of social construction, you may want to skip ahead to the implications for the nonprofit we explain later in this chapter. But if social construction is new to you, or you're still somewhat skeptical, hopefully these next few paragraphs will clarify the main ideas and provide a sufficient foundation for the key concepts that underwrite everything else in this book.

To begin, let's clarify what we mean by *social reality* or our *social worlds*. By social realities, we're talking about all the norms, values, beliefs, institutions, interpretations, understandings, concepts, etc. that govern modern life and make our day-to-day world what it is. In contrast to the natural world of mountains, rivers, lakes, and trees that is just "there" and exists independently of human activity (though human activity certainly can alter this reality), the social world is made by us and would not exist if not for human activity. Social realities like democracy, capitalism, bureaucracy, our legal system, or our education system (just to name a few) are things we made through countless human interactions and decisions. They are not natural and they would not exist if we didn't make them; they are subject to change and they could have been otherwise. For example, what counts as "legal" has changed over time and will continue to do so as long as humans are involved; legality doesn't just exist "out there" like some objective feature of the natural world that is the same for all people in all places at all times. Thus, to approach things from a social construction perspective (or upgrade to the communication-as-social construction operating system, to continue the metaphor) means to focus on the processes of human interaction by which our social realities are made, altered, sustained, and resisted. It also means understanding and explaining various phenomena in terms of communication patterns and practices, as well as foregrounding communication as a primary site for intervention and improvement. That's what we're trying to do in the remaining chapters of this book regarding the nonprofit.

Two important caveats before we move on. First, just because social realities are socially constructed does *not* mean they are easy to make or take apart, or that we're suggesting some simplistic notion of "perception is reality" or "just imagine and it will be." Not at all. Social constructions are real and consequential, and they are not easily created or dismantled. Race is certainly a social construction, for instance. Although there is no scientific basis for racial differences (what has counted as "white" or "black" in the United States, for example, has changed over the centuries), race as a concept is incredibly "real" in our society; it may not be a biological reality, but it certainly is a political, legal, and cultural reality. Certain constructions of race required a lot of time and effort to make (like how Italians in America "became" white[7]), and other constructions have proven incredibly stubborn and difficult to undo (like perceptions of black and brown men as more violent, despite much evidence to the contrary[8]). And many social constructions are much more persistent and impenetrable than actual physical constructions – sometimes it's actually easier for a company to build a new building or tear one down than it is to change the organizational culture or penetrate the glass ceiling. At the same time, the processes of social construction are always in relation to the materiality of the physical world. When you cross the street, it's you or the bus and the bus will always win, regardless of what you imagine or try to speak into existence! So it's not as easy as just talking things into or out of existence. But we *are* saying that to the extent that social realities do come into existence, they are made by people and we need to examine the social process that gave rise to their existence if we want to intervene in any meaningful way. That is our focus in this book regarding several key aspects of the nonprofit.

Second, we readily acknowledge that the boundaries between the social and natural world are a bit fuzzy. This distinction between social and natural is an *analytical* division to help clarify some of the clear differences we see in our day-to-day lives, even if some of those divisions might break down upon deeper

---

7 See Staples, B. (2019). "How Italians became 'white'." *New York Times*, October 12.
8 See Stark, E. (1993). The myth of black violence. *Social Work* 38 (4): 485–490.

philosophical investigation. After all, we humans are part of the natural world, and everything we do in the social world is somehow connected (though not necessarily reduced) to the materiality of our biology. Plus, much of what we see in the natural world is dependent on human activity, and we'll never fully know exactly how our actions affect the natural world we take for granted as just "there." Yet, at an intuitive level, there is something obviously different between the trees I'm looking at from my office window and the notion of "workplace satisfaction" that a consultant is trying to measure on a survey. Both are real and consequential in our lives, but it's helpful to distinguish trees as "natural" and concepts like workplace satisfaction as "social." Furthermore, we humans bring something unique to the table that is categorically different from anything else we see in the natural world: our capacity for language, meaning, interpretation, and symbol use have enabled us to create a realm of existence (what we're calling social reality or social worlds) that is unparalleled by anything else in the world. In particular, this capacity has helped us to coordinate our actions with other people to build societies and institutions that govern our subsequent actions. That's what the nonprofit is, and we believe it is helpful and worthwhile to distinguish nonprofit phenomena as social realities to improve our analysis and enhance our insights.

That should provide a sufficient foundation of social construction for what we're doing in this book. If you want to learn more, we highly recommend several great resources that explore these ideas in more depth. Three of our favorite books are different variations of the same phrase: Peter Berger and Thomas Luckman's seminal text *The Social Construction of Reality*, John Searle's popular book *The Construction of Social Reality*, and Dave Elder-Vass's more recent *The Reality of Social Construction*, all of which offer slightly different perspectives on social construction but share a commitment to the centrality of human communication in the making of our social worlds.[9] It's also important to remember that social construction didn't just come out of nowhere or arise naturally; it is itself a social construction (now we're getting very meta!), emerging from a history of ideas and debates across many decades and continents. The idea of social construction is rooted in early twentieth-century, Western studies of linguistics and philosophy that challenged modernist conceptions of language, knowledge, and society. These include ideas from European continental philosophy, American pragmatist philosophy, phenomenological approaches to psychology and sociology, and the so-called "linguistic turn" across the broader social sciences. Social construction is thus an important attempt to bring together many different but related ideas into a coherent framework for analysis and

---

9 Berger, P.L. and Luckmann, T. (1966). *The Social Construction of Reality: A Treatise in the Sociology of Knowledge*. Random House; Searle, J.R. and Willis, S. (1995). *The Construction of Social Reality*. Simon and Schuster; Elder-Vass, D. (2012). *The Reality of Social Construction*. Cambridge University Press.

explanation. And this refinement continues as scholars in a variety of fields appropriate the ideas of social construction in ways that are relevant for their work, while also revising key assumptions, challenging perceived limitations, and pushing the boundaries of our understanding of social constructionist thinking. This is precisely what has happened in our field of communication.

Social Construction in the Field of Communication

Now let's transition and look at how ideas of social construction have been taken up in the field of communication, which provides the foundation for what we're doing in the rest of this book. Recall the shortcomings of the transmission model of communication and the growing critique of functionalism we explained above. These challenges to the transmission model and mounting frustrations with functionalism led many communication scholars to develop alternative conceptions of human interaction across a variety of subjects and fields of inquiry (e.g. interpersonal, intercultural, organizational). As this work developed – and as is often the case in academic fields – leading scholars sought to provide additional clarity and direction by synthesizing a number of these related ideas and articulating an overarching theme to inform subsequent research and teaching. In particular, Robert Craig and Stanley Deetz[10] identified that what these ideas all had in common was a *constitutive* approach to communication. That is, we constitute – not just express – our social realities in our interactions with others. Communication is a dynamic, interactive process that involves constant negotiation over interpretation and meaning, not just the transmission of information. Social realities are not "fixed" such that they can be reflected or expressed unproblematically, and things we take for granted in the social world – organizations, institutions, relationships – only maintain their existence through sustained patterns of interaction. Communication scholars have come to call this underlying philosophical theme *communicative constitution* because communication constitutes, or makes up our social world. Basically, communicative constitution is a more precise articulation of the broad ideas of social construction, but specifically for the field of communication.[11] In a seminal essay published in *Communication Theory*, Craig

10 Craig, R.T. (1999). Communication theory as a field. *Communication Theory* 9: 119–161; Deetz, S.A. (1994). Future of the discipline: the challenges, the research, and the social contribution. In: *Communication Yearbook 17* (ed. S.A. Deetz), 565–600. Thousand Oaks, CA: Sage; Deetz, S.A. (1994). The micro-politics of identity formation in the workplace: the case of a knowledge intensive firm. *Human Studies* 17: 23–44.

11 Though with some implications and applications that go beyond (and even depart from) social constructionist thinking, but this is beyond our purposes in this book. See Ashcraft, K.L., Kuhn, T.R., and Cooren, F. (2009). Constitutional amendments: 'materializing' organizational communication. *The Academy of Management Annals* 3: 1–64 for more insights on how communicative constitution has begun to differ from social constructionism, yet with still much in common.

articulated this notion of *communicative constitution* (or communication as constitutive) as a meta-theoretical framework to encompass all communication scholarship.[12] In fact, many prominent scholars now see communicative constitution the "overarching principle that guides the discipline [of communication] today."[13] Thus communicative constitution provides the underlying philosophical orientation for our work, the way functionalism provided a similar orientation and institutional identity for previous communication scholarship. Communicative constitution gives communication scholars a broad framework to guide research, an intellectual coherence across different schools of thought within our discipline, and a clear theoretical stance in relation to other perspectives outside the field of communication.

Ok, that's a lot of scholarly material to digest, so let's step back and review where we're at before we move on to some of the implications of this alternative approach to communication for the nonprofit. Remember that we're using an operating system metaphor to understand and explain the notion of communication theory; we all have underlying assumptions about what communication is and what we're doing when we interact with people that enable or constrain our ability to do or see certain things in those interactions – just like a computer operating system humming along in the background allows or restricts our ability to run certain programs or applications. On the one hand, we have the transmission model of communication and the subsequent functionalism it entails. This approach theorizes communication as the efficient transmission of messages between senders and receivers to achieve instrumental goals. On the other hand, we have the social construction model of communication and the corresponding notion of communicative constitution. Here the emphasis is on interpretation and understanding, how our interactions with each other produce the meanings that constitute the realities of our social worlds. Table 1.1 provides a visual representation of all this and will be a handy reference for the rest of the book.

And just to clarify: we're not saying that the transmission model is completely wrong and the social construction model is absolutely right, or that functionalism is all bad and communicative constitution is all good. It's not quite that simple. We readily acknowledge that communication-as-transition is an adequate theory to understand and explain many of our communication practices, especially when we're dealing with relatively straightforward message exchanges between people who already have a shared understanding of the situation, and when issues of meaning and interpretation really aren't at stake. Just like the factory-installed operating system isn't "wrong" or "bad" – it may work just fine for the programs and applications you want to run. However, we are saying that the transmission

12 Craig, "Communication Theory," 119–161.
13 Ashcraft, Kuhn, and Cooren, "Constitutional Amendments," p. 94.

Table 1.1 Comparing theoretical approaches to communication.

Theory of Communication	Communication-as-Transmission	Communication-as-Social Construction
Underlying philosophy	Functionalism	Communicative constitution
Key terms and relevant vocabulary	Informational, instrumental, message effects, clarity, efficiency	Meaning, interpretation, understanding, production, pluralism, social worlds

model of communication is often inadequate to understand and explain the complexities of human interaction and to inform our communication practices, especially for many key aspects of the nonprofit. Plus, working from the assumptions of the transmission model can inhibit our ability to accomplish certain things in our communication, and may in fact prove harmful or ineffective. In that case, we should upgrade to a new operating system and learn more about how to run the more sophisticated programs and applications needed to accomplish our goals.

That's what we're going to do throughout the rest of this book. We're going to demonstrate how the ideas of communicative constitution can influence our thinking and actions across several key aspects of the nonprofit (what we call "taking a communication approach" or "thinking communicatively"). We recognize that the lines between communication-as-transmission and communication-as-social construction can be a bit fuzzy (that's why we put a fuzzy line in the table!), so the point is not to get too caught up in the technicalities – this is not the periodic table of communication theory elements. Instead, we have two different orientations toward how we think about communication and what is happening when people interact with each other. Social construction provides a broad perspective to inform our understanding of the nonprofit; it moves us away from mechanistic and instrumental approaches toward organizational communication and reorients us toward communicative constitution and the processes of meaning production that make up our social realities. With all this in mind, let's begin wrapping up this chapter with a look at some of the key implications of communicative constitution for the nonprofit, followed by a preview of the upcoming chapters.

Implications of Communicative Constitution for the Nonprofit

Our purpose isn't simply to review scholarship about a constitutive approach to communication – that has already been done very well by many other great writers.[14] Instead, we explore two key implications of communicative constitution, both of which involve a rethinking of nonprofit concepts and organizations. Together these implications move us toward seeing communication as a *mode of explanation*, and thus a distinct "communication perspective" that that both complements and challenges other disciplines and approaches to enhance our understanding of nonprofit work.

Rethinking Core Concepts

A first implication of a constitutive approach to communication involves challenging the taken-for-granted or "natural" character of nonprofit concepts and phenomena. We often take for granted terms like *volunteer*, *nonprofit*, *mission*, *faith-based*, and *sector*. A functionalist approach to communication (where social realities are pre-existing and exchanged/transmitted as information) lures us into accepting these concepts as given or natural, when in fact they are quite fragile, artificial, and political, and arise from very particular social circumstances. But a communication perspective helps us see that language matters because it calls into being specific social realities that enable or restrict social action with real material consequences – it is not just a matter of perception. Volunteers do not simply "exist" but rather are created and sustained through how we use this term. Labeling someone as a volunteer or categorizing specific actions as voluntary has important consequences, especially if this is done by certain kinds of people or organizations. Rather than asking what things "are" a communication perspective asks how things are constituted communicatively, whose interests are represented in these constructions, how they are sustained or transformed through interaction, what identities are produced or suppressed, and what kinds of actions are supported or constrained. An example of this is Dorothea's Hilhorst's study of

14 See, for example, Ashcraft, Kuhn, and Cooren, "Constitutional Amendments," 1–64; Craig, "Communication Theory," 119–161; Craig, R.T. and Muller, H. (eds.) (2007). *Theorizing Communication: Readings Across Traditions*. Thousand Oaks, CA: Sage; Deetz, "Future of the Discipline," 565–600; Littlejohn, S.W. and Foss, K.A. (2010). *Theories of Human Communication*. Long Grove, IL: Waveland Press.

nongovernmental organizations (NGOs) in the Philippines.[15] She demonstrates how the term *NGO* should not be understood as a neutral characterization, but rather as a claim-bearing label that activates particular assumptions about legitimacy, power, and identity. By using the term *NGO*, workers assumed certain relations of power, gave themselves specific identities, and made possible particular modes of development work. When we understand communication as the production (not just the expression) of meaning we gain valuable insights into *how* important aspects of the nonprofit sector are constituted versus merely explaining *that* they exist. A communication perspective helps us see how the social realities we often take for granted are actually created, sustained, and/or transformed depending on how people interact with each other.

One area where this is especially relevant is the ongoing discussions in the literature about whether or not nonprofits should be more "business-like."[16] Terms like *efficiency*, *bottom line*, or *effectiveness* may have common dictionary definitions, but they do not refer to a neutral or natural state of affairs. Instead, they are used in practice to constitute particular social realities that may favor certain interests and marginalize others. Taking a communication perspective toward various nonprofit phenomena means exploring the processes and patterns of human interaction that constitute specific social realities and not just accepting them as given or inevitable. Our own Matthew Sanders' study of the mission-market tension facing many nonprofits does just this. As he describes, "The notion of being business-like in the nonprofit sector can be understood as a communicative construction whose meaning is not fixed but is negotiated and transformed in practice."[17] He goes on to explain how specific understandings of "business-like" enable or restrict nonprofit's pursuit of their social missions. Sanders' study is the lone example in the nonprofit literature that explicitly works from a constitutive model of communication. It demonstrates the value of a communication perspective for understanding important

---

15 Hilhorst, D. (2001). Village experts and development discourse: 'progress' in a Philippine Igorot village. *Human Organization* 60: 401–413.

16 See, for example, Bush, R. (1992). Survival of the nonprofit spirit in a for-profit world. *Nonprofit and Voluntary Sector Quarterly* 21: 391–410; Dart, R. (2004). Being 'business-like' in a nonprofit organization: a grounded and inductive typology. *Nonprofit and Voluntary Sector Quarterly* 33: 290–310; Ruud, G. (2000). The symphony: organizational discourse and the symbolic tensions between artistic and business ideologies. *Journal of Applied Communication Research* 28: 117–143; Eikenberry, A.M. (2009). Refusing the market: a democratic discourse for voluntary and nonprofit organizations. *Nonprofit and Voluntary Sector Quarterly* 38: 582–596; Maier, F. and Myer, M. (2011). Managerialism and beyond: discourses of civil society organizations and their governance implications. *Voluntas* 22: 731–756.

17 Sanders, M.L. (2015). Being nonprofit-like in a market economy: understanding the mission-market tension in nonprofit organizing. *Nonprofit and Voluntary Sector Quarterly* 44 (2): 205–222, p. 2.

aspects of the nonprofit sector and exemplifies the kind of scholarship we are advocating. And he has much more to say about all this in Chapter 3.

Rethinking Organizations *as* Communication

A second implication of a constitutive approach to communication involves rethinking how we conceptualize nonprofit organizations. In common vernacular we talk about communication that happens *within* organizations, which is consistent with an informational approach to communication that emphasizes message transmission inside pre-existing systems. This container metaphor (which we explained above) implies that communication flows depend on the literal or figurative shape of the organization.[18] And by the shape of the container we can mean the physical shape of the organization, like if you have to take the elevator up ten floors to deliver a report to your boss, or more of a symbolic shape, like where you are in the organizational hierarchy and how this influences the way you communicate with other organizational members. The key is that communication is seen as something existing separately from the organization itself.

But this is problematic because it requires us to account for the ontological status of organizations – their underlying character or the nature of their being – apart from human interaction.[19] In contrast, a constitutive approach to communication encourages us to think about organizations *as* communication. This ontological shift challenges our conventional wisdom about what nonprofit organizations are, based on the lived experiences of those involved. We know that nonprofit organizations are not simply the physical structures or material resources we encounter in their operations, nor are they merely the legal charters that give them a virtual existence in our tax system. What makes a nonprofit organization truly an *organization* are the specific processes, practices, and procedures that set them apart from other collections of people. An organization is basically an ongoing assemblage of interactions, decisions, interpretations, symbols, negotiations, agreements, contracts, relationships, and so forth; what communication scholar

---

18 Putnam, L.L. and Boys, S. (2006). Revisiting metaphors of organizational communication. In: *The SAGE Handbook of Organizational Studies*, 2e (ed. S.R. Clegg, C. Hardy, T.B. Lawrence, and W.R. Nord), 541–576. London: Sage.

19 Communication scholar Timothy Kuhn does a nice job of explaining this issue of organizational ontology, which is the philosophical investigation of what organizations *are*. See Kuhn, T.R. (2008). A communicative theory of the firm: developing an alternative perspective on intra-organizational power and stakeholder relationships. *Organization Studies* 29: 1227–1254.

W. Barnett Pearce called "temporary configurations of a continuous process".[20] These processes are made visible in temporary structures, which often take so much time, effort, and attention that it's hard not to want them to be permanent.[21] But a communication perspective draws our attention to connections and relationships and patterns of interaction, not static notions of what things are but rather what they are doing. Organizations are not neutral structures that exist apart from human interaction; they are the visible manifestations *of* human interaction (i.e. communication) – thus the shift from thinking about communication *within* organizations to understanding organizations *as* communication.

After all, few people experience nonprofit organizations as financial entities, and the most fundamental aspects of the nonprofit sector cannot be reduced to legal abstractions. For most people what constitutes their experience of nonprofit organizations is fundamentally social, relational, interactive, and meaningful – in short, *communicative*. We cannot fully account for what a nonprofit organization *is* by just reading its articles of incorporation, reviewing its organizational chart, or going through its financial statements. That misses the true character of the organization and tells us nothing about the actual experience of being part of the organization as a volunteer, employee, client, or donor. The spirit of the nonprofit sector is grounded in social entrepreneurship, civic and political engagement, service delivery, and even religious faith, and these essential aspects of the nonprofit are created and sustained through ongoing patterns of human interaction.[22] Therefore communication is much more than mere information transmission; communication is indeed a *way of being* for nonprofit organizations.

The point, then, is that a constitutive view of organizations *as* communication enables us to question and investigate key organizational realities, not just accept them as given. We can question the existence of the organization – its structure, its forms of power, its guiding assumptions, its norms of operations – and so on. If these organizational features are not "natural," but rather came into existence through specific communication processes, then we can examine the implications of those communication processes and explore ways of communicating that lead to more favorable organizational outcomes for more people. We can examine, for example, how certain patterns of interaction give rise to norms of conflict resolution, or how the taken-for-granted values of a particular industry or sector shape the practice of leadership, or how interpersonal dynamics affect the success

20 Pearce, W.B. (2009). *Making Social Worlds: A Communication Perspective*, 49. Wiley.
21 Organizational consultant and scholar Margaret Wheatley has a great book on this idea of organizations as processes, not "things": Wheatley, M. (2006). *Leadership and the New Science: Discovering Order in a Chaotic World*. Berrett-Koehler.
22 We highly recommend Peter Frumpkin's insightful book for more insights about the character of the nonprofit sector: Frumkin, P. (2002). *On Being Nonprofit: A Conceptual and Policy Prime*. Cambridge, MA: Harvard University Press.

of an organizational change initiative. We can look at how certain views of masculinity or femininity are related to communication practices, or how our very identities are often created and sustained through organizational communication. We can uncover hidden forms of power and control that are embedded within communication processes. We can explore ways to make organizations more equitable and inclusive by surfacing alternative voices. We can figure out how to make organizations more productive, adaptive, and responsive through organizational communication that encourages innovation and collaboration. Whatever the case, a constitutive view of organizations *as* communication provides a much stronger explanatory framework to understand the complexities of nonprofit organizing and communicating.

What does this mean for nonprofit scholarship, and how can it enhance our knowledge of the nonprofit sector? When we see that organizations exist as the very communication processes by which they are constituted we gain a fuller understanding of what nonprofits are, based on how people experience these interactions. Organizational communication scholars Pamela Lutgen-Sandvik and Virginia McDermott demonstrate this in their study of dysfunctional relationships at a nonprofit women's community center.[23] Working from a constitutive approach, these communication scholars argue that we should rethink what this particular nonprofit is, based on the communication patterns that constitute the organization. Accordingly, they claim that this nonprofit should be understood as an "employee abusive organization" because of the ongoing patterns of negative interactions that made up this organization. Calling this a "nonprofit organization" tells us very little about what this organization actually was for the people involved. In fact, the term *nonprofit* was misleading in this case because it suggested a level of altruism, charity, and motivation beyond financial concerns that was not true of this organization. But analyzing this case from a communication perspective enabled these researchers to develop insights about workplace bullying and abuse that are not accounted for through other theoretical frameworks. When we privilege the financial and economic status of organizations we can miss important insights about the actual lived experiences of the people involved.[24]

We recognize that it may seem unusual to conceptualize organizations based on their communicative versus legal or economic constitution, but that is exactly the point. In order to advance our knowledge of nonprofit organizations and the nonprofit sector we need to explore new ways of thinking and alternative

---

23 Lutgen-Sandvik, P. and McDermott, V. (2008). The constitution of employee-abusive organizations: a communication flows theory. *Communication Theory* 18: 304–333.
24 And yes, this does imply that the term *nonprofit* may be inherently problematic for the perspective we're developing and for what we're trying to accomplish in this book. This tension will show up throughout the subsequent chapters and is something we will revisit more explicitly in our concluding chapter.

perspectives that can enhance our understanding. We are not claiming we should jettison economic, financial, or legal theorizing – clearly these approaches have fostered tremendous insights and are essential for understanding the nonprofit sector. Nevertheless, understanding organizations *as* communication complements these established approaches and can help advance our thinking about nonprofit work.

Communication Among the Disciplines

So, how does this alternative conception of communication relate to other fields of study that inform our understanding of the nonprofit? There already exists an extensive body of research and writing from several disciplines – particularly economics, sociology, and psychology – that constitutes most of the nonprofit scholarly literature, so what does a communication perspective offer that we don't already know? How is a communication perspective different from these other perspectives? What does it contribute?

The wrong way to answer these questions is to focus simply on objects of study. That is, economics studies the economy; sociology studies society; psychology studies the human psyche; and consequently the field of communication studies, well, communication. But that puts us right back to a message-centered, transmissional understanding of communication that we critiqued above. Plus, it doesn't account for what these areas of study are actually doing in their research or how they seek to shape our understanding of the nonprofit. Instead, we want to differentiate a communication perspective from other fields of study in terms of their *modes of explanation*. This is the most significant implication of the constitutive approach to communication we've explained throughout this chapter: *elevating communication from a unit of analysis to a mode of explanation*. This means that communication is not just a phenomenon to be explained, but rather provides an explanatory framework from which to understand a host of other social phenomena.

Now at first, it may seem odd to think of communication as a mode of explanation, but we certainly appreciate this move in other academic fields. Biologists, for example, do not only study biology but also develop biological explanations for many aspects of the social world. The same with chemists and physicists. Various disciplines do not just study different objects, but also offer different explanatory frameworks to make sense of our experiences. The field of economics does not just study the economy, for example, it also develops economic explanations for a whole host of social and financial phenomena. Similarly, sociology and psychology do not only study society and the human psyche, respectively, they also develop sociological and psychological explanations for a wide range of behaviors and actions that might seem beyond the narrow purview of their objects of study.

Likewise, if our social realities are constituted in and through human interaction then it stands to reason that communication can provide a framework from which we understand and explain the social world, what communication scholar Robert Craig calls a "communicational perspective on social reality."[25]

Traditionally, communication has been understood as a unit of analysis – instances of talk and message exchange that happen in certain contexts. Thus scholars focus on different kinds of communication (e.g. superior–subordinate communication, instructional communication, family communication, crisis communication, volunteer communication), but which are formed and explained psychologically, sociologically, or economically. For example, family communication may examine instances of talk and text between parents and children as units of investigation, but the "real" analysis will focus on the psychological factors shaping the interaction, and thus result in a psychological (not communicative) explanation.

Conversely, a constitutive approach to communication reverses the explanatory direction: studying psychological, sociological, or economic phenomena as formed and explained communicatively or communicationally. Communication scholar Stanley Deetz clarifies this idea nicely:

> What we need is an understanding of disciplines as holistic but complementary. Disciplines are attempts at explaining a totality: There are not psychological or sociological things; there are things that are constituted by thinking and talking about things psychologically or sociologically.[26]

He goes on to say:

> If psychological explanations explain individual behavior using goals, reinforcements, needs, and drives, and sociological explanations explain collective action using economic class difference, social structures, and forms of integration, then communication explanations explain [social] practice by showing how goals, needs, reinforcements, drives, economic class, social structures, and forms of integration are produced and reproduced in interaction.[27]

This is how we are conceptualizing communication, as a *mode of explanation*. Not simply a thing to be explained, but rather a way of explaining multiple aspects of

---

25 Craig, "Communication Theory," p. 124.
26 Deetz, "Future of the Discipline," p. 571.
27 Deetz, "Future of the Discipline," p. 577.

human behavior and organizational life. Not just explaining different things, but explaining things differently.

By advancing a communication perspective, our goal here is to expand the explanatory resources we have to understand and improve nonprofit work. For example, people are obviously biological creatures, but there are limits to biological understandings – you simply cannot comprehend and appreciate the fullness of the human experience merely through biological dissection and reduction (even if they still lead to some valuable insights). Just like you cannot fully understand poetry through analyzing the chemical composition of the ink and paper. Likewise, when we reduce the nonprofit to a singular perspective, we then paint ourselves into a corner of having to explain all phenomena from this perspective. Nonprofits are certainly legal, financial, and economic entities, but they are also fundamentally communicative, and surely we miss something important if we forgo a communication perspective, and are likely to gain much from incorporating a communication perspective. Our concern here is reductionism and the insights we lose if we insist on shoehorning all phenomena into a particular framework or perspective.

Elsewhere we've written about how most current thinking about the nonprofit is dominated by economic thinking, which attempts to explain why nonprofits exist and how they function in a market economy.[28] However, economics represents only one way to understand the nonprofit sector, and assuming the primacy of the market economy to develop theoretical explanations has notable limitations. Economic theorizing tends to "black box" social interaction and assumes human behavior is primarily about consuming goods and services and acquiring resources. Furthermore, economic theories tell us very little about the lived experiences of the nonprofit sector or the processes of organizing. This is not to deny the value of economics, but merely to recognize its limitations for explaining the fullness of the nonprofit sector. To address these limitations we do not just need better economic theories because the shortcomings of economic theorizing are outside the logics of economic thinking.[29]

Instead, why not start from different assumptions about the nature of collective experience to understand and explain certain aspects of the nonprofit? This is what a constitutive approach to communication can provide. Nonprofit

28 Koschmann, M.A. (2012). Developing a communicative theory of the nonprofit. *Management Communication Quarterly* 26: 139–146. Also see Anheier, H.K. (2014). *Nonprofit Organizations: Theory, Management, Policy*. New York: Routledge on this point.

29 For further insights on these ideas see Dempsey, S.E. (2012). Nonprofits as political actors. *Management Communication Quarterly* 26: 147–151; Priem, R.L. and Butler, J.E. (2001). Is the resource-based 'view' a useful perspective for strategic management research? *Academy of Management Review* 26: 22–40; Kuhn, T.R. (2008). A communicative theory of the firm: developing an alternative perspective on intra-organizational power and stakeholder relationships. *Organization Studies* 29: 1227–1254.

scholar Roger Lohmann argues that the central economic facts of the nonprofit sector are "episodes of communicative interaction" because services are primarily "social acts and not physical objects."[30] If this is the case then we should also pursue communicative explanations of nonprofit organizations and the nonprofit sector to complement economic theories and explanations. For example, in his study of homelessness in Denver, Colorado, emeritus communication professor Philip Tompkins argues that homelessness is not only an economic problem, but also a communicative problem stemming from a breakdown of communication networks that supply social capital.[31] He reconceptualizes homelessness and poverty from a communication perspective in order to explain homeless service providers as organizational links that restore breakdowns in social capital. There are even hints in the nonprofit research literature that portray communication as a mode of explanation. Studies by Eikenberry, Ebrahim, Fry, Maier and Myer, and Martinez highlight the importance of language, discourse, and underlying assumptions to understand issues such as marketization, democracy, international development, and civil society governance.[32] The key difference is that these studies do not depict communication only as something to be investigated, but rather move toward understanding communication as a vantage point from which to comprehend a host of nonprofit phenomena. Of course, communication is not always the best way to understand or explain everything. Some situations call for legal, economic, or psychological perspectives, for example. But even here a communication perspective can help complement existing explanations to give us fuller, more insightful understandings by exploring the communicative aspects of the law, the economy, or the human psyche. We are not calling for uniformity or standardization, but rather an overarching framework to orient and define our work and a rationale that enables us to clearly articulate the value of communication to those in other fields. In saying all this, we also recognize the difficulties of interdisciplinary work, and the challenge of synthesizing intellectual positions and learning alternative disciplinary perspectives. Yet the diverse nature of

---

30 Lohmann, R.A. (2001). And lettuce is nonanimal: toward a positive economics of voluntary action. In: *The Nature of the Nonprofit Sector* (ed. J. Steven Ott), 200. Boulder, CO: Westview Press.
31 Tompkins, P.K. (2009). *Who Is My Neighbor? Communicating and Organizing to End Homelessness*. Boulder, CO: Paradigm Publishers.
32 See, for example, Eikenberry, A.M. (2009). Refusing the market: a democratic discourse for voluntary and nonprofit organizations. *Nonprofit and Voluntary Sector Quarterly* 38: 582–596; Ebrahim, A. (2001). NGO behavior and development discourse: cases from Western India. *Voluntas* 12: 79–101; Fry, M.-L. (2011). Discourses of consumer's alcohol resistant identities. *Journal of Nonprofit & Public Sector Marketing* 23: 348–366; Maier, F. and Myer, M. (2011). Managerialism and beyond: discourses of civil society organizations and their governance implications. *Voluntas* 22: 731–756; Martinez, B.R. (2009). Structure, power, and discourses of development in Spanish NGOs. *Nonprofit Management & Leadership* 20: 203–218.

nonprofit research and the complexity of the nonprofit sector itself necessitate such engagement because that is where the greatest insights emerge.

Biologists and geographers use the term *ecotone* to describe the area where two different ecosystems intersect and integrate. It is a place of tension, but it is also the place where more diversity and more new life forms exist than anywhere else on earth. This is the value of interdisciplinary scholarship – an intellectual ecotone where different approaches converge to create fresh and innovative ways of thinking. We believe that communication scholarship can and should play an important role in this ecology to enhance our understanding of the nonprofit sector and we offer this chapter as the intellectual foundation to guide our endeavor in this book. Overall, our hope is that more often people would say things like "Let's think about this *communicatively*" or "What if we take a *communication perceptive* on this issue?" when they are trying to understand, explain, and make decisions about a variety of nonprofit issues – and that people would know what this means and what they could do in response.

Preview of Chapters

In order to realize this hope and accomplish our goals in this book, the remaining chapters explain what it can mean to "think communicatively" about a number of relevant nonprofit issues. But we are not going to run through a list of common nonprofit topics – volunteers, fundraising, boards – and simply add a communication twist. Instead, we will focus on higher-level phenomena that are unique or distinct in the nonprofit sector where the underlying challenges are manifestly communicative. That is, areas of nonprofit work where issues of meaning, interpretation, understanding, and interaction are especially prevalent and significant, and thus areas where thinking communicatively can make a notable difference. In addition to our research and personal nonprofit experiences, we've assembled some of the best thinking and scholarship about organizational communication and applied these insights to develop a unique understanding of the nonprofit, highlighting key areas where this approach is most relevant and applicable. These include leadership-management-governance, marketization, collaboration and organizational partnerships, international work, and the nature and meaning of nonprofit work itself. Each of these chapters provides a communicative explanation or understanding of the subject, with further implications for action and practice when we think communicatively about these issues. So consider this more of a *demonstration* of communicative thinking for the nonprofit, not an encyclopedia of nonprofit issues and topics.

We begin in Chapter 2 with the related topics of leadership, management, and governance (L-M-G). In fact, we think they are so related that we depart from the conventional wisdom that sees L-M-G as discrete concepts with clear boundaries and definitions. Instead, we advocate a more relational approach, where L-M-G are integrated, and the meaning and practices of each are always understood in connection with the associations and interactions that constitute these concepts. Our goal is to demonstrate how a communication perspective on nonprofit L-M-G – what we call *communicative L-M-G* – offers a useful corrective to existing thinking that portrays L-M-G as mental, individual, positional, mechanistic, and situational; thus enhancing our understanding and practice of nonprofit L-M-G.

Next in Chapter 3, we turn to the topic of marketization, or how it is that nonprofits manage the tensions of existing as mission-based organizations that have to function in a market economy. This relates to how nonprofits manage their money, build organizational capacity, ensure financial viability, price their goods and services, and respond to donor preferences. Nonprofits must navigate a complex fiscal and legal landscape that is further complicated with social expectations and public pressures that are often unreasonable and uninformed. To operate, they rely on donations, grants, and revenue from often underpriced or underwritten products and services. Nonprofits must use this revenue to fulfill privately unprofitable, but socially beneficial, community missions. As they spend these funds in pursuit of their missions, they must do it in ways that meet the expectations of those they serve, donors and members of their organizations, and the public at large – who often have divergent or contradictory interests and preferences. There is a fine line that exists between excess and frugality, between overhead and charity, between addressing immediate needs and long-term sustainability. In short, nonprofits must live and operate within a market economy while serving the public good. In response to all this, many nonprofits have pursued strategies to become more "businesslike" as a way to manage the tension of being mission-oriented in a market economy. Accordingly, nonprofit marketization refers to adopting the methods and ideology of the market and applying them to guide policy and management decisions. But what are the consequences of this strategy, and is this even the best way to frame the issue? In this chapter, we explore how a communication perspective can enhance how we think about nonprofit marketization, challenging some of the taken-for-granted assumptions that dominate our conventional wisdom, and offering new insights to inform alternative strategies and policies.

In Chapter 4, we focus on collaboration and organizational partnerships, which are a key aspect of nonprofit work. This includes a variety of organizational arrangements, partnerships, and alliances across sectors that vary in scope and degree of formality, and are born out of necessity and/or opportunity. Collaboration is especially relevant for the communication perspective we are developing in this book because collaborations lack many of the key features of "normal" organizations we take for granted – physical structures, clear lines of authority, contractual relationships, etc. – and thus are better understood as communicative phenomena that exist in and through specific communication practices. Accordingly, we employ the term *collabrocation* to signify and describe the inseparability of collaboration and communication – to *be* a collaboration means to communicate in certain ways, and communicating in certain ways is how we create and sustain collaboration as both a process and structure of organizing. Collaboration also magnifies key issues of authority, identity, agency, and value that we argue are best understood communicatively, which reinforces our broader project in this book of developing a communication perspective on the nonprofit.

Then in Chapter 5, we'll explore the meaningfulness of nonprofit work. Nonprofits operate in resource-scarce environments, they usually cannot incentivize work with market-rate compensation, and they rely on an extensive amount of voluntary labor. Therefore, nonprofits need to encourage participation through mission and purpose – there has to be a greater sense of meaning that motivates nonprofit work. But how does this happen, and how is it that nonprofit work becomes meaningful? In contrast to economic, managerial, and psychological perspectives that dominate our conventional wisdom about the meaning of work, a communication perspective demonstrates that meaning is not "in" nonprofit work as an objective feature of the work itself, nor is it merely a psychological state of personal perception. Instead, we explain how meaningful work is a *discourse*, a way of talking about work that creates deep structures of meaning that shape how we make sense of our experiences. This has important implications for how we talk about nonprofit work, how we frame our interactions with other people, and how we legitimate and compensate work that people are doing across the nonprofit sector. This chapter also explains specific communication practices that constitute meaningful work and examines the ethical implications of constructing various understandings of nonprofit work.

Chapter 6 is our last topical chapter, and shifts our attention to international nonprofit work. Admittedly, a fair amount of nonprofit work is similar across geographic locations: fundraising, volunteer work, civic engagement, and helping vulnerable populations – just to name a few – are prevalent everywhere. But when we look at nonprofit work in other "developing" countries, we also see a number of features that are either unique or magnified in these international contexts. Things like language and terminology, knowledge and knowing, religion, and financial arrangements. Each of these draws our attention to processes of social construction and meaning negotiation, and thus magnifies the significance of communication. The big idea running through all these themes is that each has a substantial impact on how people communicate while simultaneously being shaped and changed through those same communication processes, and each sets the stage for how nonprofit work is organized and practiced in other countries. Therefore, our goal in this chapter is to explore these features and see how a communication perspective can influence how we think about these aspects of international nonprofit work. Of course, the term *international* is relative and depends on one's initial point of reference; and what constitutes an issue (things that are difficult for international workers may not be problematic for locals). So in this chapter we'll talk about nonprofit work outside of the United States being done by people who are not from the countries where the work is taking place. Additionally, we'll concentrate on nonprofit work in so-called developing nations, which we think is what most Westerners have in mind when we consider international nonprofit work, and is the kind of work that many readers of this book are more likely to engage in.

Our concluding chapter brings it all together, looking back at the previous chapters and synthesizing what we learned about organizational communication and the nonprofit. We also push the implications of communicative thinking for the nonprofit and develop further insights into what it means to be nonprofit and do nonprofit work. The result, we hope, is a robust understanding of nonprofit work from a communication perspective to better inform your engagement with the nonprofit. Whether you are a nonprofit manager or practitioner, board member or volunteer, scholar or student, or any number of positions that interact with the nonprofit, the ideas we develop in the ensuing chapters will help improve your efforts and enhance your understanding of nonprofit work.

2

Communicative L-M-G

Leadership, Management, and Governance

Matthew A. Koschmann

Introduction

This chapter focuses on the related topics of nonprofit leadership, management, and governance and how a communication perspective can influence our understanding and practice of this work. I depart from the conventional wisdom that sees leadership, management, and governance as discrete concepts with clear boundaries and definitions. Instead, I advocate a more relational approach, where leadership, management, and governance are integrated, and the meaning and practices of each are always understood in connection with the associations and interactions that constitute these concepts. My goal is to demonstrate how a communication perspective on nonprofit leadership, management, and governance – what I call *communicative L-M-G* – offers a useful corrective to existing thinking that portrays leadership, management, and governance as mental, individual, positional, mechanistic, and situational; and thus enhancing our understanding and practice of nonprofit leadership, management, and governance.

***

If you spend any time talking to people who work for nonprofit organizations, or listen in on nonprofit professionals talking about their work, a few things become very apparent: funding is always a concern; tax and regulatory stuff is complicated; and virtually everything comes down to some issue of leadership, management, or governance. These three terms – leadership, management, and governance – make up the triad of running a nonprofit organization. Almost every administrative task involved in operating a nonprofit organization falls under the purview of one or more of these concepts. When people want to change,

Understanding Nonprofit Work: A Communication Perspective, First Edition.
Matthew A. Koschmann and Matthew L. Sanders.

improve, or otherwise enhance nonprofit organizations they are usually implying some aspect of leadership, management, and/or governance that needs to be addressed (or at least something they would label as a leadership, management, and/or governance issue). When people launch a nonprofit organization, they often begin with some notion of leadership, management, and/or governance needed to get things started. And when nonprofit organizations fail, it is often attributed to some shortcoming of leadership, management, and/or governance.

Yet because of their importance, the concepts of leadership, management, and governance are also often the most problematic. When I talk to nonprofit professionals, many conversations quickly turn to issues of leadership, management, and/or governance – there's something not quite right about one or more of these concepts in their organization (or more accurately, some practice that is labeled or attributed to one of more of these concepts). Accordingly, the overwhelming majority of nonprofit books and seminars and workshops are on issues of leadership, management, and/or governance. We certainly have made some progress, especially in terms of expanding our understanding of what leadership, management, and governance should entail and who can be involved. But despite decades of research, countless hours of training, and millions of pages of insights, we are still no closer to anything resembling consensus on what leadership, management, and governance are, let alone how they should be taught – or even if they can be taught in the first place (though maybe this isn't such a bad thing, especially if it motivates us to find and develop new ways of thinking).

Surely part of this lack of integration is because the challenges of leadership, management, and governance are continually new and changing and different for each nonprofit organization. Fresh insights are always welcome, and there is much value in adapting previous thinking to contemporary developments. So we should expect a certain level of churn as ideas about leadership, management, and governance are repackaged, replicated, and recycled for new audiences, resulting in a landscape of thinking that may seem fragmented and adrift at times. But that's not the problem. My concern is deeper – that the general orientation of most work on leadership, management, and governance is skewed and based on a number of unhelpful assumptions. Not completely wrong or detrimental, but misguided such that we stay on an endless cycle of trying to define a new version of what leadership, management, and/or governance really is, and the corresponding strategies and lists of best practices that should be employed. How we lead, manage, or govern depends on what we think we're doing (or supposed to be doing) when we're engaged in those activities. If leadership, management, and governance continue to be challenging and problematic – which so many headlines, books, and workshops suggest – then perhaps we should rethink our understanding of these concepts in the first place.

My contention is that much of the conventional wisdom about leadership, management, and governance is problematic, and that a communication perspective can offer a useful path forward. Not to resolve all these complications per se, but rather to sidestep some of the issues altogether and reorient us to a different set of questions and concerns that might be more relevant for the actual practices of nonprofit leadership, management, and governance. Rather than continue the never-ending quest to discover and classify the principles, variables, tactics, or models of "effective" leadership, management, and governance (which seems to be the holy grail of so much work in this area, especially for the topic of leadership), why not embrace the inherent interconnectedness of these concepts and get on with the important work of running our nonprofit organizations and helping the people these organizations exist to serve? My goals in this chapter are to help nonprofit professionals do just that, and to help scholars see how they can study and advance this work.

To accomplish all this, I begin by challenging the conventional wisdom that leadership, management, and governance are distinct "things" that can and should be understood separately, and I call into question the idea that we need to reach some sort of overarching consensus on what these things "are" so they can be taught and learned appropriately (though I certainly recognize that we need some level of definitional clarity on what we mean when we discuss leadership, management, and governance). Next, I surface some additional assumptions about so much leadership, management, and governance thinking that I believe are problematic. Along the way, I'll introduce and apply a number of ideas from an extensive – but comparatively less known – research literature on leadership, management, and governance that is rooted in communication, discourse, and social construction – versus psychology and economics. These ideas haven't quite trickled down (or bubbled up?) to more popular outlets, but they help us address the shortcomings that are inherent to the conventional wisdom about leadership, management, and governance. Rather than advocate one particular model or definition, which would be antithetical to our overall approach in this book, my goal is to marshal these intellectual resources in order to articulate a broader communication perspective, and explore the implications of putting these ideas into practice. I want to invite people to "think communicatively" about nonprofit leadership, management, and governance and consider what this might mean for their nonprofit work.

Finally, I'll explore several aspects of the nonprofit sector and nonprofit organizations that are especially relevant and challenging for nonprofit leadership, management, and governance. Things like board relationships, volunteer management, donor relations, mission orientation, and accountability. Not that these are fundamentally different from the leadership, management, and governance challenges of other sectors, but they take on a different feel or character in the context of nonprofit organizing. In the end, I hope to shift your understanding of leadership, management, and governance to a different set of assumptions about organizing and human interaction that have important implications for the nonprofit.

What's the Difference?

From now on, I will frequently use the term L-M-G instead of leadership, management, and/or governance to signal the inherent interconnectivity of these concepts (plus it's a lot easier to type and read!). I am not trying to conflate these terms, as if there aren't any meaningful differences between them and they can be used interchangeably (although when you listen closely to how many people talk about L-M-G and the actual practices people are referring to with those terms, it often *seems* like they are interchangeable). Of course, if they were identical we wouldn't have three different words in the first place, so there are some important differences here. But as we'll see, the differences in L-M-G are more differences of *degree* or *practice*, not necessarily differences of *kind* or *essence*, and the differences are more about the contexts in which these terms are used versus anything intrinsic to the terms themselves. *Leadership* suggests some sort of visionary or direction-setting role, something about being out in front for others to follow (though this is complicated by books and articles about "leading from behind" and "followers as leaders"). *Management* usually implies something about day-to-day administration (though leaders certainly do a lot of managing, and managers are often tasked with responsibilities that sure look a lot like leadership). And *governance* often refers to the board of directors for an organization (though governance is a function, whereas a board is a structure; and boards are often tasked with providing strategic leadership).

By using the term L-M-G I'm signaling the inherent interconnectivity of these concepts, that you can really only comprehend them in relation to each other. Understanding these relations – and the language used to create and sustain them – is key to practicing better nonprofit L-M-G. I'm also suggesting that the conceptual differences among these three terms just doesn't matter in the way they seem to matter in so many of the books and workshops and advice about L-M-G. There is so much overlap among L-M-G practices that things quickly get so convoluted, and trying to parse everything out takes us off track, tempting us to think we're almost there if we just keep trying, that if we just keep refining the concepts we'll finally figure out how best to lead, manage, and govern our nonprofit organizations. But this is merely a conceptual hamster wheel – it never stops and we never really get anywhere.

It would be much more helpful if we dropped the idea that L-M-G are discrete "things" altogether, and that we need to reach some sort of consensus on what they "are" in order to have more effective nonprofit organizations. If you ask 50 different scientists from 50 different countries what plutonium is, for example, you will get pretty much the exact same answer from everyone, every time. Conversely, if you ask 50 different people *from the same organization* what leadership or management are, you're likely to get 50 different answers – and you might get an additional 50 different answers if you asked the same people a year later. The point is that the meaning of these concepts is a moving target because they do not refer to an objective, independent reality we all have in common. Instead, these concepts are used to explain and justify and make sense of our experiences in particular contexts with specific people. (When I talk to various nonprofit professionals about leadership, for example, I'm struck by how often people begin by saying, "To *me*, leadership is ..." Conversely, consider how unusual it would be for a scientist to say, "To *me*, plutonium is ...")

Scholars use various terms to describe this idea, such as "negative ontology," "empty" or "floating" signifiers, "blurred" or "contested" concepts, or even "shell terms." What all these terms suggest is that certain concepts (like L-M-G) really exist at a level of abstraction, waiting to be infused with meaning by specific people in various contexts, rather than functioning as neutral or straightforward descriptions of "things" that exist independently of human interaction. This is especially true for the concept of leadership, which has achieved near mythical status in our society, used to explain or justify any number of events, behaviors, or phenomena (similar to how the terms "freedom," "justice," or "equality" are used).

Of course this does not mean that there aren't any common, shared aspects of these terms that transcend any one person or situation. In many situations we have certain contextual features in common with many of the people we interact with, and our individual social realities often have a lot of overlap – we share common assumptions, values, and beliefs. And we often will use different terms in different situations. Not necessarily because we are referring to different things, but rather because different terms help us accomplish particular outcomes in certain situations. Different terms have varying consequences depending on the context – not because they refer to a different independent reality, but rather because certain terms mean different things to different people (or even the same people) in different situations and are used for different purposes.

Communication scholar Stanley Deetz wrote an insightful essay on these issues called "Words without things," where he explains that rather than merely describing objective reality, language instead makes things into possibilities of experience. As he puts it, concepts like leadership, management, or governance are:

> Essentially ambiguous and without a nature outside of the human encounter and in a specific pre-predicative constitutive activity. The object is constituted – given its specific nature – only in the human encounter. Its very permanence as object comes from already being understood in a specific modality of activity.[1]

1 Deetz, S. (1973). Words without things: toward a social phenomenology of language. *Quarterly Journal of Speech* 59 (1): 40–51.

Now that's a mouthful of academic jargon, but the main point here is that our understanding of L-M-G is created and sustained through our interactions with other people. Not a neutral definition referring to a tangible entity; not even a personal mental concept that we "apply" to a situation. Instead, following the philosopher Hans-Georg Gadamer, we can say that words belong to situations or contexts, not to people.[2] Similarly, we can appropriate J.L. Austin's famous illustration to say that the question "What is leadership?" is significantly different from the question "What is the meaning of the term leadership?" The second question is completely disconnected from the experiential reality of ongoing communication, separating the word from what it supposedly represents; whereas the first question reveals language as primary for our experiences.[3] Language as experienced, language as non-object, in the words of Deetz: "Language experience can be explained only by exemplification and not by systematic delineation."[4]

Accordingly, I'm arguing that we should get out of the business of trying to figure out what L-M-G "are" and what the differences between them "are" so we can then figure out what to "do." Instead, I'm suggesting we focus on what we already do and what we want to accomplish – what we experience – and explore how our language and interactions can help us do that better. That's what a communication perspective is all about. Most nonprofit professionals are focused on what should be done in a particular situation – what actions should be taken, what decisions should be made – and framing or explaining something as leadership, management, and/or governance can make all the difference. L-M-G is not an algorithm to be perfected, but rather a discursive or rhetorical resource we draw upon to accomplish particular social goals and justify certain activities in various situations.

So how do we make this shift away from much of the conventional wisdom about L-M-G and move more toward a communication perspective? That starts by questioning some of the underlying assumptions about L-M-G we often take for granted.

Questioning Underlying Assumptions

In addition to the primary (and faulty) assumptions that L-M-G are discrete "things," and that to do them well we need to first define and classify them better, there are additional assumptions that further underwrite much of the current

---

2 Gadamer, H.-G. (1960/2004). *Truth and Method* (trans. J. Weinsheimer and D. G. Marshall). Continuum.

3 See Austin, J.L. (1961). *"The Meaning of a Word," Philosophical Papers*, (ed. J.O. Urmson and C. J. Warnock) Oxford: Clarendon Press.

4 Deetz, "Words without things," p. 42.

teaching and practice of L-M-G we should reexamine. In general, these interrelated assumptions portray L-M-G as work that is mental, individual, positional, mechanistic, and situational. And although these assumptions are not completely false – something must be working at some level or we wouldn't have made any progress – they also are not always helpful (and may even be detrimental) as we think about the challenges and complexities facing the nonprofit here in the twenty-first century. My goal in this section is to surface these additional assumptions about L-M-G and expose their key shortcomings, setting the stage for alternative ideas to ground our understanding of L-M-G for the nonprofit.

Assumption #1: L-M-G Is Primarily Cognitive

First, a common assumption is that L-M-G is primarily *mental* work – planning, organizing, coordinating, controlling – and that L-M-G is best understood *cognitively*. Communication is still seen as important, but only as the input and outcome of the "real" work of L-M-G: thinking and figuring stuff out. In her book on leadership, communication scholar Gail Fairhurst goes to great lengths to demonstrate this fundamental *psychological orientation* of most research and writing on leadership (and by extension, management, and governance). She quotes management scholars Carroll and Gillen (1987) in the prestigious journal *Academy of Management Review* as validating this point: "Managerial work is really mental work and the observable behaviors such as talking to others, reading, and writing serve as inputs and outputs to neurophysiological activities".[5] Notice how this approach privileges cognitive activity as primary and downplays social processes as derivative or complementary. But it begs questions about the initial grounding of that mental activity, as if our thinking involves us standing independently from the social world and merely assessing and describing our experiences, rather than being embedded and enmeshed in the social world. But why do we think what we think in the first place? And what motivates us to think about some things and not others?

It is a mistake to assume that people make rational, self-interested calculations about their circumstances – or the circumstances of their nonprofit organizations – using all the relevant and available information (in fact, since the 1970s, three Nobel prizes have been awarded for proving this very point). And although few people would articulate such a strong rationalist position today, much of the conventional wisdom about L-M-G still privileges mental work in ways that certainly lean in this direction. I'm not trying to establish an either–or

---

5 Carroll, S.J., and Gillen, D.I. (1987). Are the classical management functions useful in describing managerial work?. *Academy of Management Review* 12 (1): 38–51 as quoted in Fairhurst, G.T. (2007). *Discursive Leadership: In Conversation with Leadership Psychology*. Thousand Oaks, CA: Sage.

dichotomy between mental and social processes here. Of course L-M-G involves thinking and cognitive activity – to deny that would simply be absurd. Instead, like so many other scholars and L-M-G experts as we'll see below, I'm trying to create or restore more of a balance between mental work and social processes, recognizing that our thinking takes place in an already-given, already-existing social landscape that we are "thrown" into (using the language of philosopher Martin Heidegger and other phenomenologists), and most of our mental work is figuring out how to adapt, adjust, and otherwise cope in response to this complex social world. Without this balance, most of the research, training, and advice about L-M-G communication is reduced simply to what people in leadership, management, or governance positions say, or what messages they craft and transmit to others. Important stuff, to be sure, but this misses the key point that the overall practice of L-M-G is fundamentally communicative.

For example, when the executive director of a nonprofit is working to develop a new strategic plan for the organization, this is not primarily a cognitive task divorced from communication, where the "real" work of leadership is (mentally) figuring out the plan and where communication only enters the picture when the plan is done and needs to be articulated to other stakeholders. No, strategic planning is inherently communicative, constituted through ongoing cycles of talk and text until various interpretations converge on a final understanding of a plan and its relation to the organization.[6] And thus executive or managerial communication about the strategic plan is not simply the transmission of pre-existing mental states (something for the communication professionals to do after the real L-M-G work is done), but rather is a key part of the plan itself, further shaping what the plan is and how it sustains (or loses) authority over time. The key point here is that privileging mental work over social processes causes us to miss a lot of important stuff that could help enhance our understanding and practice of nonprofit L-M-G.

Assumption #2: L-M-G Is Individualistic

Stemming from this psychological orientation comes a second conventional assumption about L-M-G as largely *individual* work. If we assume that the real work of L-M-G is primarily mental, then it would make sense for that work to be carried out individually by separate people. Thus in much of the popular L-M-G literature we see a strong focus on individual agency and the capacity of individual leaders or managers to act. Scholars often refer to this as "heroic leadership" because it portrays individuals as solely responsible for the positive or negative

6 Spee, A.P., and Jarzabkowski, P. (2011). Strategic planning as communicative process. *Organization Studies* 32 (9): 1217–1245.

outcomes in their organizations. Even if the authors wouldn't claim this is their intention, it certainly is implied by the way stories are told and the images used on book covers, as if Jack Welch was solely responsible for turning G.E. around, for example, or Abraham Lincoln was solely responsible for winning the Civil War. I don't think anyone really believes this, but it's a much easier story to tell than accounting for all the people and complexities involved in a given situation, and it certainly sells more books ("Lincoln on Leadership" rolls off the tongue much easier than any title conveying the complicated history of the Civil War, the complex relationships surrounding Abraham Lincoln, and the social processes we would recognize and attribute as leadership in that particular context).

The truth is, we long for simplicity and straightforward ways to makes sense of complexity, especially in the complicated organizational landscape of the nonprofit, and naming an individual hero (or scapegoat) certainly helps us do this. But it also overlooks the nuance and gradation involved in any situation, and often causes us to miss the full range of factors actually involved in organizational success or failure. If we assume that L-M-G is largely individual work, we will overemphasize personal agency over institutional forces, and underestimate key factors that shape L-M-G. This does not mean we should ignore or excuse individual behavior and simply blame "the system," but it does mean we should recognize how individual agency is both empowered and inhibited by larger systemic influences, that L-M-G is always practiced within a particular social context that has real power to enable or constrain. When we see the public scandals that unfortunately embroil nonprofit organizations it is a mistake to think it's just a problem of bad apples that can be fixed if we simply remove or replace a few individuals. Conversely, we make the same mistake in thinking that organizational success will come if we just hire the right individual but ignore larger systemic or institutional forces that can limit even the most talented leaders, managers, or board members. A communication perspective certainly recognizes the importance of individual behavior, but places equal (sometimes more) emphasis on broader social and interactional contexts that shape individual behavior.

Furthermore, as we look beyond individualism we can also question exactly who or what is exercising agency in any particular situation. Clearly, human intentionality is a key factor in the practice of L-M-G. But when we look more closely, we see that any instance of nonprofit L-M-G involves a complicated web of both people and material artifacts, from signs and memos to clothing and technology. These artifacts aren't just *matter* in a physical sense, they also *matter* in a social sense – they participate in the accomplishment of organizational action.[7] For example, when you observe any situation where individuals are assumed to be

---

7 See Koschmann, M.A. and McDonald, J. (2015). Organizational rituals, communication, and the question of agency. *Management Communication Quarterly* 29 (2): 229–256.

demonstrating L-M-G (such as a board meeting, a weekly staff meeting, a fund-raising event, or some sort of advocacy or lobbying presentation), you quickly notice how several non-human objects are integral to the practice and accomplishment of effective L-M-G. From PowerPoint slides and functional audiovisual equipment to appropriate clothing and documents, nonprofit L-M-G depends on a variety of non-human agents to be successful (and we see just how dependent when these things break down and success is limited). As communication scholars Gail Fairhurst and Stacey Connaughton poignantly observe in their research about leadership, leaders without clothes, friends, money, or technology usually aren't very effective. All the various competencies that conventional wisdom attributes to leaders or managers or board members have to be *materialized* in some way to be realized and recognized, and we should appreciate how this materiality is vital to effective L-M-G.[8]

We also see this in the way people ascribe agency to non-human objects in their everyday conversations. How often have you heard people say things like, "The bylaws won't let us do that ..." or "The memorandum of understanding enabled us to accomplish ..." or "The regulation told us ..." or "The layout of the room prevented us from ..." More than just mere personifications, these instances tell us something about the complicated networks of both human and non-human artifacts that participate in the accomplishment of organizational action.

This is a key contribution of a communication perspective: elevating the role of materiality to understand the fullness of human interaction.[9] A communication perspective decenters the role of individual people in favor of a hybrid approach that recognizes the networks of both human and non-human actors (or "actants" as scholars like to say) that make a difference in any particular situation. The material objects themselves are actually doing something; they are more than just carriers of human intentionality. As communication scholar François Cooren has explained in a number of publications, people certainly "use" objects like signs and memos to accomplish their work, but equally important is how these objects facilitate their own appropriation (i.e. how they also "use" us).[10] Once it is signed,

---

8 Fairhurst, G.T. and Connaughton, S.L. (2014). Leadership: a communicative perspective. *Leadership* 10 (1): 7–35.

9 See Ashcraft, K.L., Kuhn, T.R. and Cooren, F. (2009). Constitutional amendments: "materializing" organizational communication. *Academy of Management Annals* 3 (1): 1–64 for an extensive discussion about materiality and communicative constitution, especially in regards to objects, bodies, and sites.

10 Cooren, F. (2004). Textual agency: how texts do things in organizational settings. *Organization* 11 (3): 373–393; Cooren, F. (2006). The organizational world as a plenum of agencies. In: *Communication as Organizing: Empirical and Theoretical Explorations in the Dynamic of Text and Conversation* (ed. F. Cooren, J. R. Taylor, and E. J. Van Every), 81–100. Lawrence Erlbaum: Mahwah, NJ.

a memorandum of understanding (MOU), for example, compels people toward certain behaviors, it actually *does* something. Certainly MOUs never act alone (people have to mobilize them). But neither can nonprofit members act without the MOU. If human agency is *always* constrained by a number of material factors, then we need to incorporate those factors into any understanding of L-M-G (rather than just focusing on the attributes of human actors). Therefore nonprofit L-M-G is best understood as a configuration of human and non-human representatives who together exercise agency in various situations.

Assumption #3: L-M-G Is Positional

Building off the mental and individualistic orientations discussed already, a third conventional assumption is that L-M-G is *positional*. By this I mean that L-M-G is exercised in and from a particular location in an organizational hierarchy or structure, and this location is often assumed to be a person or specific collections of people. Again, this is what we would expect if we assume that L-M-G is largely mental and individual: we would look for L-M-G in people who are in certain positions. Of course at some level this certainly is true – organizational charts do exist and play a helpful role in understanding how nonprofits are structured, and certain roles are given the power to exercise authority throughout the organization. And it is understandable that our thinking would gravitate toward the positionality of L-M-G. After all, if L-M-G is so important – for the nonprofit and beyond – it would make sense that we would want to know "where" it is. But it would be a mistake to conflate the *positionality* of L-M-G with the *practice* of L-M-G, which is what we really want to understand. We don't want to confuse the map for the territory.

So where exactly is nonprofit L-M-G? Conventional wisdom generally states that leadership is in certain people, management is in hierarchical roles, and governance is in the board of directors. And certainly if we look in these places we're likely to find something that resembles nonprofit L-M-G. But we're also just as likely to see some things that complicate our conventional wisdom, like leaders who don't actually lead, managers who aren't managing, and boards that don't seem to govern. Plus, we'll also miss key instances of L-M-G because nonprofit L-M-G doesn't always happen in these specific locations. Leadership is elusive and seems to show up in a lot of places, management is rarely limited to certain hierarchical positions, and governance is a broader function that often goes beyond just the board of directors. So if we want to understand and practice nonprofit L-M-G better we have to challenge the assumption that L-M-G is positional, at least in the conventional sense.

Instead, a communication perspective challenges us to consider a more complicated (but also more helpful) understanding of where L-M-G may be found. Not that we would eschew the idea of positionality altogether (L-M-G still has to exist or materialize somewhere), but rather we should think differently about the idea of "location" for social phenomena like L-M-G. As we move away from the mental and individualistic underpinnings of most L-M-G thinking, we see that what we recognize as nonprofit L-M-G is much more of a performance or enactment that exists in the spaces *between* people, involving a continuous flow of human interaction that is difficult to pin down. The point is that nonprofit L-M-G is not in consciousness or an objective organizational position, but it is to be found in both momentary and ongoing communication practices among relevant people who constitute L-M-G through their interactions in certain contexts and recognized as such.

Think of it like trying to locate a river out in nature. Yes, we can point to certain physical manifestations of the river, but often what we identify are actually the banks or other features of the river, not the river itself. The actual flow of water is much more difficult to locate, because it's always moving and integrating with its surroundings, though also always with particular boundaries. That's why you can never technically step in the same river twice, as the saying goes. And this isn't a new idea; it's actually the way some of the ancient Greeks understood various social phenomena. Heraclitus was a pre-Socratic philosopher who first used this river analogy (as far as we know) to develop his understanding of being and ontology, claiming that things are always in flux and should be understood as continuous flows, not static objects.[11] This is also the case for nonprofit L-M-G. But it doesn't mean L-M-G is some abstract concept we can never grasp. After all, we can still identify, navigate, and harness the power of rivers, despite their uncertain natures, and we can do the same for nonprofit L-M-G.

Management professor Keith Grint offers some of the most insightful thinking on this topic to help us make sense of locating L-M-G if we are to look beyond specific people or hierarchical roles. He develops a framework showing that we can understand L-M-G as a nexus of people (who), results (what), positions (where), and processes (how).[12] L-M-G certainly involves people, and those people always have some sort of organizational position (even if not formally recognized in a chart). But this is never enough to fully comprehend L-M-G; we also have to appreciate how L-M-G is always understood in relation to organizational outcomes (however formal or informal those may be), and that L-M-G is always processual and unfolding over time (and thus always involves some sort of temporal bracketing for when things begin and end). L-M-G is never located in just one

11 See Stern, D.G. (1991). Heraclitus and Wittgenstein's river images: stepping twice into the same river. *The Monist* 74 (4): 579–604.
12 Grint, K. (2005). *Leadership: Limits and Possibilities*. Macmillan International Higher Education.

of these places, but always at their *intersections*. If it's just a person or only a process, it's probably not L-M-G (though it may still be quite important). Instead, L-M-G always involves certain people pursuing specific results from definite positions through particular process. Thus nonprofit L-M-G is best understood as a *social accomplishment* that emerges at the nexus of people, results, positions, and processes, and cannot be reduced to any one component. And if something changes or becomes absent in the arrangement of people, results, positions, and process, then L-M-G changes or perhaps disappears – it's no longer "there" (like a board of directors that exists on paper and may even have people in various roles, but no longer provideds any actual leadership or governance). Conceptually, this is a little more difficult to pin down; it pushes us to forego our mechanistic approach to the social world that longs for the blueprint of the machinery of L-M-G so we can isolate and fix the component parts. But this is a much more accurate depiction of where L-M-G is located. And if we have a better sense of where nonprofit L-M-G is, we're in a better position to practice and improve nonprofit L-M-G in a variety of situations and organizational contexts.

Assumption #4: L-M-G Is Mechanistic

A key aspect of all our thinking about L-M-G involves our assumptions about organizations – what organizations are and how they work. After all, most aspects of L-M-G happen within some sort of organizational context, and this certainly is the case for nonprofit L-M-G. And the most common assumption about organizations – both explicitly and implicitly – is that organizations are some kind of *machine*. Think of how many times you've heard someone refer to an organization as a "well-oiled machine" or critically referred to some organizational members as "cogs in the machine." Or even how so many organizational change initiatives are called "reengineering." These all imply a mechanistic approach to organizations and organizing. The idea here is that organizations are like a big engine with lots of interlocking components, each doing their separate part so that together they accomplish some form of productivity or output. And it's easy to see how we would absorb this assumption, especially with the visual representations of organizational charts that resemble the owner's manual for our cars or electronic devices. Mechanistic thinking arose out of the industrial revolution, when large factories (really the first "organizations" in the modern sense) seemed to resemble the very machinery they utilized to manufacture various products. Workers were seen as interchangeable parts with individualized functions that could be made more efficient through "scientific" analysis, and thus the birth of *scientific management* and modern management theory (I say "scientific" in quotes because history has shown that the whole enterprise really wasn't very scientific, at least in terms of replication, falsifiability, generalizability, and prediction, despite the prevalence of time-motion studies and countless investigations of worker productivity).[13]

The idea here was that the emerging field of management needed to be "scientific" to gain credibility, and what better way to do this than by connecting management to the best science of the day, especially the field of physics, which at the dawn of the twentieth century was revolutionizing how we understood the physical world. Were not organizations and their workers another physical system that followed Newton's laws of motion, inertia, and linear causality? If so, then it makes perfect sense to study organizations (and by extension L-M-G) through the science of machines, classical/Newtonian physics. And that's exactly what we've seen throughout the twentieth century and the study of organizations in our industrial economy. And even now in the twenty-first century with our focus on "knowledge work" and a "post-industrial economy," scientific management and mechanistic thinking still cast a long shadow across many aspects of professional work and how we understand organizational life. Organizational scholar and consultant Margaret Wheatley puts it clearly:

> Each of us lives and works in organizations designed from Newtonian images of the universe. We manage by separating things into parts, we believe that influence occurs as a direct result of force exerted from one person to another, we engage in complex planning for a world that we keep expecting to be predictable, and we search continually for better methods of objectively measuring and perceiving the world. These assumptions come to us from seventeenth-century physics, from Newtonian mechanics. They are the basis from which we design and manage organizations, and from which we do research in all of the social sciences.[14]

If we believe that organizations are machines governed by the laws of Newtonian physics, then we will assume a mechanistic paradigm and look to these laws to understand and improve our organizations, especially in terms of how we lead, manage, and govern. Again, Margaret Wheatley:

> This machine imagery leads to the belief that studying the parts is the key to understanding the whole. Things are taken apart, dissected literally or figuratively (as we have done with business functions), and then put back together without any significant loss. The assumption is that the more we know about the workings of each piece, the more we will learn about the whole.[15]

---

13 Stewart, M. (2009). The Management Myth: Why the Experts Keep Getting it Wrong. New York: Norton. The Trouble with Scientific ManagementBy: Livia Gershon September 9, 2015. Retrieved from https://daily.jstor.org/trouble-scientific-management/ on March 18, 202.
14 Wheatley, M.J. (2006). *Leadership and the New Science: Learning About Organization from an Orderly Universe*, 7–8. Berrett-Koehler.
15 Wheatley, *Leadership and the new science*. p. 10.

And isn't this what we see with so much L-M-G training, practice, advice, and consultation? Break things down, get to the bottom of it, isolate the key issues, etc. Understand the organization by understanding the component parts. Map, chart, or diagram the system. Indeed, this has led to some tremendous insights and advancements for organizations across many sectors of our society (especially in terms of the *physical* aspects of those organizations), and mechanistic thinking wouldn't be so entrenched if it didn't have some benefits (at least for certain people who benefit from mechanistic conceptions ... follow the money). Furthermore, the main implication of mechanistic thinking for L-M-G is an emphasis on *control*. Newtonian science provides the physical laws that enable us to control our machines. Consequently, if organizations are machines then most of our L-M-G efforts should be aimed at controlling the component parts of the machine.

But what if organizations *aren't* machines, and Newtonian physics *isn't* the best science to understand organizations? In fact, that's the growing consensus of scholars in many different fields, and it should shape our understanding of nonprofit L-M-G as well. For too long we've shoehorned human systems (i.e. organizations) into the sterile, mechanistic world of physical systems and Newtonian science, forcing people to conform to the constraints of classical physics instead of adapting our paradigms to the realities of living systems. Thankfully, insights from an alternative scientific paradigm – *quantum physics* – is radically changing how we comprehend they physical world and has significant consequences for our understanding of organizations and L-M-G.

Newton was a genius. His discoveries changed the world and the laws of Newtonian physics underwrite so many important aspects of our modern society. But the subatomic world was nonexistent to him and did not factor into his theories. All this changed in the early twentieth century when physicists looked into their microscopes and discovered the strange activity of electrons, photons, neutrons – the quantum world. At the quantum level (smaller than the atom) things didn't behave as expected, they didn't follow the laws of Newtonian physics. Objects in motion *didn't* stay in motion unless acted upon by an outside force; motion and acceleration *weren't* directly related to force and mass; and for every action there *wasn't* an equal opposite reaction. Light behaves as both a particle and a wave. Subatomic particles can exist in different states simultaneously (quantum superposition). What things "are" at any time depends on how we observe them. The position, trajectory, and momentum of quantum objects is fundamentally uncertain. Simply put, the laws of Newtonian physics did not apply neatly (or even at all) to the quantum world.

The rise of quantum physics is well-documented elsewhere, and is much more complicated and extensive then we can pursue here. And a substantial amount of academic and popular literature has appropriated the insights of quantum physics for the social sciences. For our purposes, the main takeaways are that the science of scientific management has changed, and quantum physics is proving to be a better scientific paradigm for understanding organizations and other social systems – the world of organizations is much more like the quantum world than the world of classical physics. People have multiple (even conflicting) motivations and "positions;" cause–effect relationships tend to be nonlinear and exponential (small causes can have disproportionate effects); what we "see" in organizations depends on how we observe; key outcomes tend to be emergent, system-level properties that cannot be reduced to component parts; and everything is characterized by pervasive interdependencies. All this relates to communication because everything is about the *interactions* and *relationships* within a system, not the individual agents themselves (i.e. the component parts).

Classical physics tells us that "things" exist and then relationships are formed, like the distance (relationship) between a rocket and its target (things). But quantum physics shows the reverse. "Things" emerge from relationships and come into temporary existence through associations. Electrons and protons don't exist in isolation; their existence as negatively and positively charged particles only make sense in relation to each other, and within the broader context of an atom. In the quantum world, relationships, not things, are primary. And doesn't this sound more like the world of organizations and L-M-G that you and I experience? A volunteer, for example, doesn't just exist, isn't just a thing. Volunteers only exist in relation to certain kinds of institutions involved in specific kinds of work. What we understand as "volunteering" is best understood as a relationship, not a thing. And thus to improve our volunteer recruitment, productivity, satisfaction, or any other aspect of volunteering we should focus on the relationships (i.e. communication) that constitute the concept of volunteering. Organizations are not machines, understood by isolating the component parts and then charting the relationships between things. Instead, organizations are temporary manifestations of ongoing processes, a snapshot of extensive human activity made visible in temporary structures. What we call "the organization" is a particular way of making sense of (some) aspects of human activity at a specific moment in time and for a specific purpose – not an objective reality that exists "out there" independent of our observations and classifications (despite any physical or material manifestations). And if we want to lead, manage, and govern more effectively this has to be our underlying assumption.

Margaret Wheatley is right when she says we have confused order with control, assuming that organizations are machines and the order we rightfully seek is accomplished through ridged structures of control. "If people are machines," she writes, then "seeking to control us makes sense."[16] But if we live with the same

16 Wheatley, *Leadership and the new science*.

forces intrinsic to all other living systems, then seeking to impose order through control is detrimental – we will eliminate the very life needed for survival and growth. Instead, we need to align our thinking about the social world (i.e. organizations and L-M-G) with a better understanding of the realities of the physical world, or in the words of physicist Karen Barad, we have to meet the universe halfway.[17]

Practically speaking, what does this look like? Overall, it means L-M-G practices that focus more on shaping patterns of interaction that foster emergent properties, instead of imposing order through rigid control systems. It means embracing diversity as a source of insight and value, rather than pursuing conformity and predictability. It means developing boundary conditions and decision rules that foster adaptation, rather than systems that are unresponsive to outside environments. And it means elevating communication as central to all aspects of L-M-G because nonprofits only exists as temporary manifestations of the interactions and relationships of people that constitute the organization. We should still practice "scientific" L-M-G, but our practices should be aligned with the best science of our day. Not the mechanistic world of Newtonian physics, but the quantum world of relationships, nonlinearity, adaptation, observer dependency, emergent properties, and the significance of agent interactions – this is a better foundation for understanding and practicing nonprofit L-M-G.

Assumption #5: L-M-G Is Situational

Finally, much of our conventional wisdom about L-M-G is that it is situational or contingent – what we do depends on the context or situation. At first this may seem more in line with the communicative approach toward L-M-G that I'm advocating, and to some extent it is. But there is a key distinction we need to be aware of. As L-M-G research and writing has developed over the years, much of that work has settled on the idea that effective L-M-G should be understood situationally. That is, what counts as "effective" L-M-G is dependent or conditional on the particular circumstances involved in a given context. Thus "contingency theories" tend to dominate the L-M-G research literature (along with charismatic approaches to leadership). This is all well and good, and marks an important advancement beyond traits and styles approaches that characterized early L-M-G thinking. However, we need to examine what exactly is meant by "the situation" in these contingency approaches to L-M-G.

Are situations objective, independent features of our social world that simply exist "out there" for us to define, analyze, and respond to? If you survey most of the popular L-M-G literature these days the answer would likely be a resounding "yes."

---

17 Barad, K. (2007). *Meeting the Universe Halfway: Quantum Physics and the Entanglement of Matter and Meaning*. Duke University Press.

Not that all authors and consultants put it this explicitly, but it sure is the clear implication of much L-M-G teaching and training. We are taught to read the context, get a sense of the environment, study the landscape, and respond with an acute understanding of the situation. And certainly this is good advice, especially as it moves us past any notion of a one-size-fits-all approach to nonprofit L-M-G. But it also reveals a key shortcoming: ignoring or underestimating how we play an active role in creating or constructing the situation in the first place, and what we usually mean by "the situation" is really our interpretation or understanding of particular events and phenomena, which are often different for different people. It is not the case that we all agree on what the situation is, and we just have different perspectives on how to respond. No, we often disagree on the nature of the situation in the first place, and our preferred responses are usually arguments for how we think the situation should be understood. Therefore "situational" L-M-G is not about taking situations as given and developing appropriate responses, but rather playing an active role in constructing the situation in the first place in order to justify certain responses and facilitate the ways in which various people make sense of what is happening.

For example, consider the ongoing debate about how much money nonprofit organizations allocate to "overhead" or "administration" versus the amount they spend directly on "relief" or "clients" or "those in need," in the language that often shows up in both fundraising materials and critical reports. As I write this chapter, the American Red Cross is in the news again for the way it distributed funds, this time for its response to Hurricane Harvey in the Gulf Coast area of Texas back in 2017. The concern is that not enough money went "directly to relief efforts" and too much was spent on "internal expenses." A reporter from National Public Radio pressed a Red Cross executive to explain why "such a substantial percentage of donations [was] going to internal administrative costs, rather than to relief."[18] The Red Cross executive clumsily explained that he really didn't know exactly what portion of revenue streams is for relief versus administrative expenses, giving the story a clear angle that the Red Cross mismanaged funds (again). And surely we can think of many other examples where nonprofit L-M-G has had to react to the "situation" of financial mismanagement in response to inquiries about allocation of donor funds.

What should L-M-G responses entail? Well, that probably depends on what the situation is. But what exactly *is* the situation here? Financial mismanagement? Ignorant press? Misconceptions about nonprofit operations and revenue allocations? A combination of several things? Something else? It would be a mistake to accept

18 Gonzales, R. (2017). Red Cross Exec Doesn't Know What Portion Of Donations Go To Harvey Relief, The Two-Way, August 30. Retrieved from https://www.npr.org/sections/thetwo-way/2017/08/30/547435136/red-cross-exec-doesn-t-know-what-portion-of-donations-will-go-directly-to-harvey.

certain features of this event as given or objective, rather than a complicated mix of alternative perspectives and imposed interpretations. After all, things like "relief" and "overhead" are not components on the nonprofit periodic table of elements, as if they have clear, defining properties that make them distinct concepts. No, there are fuzzy boundaries that make it difficult to distinguish them in practice, and what counts for each depends more on the rhetorical force of those explaining the differences, rather than anything inherent to any particular item on an accounting ledger. And even various charity watchers that indicate the "right" amount of money that should be allocated to "services" versus "overhead" are doing so based on a general social or professional consensus that seems correct based on a number of factors that are valued over others, not anything that is "natural" or purely objective.

When we look at effective L-M-G, it's not that people are simply responding appropriately to "the situation," but rather they are also actively constructing the situation itself in ways that justify and validate their chosen responses, and the responses themselves in turn further define the situation. Again, management scholar Keith Grint (2005) offers an insightful take on this issue:

> I am not suggesting that the correct decision-making process lies in the correct analysis of the situation, but that decision-makers tend to legitimize their actions on the basis of a persuasive account of the situation. In short, the social construction of the problem legitimizes the deployment of a particular form of authority.[19]

He concludes that effective L-M-G is not *situational*, but *situated*. This moves us away from essentialist notions of context, where the social landscape is taken as given and unproblematic, in favor of an approach that sees "the situation" of L-M-G as fundamentally communicative (i.e. created, sustained, and altered in processes of human interaction). Of course this does not mean that things don't actually happen, that there's no shared reality, and everything is simply a matter of interpretation. No, things happen that have real material consequences for real people, no matter what our perceptions or interpretations. But what those things *mean* and how we justify various responses as effective or inappropriate are all about perspective and sense-making and cannot be judged by purely objective criteria.

***

To summarize, we have seen that most of our conventional wisdom portrays L-M-G as work that is mental, individual, positional, mechanistic, and situational. This should be expected: if you think L-M-G is a thing (or discrete things) that

---

19 Grint, K. (2005). Problems, problems, problems: the social construction of 'leadership'. *Human Relations* 58 (11): 1467–1494, p. 1475.

exists independently and objectively, it would make sense that most of your efforts would involve definition and classification, figuring out the right cognitive processes involved, pinning it down in its right place, controlling the component parts, and developing best practices in relation to the current situation. And although this isn't completely wrong, it does lock us into a narrower conception that limits our understanding of the full scope of nonprofit L-M-G. Like the guy who only looks for his lost keys under the lamppost because the light is better, we need to venture beyond the convenient illuminations of conventional wisdom if we are to enhance our knowledge and practice of nonprofit L-M-G. But all this does require a shift to an alternative set of assumptions and intellectual resources to guide our thinking.

Thankfully, there is a wealth of conceptual, empirical, and practical resources we can draw upon to develop a communicative understanding of nonprofit L-M-G. You wouldn't know it from searching for leadership, management, or governance on Google or Amazon, but there is a notable (and growing) research literature on L-M-G that is distinctively communicative, discursive, and social constructionist. And a robust academic conversation about "rethinking" L-M-G is taking place among scholars across the world from several different disciplines. This work moves away from any grand theory of L-M-G in favor of a broader approach that conceives L-M-G as a constellation of language games oriented toward organizational power and influence.[20] For simplicity, we can call this *communicative L-M-G*. In relation to the conventional wisdom, communicative L-M-G balances the cognitive aspects of L-M-G with an emphasis on social processes; it challenges an individualistic orientation in favor of a relational approach that expands our understanding of human agency; it reimagines the location of L-M-G as emerging at the nexus of people, results, positions, and processes; it sees organizations as more like ecosystems or even a complex mind instead of a machine; and it assumes we play an active role in socially constructing the situations of L-M-G. Now let's explore how communicative L-M-G can make a difference for a number of issues that are central to the nonprofit.

Communicative L-M-G and the Nonprofit

Even if you're with me so far and can see the value of "thinking communicatively" about nonprofit L-M-G, I bet you're still thinking: "OK, but what exactly would I do differently as a nonprofit director or board member? How does communicative L-M-G change what I actually do in my daily work?" This is the right

20 See Fairhurst, G.T. and Connaughton, S.L. (2014). Leadership: a communicative perspective. *Leadership* 10 (1): 7–35.

response, because if communicative L-M-G can't provide answers to questions like these, then this is nothing more than an intellectual exercise resulting in little more than a new vocabulary with no further substantive contribution. So in this final section I want to address the issue of how communicative L-M-G can make a practical difference in the day-to-day operations and decisions of the nonprofit.

However, I do want to take a slightly different approach than simply concluding with an inventory of best practices or providing a to-do list of 10 things you should say or not say in various situations. Hopefully by now you realize this would be antithetical to everything communicative L-M-G is about. After all, communicative L-M-G involves understanding the unique contextual factors and interaction patterns that constitute our social worlds, so any advice that would be specific enough for you and your organization wouldn't be relevant for many others reading this book, and any advice that is broad enough for the majority of readers would be too generic and probably be stuff most of you already know (e.g. cultivate good relationships with key stakeholders, find ways to appreciate your volunteers, pay attention to regulatory changes that affect your organization, etc.). Instead, I want to explain how the key aspects of practicing communicative L-M-G involves how we *approach* any particular situation, and what we think is *actually happening* when we interact with other people.

Think about the kinds of interactions likely to take place in nonprofit organizations, interactions that seems particularly relevant for leadership, management, or governance. Things like board relationships, volunteer coordination, donor relations, mission, and vision planning, or even being accountable to funders, regulators, or the general public. At a basic level, how would you describe or explain what is happening in these situations? I think for many people the answer would be: "Well, in all of these situations people are sending or exchanging relevant information about their work in accordance with the nature of their relationship." Or something like that. And to some extent this is true (or at least it certainly looks like that is what is going on). When a nonprofit executive director gives a quarterly update at a board meeting, when a nonprofit manager meets with a group of volunteers to explain the work that needs to be accomplished, when a nonprofit development director meets with a potential donor, when a team of nonprofit professionals meets to develop a new mission and vision, or when a nonprofit organization delivers an annual report to a government funding agency, information is certainly being sent and exchanged. But so much more is happening as well.

It is not the case that all these relationships simply just "exist" and then communication takes place as people interact with each other. No, communication is central to the existence of these relationships in the first place – these relationships only exist as the patterns of interactions among people involved. Communication isn't epiphenomenal, it's essential. This means that executives and board members and donors and volunteers and managers are creating and recreating their relationships every time they interact with each other. A communication perspective doesn't take these relationships for granted, treating them as given, but rather sees every interaction as a moment of constitution where relationships are produced and sustained. Of course this doesn't mean we have to micromanage every discussion and stress about the outcome of every conversation – many of our relationships are fairly stable and resilient, and many of our interaction patterns with certain people are fairly consistent. But it does mean that we should approach these relationships differently; not as given realities or fixed boxes in an organizational chart, but as precarious social constructions, always in motion and subject to significant changes depending on how we interact with each other. Therefore *what is actually happening* in all the interaction examples I listed above is the ongoing social construction of nonprofit relations through the continuous flow of interaction, not simply the transmission or exchange of information.

Consequently, the approach that communicative L-M-G suggests is to see how all these relationships and interactions happen in a *realm of probability*. This means that we should approach these situations with an eye toward *increasing the likelihood* of favorable outcomes. Nothing in the social world has a final or permanent identity, but rather exists in states of potential, waiting to be realized through relations that evoke these potentials. And how we interact with people, how we communicate with each other, constitutes these relationships. We can't predict or control favorable outcomes with certainty, but we can act in ways that make their likelihood more probably. We can study the patterns of interaction that foster the emergence of positive consequences, while also cultivating a mindset of continuous learning and adaptation when we fail.

Communicative L-M-G focused on increasing the likelihood of favorable outcomes also means approaching key situations with a series of questions (rather than imposing answers). Rather than a list of best practices, the practical application of communicative L-M-G looks more like a list of best questions, as summarized in Box 2.1. First, consider approaching situations by asking yourself "What do I want to *accomplish*?" not just "What do I want to *say*?" The idea here is to focus more on production, not just expression when communicating with other people. Someone who is thinking communicatively about L-M-G will see their communication as part of a broader process of making social realities, not just a moment for personal expression that is disconnected from other factors. Second, think about the question "What are we *making together*?" Here the emphasis is on seeing L-M-G communication as something we do *with* people, not just *to* people – social construction not just message transmission. Third, ask yourself "How can I facilitate *order* in this situation?" rather than "How can I take *control*." As we saw above, we often confuse control with order, thinking that the stability we seek comes from imposing our authority over other people. But if organizations

Box 2.1 Best *questions* of communicative L-M-G

- What do I want to *accomplish* in this situation? (not just what I want to *say*)
- What are we *making together*?
- How can I *facilitate order* in this situation? (versus take control)
- How can I focus more on *relationships* and less on *things*?
- How can we increase the number of *perspectives* in this situation so that we can be a more *intelligent* organization?
- How could I *frame* things differently in this situation?
- What *question* can I ask as an initial response?

are living systems and not static machines, then order is an emergent property that arises from smaller-scale interactions, not something we can impose from the top down. Good leaders and managers realize they can participate in those interactions even if they cannot control the outcomes. Leaders, managers, and board members have more power than others to shape the boundary conditions, decision rules, and interaction patterns of organizational communication.

Fourth, when trying to make sense of various phenomena, communicative L-M-G entails asking, "How can I focus more on *relationships* and less on *things* here?" Concepts like "organizational culture," "volunteer commitment," "client satisfaction," "regulatory compliance," or "financial accountability," for example, aren't just "things" that exist independently from the social process that created them. Instead, it's better to understand these concepts as a nexus of relations that incorporate multiple interests that change over time and thus are subject to ongoing reconfiguration. Rather than focusing on the abstract concepts themselves as if they were "things" that could be tinkered with, communicative L-M-G means examining the relationships that bring these concepts into being and sustain their existence. Fifth, consider asking, "How can we increase the number of *perspectives* in this situation so that we can be a more *intelligent* organization?" Again, if organizations are living systems and not static machines, then there is no neutral vantage point from which leaders, managers, and board members can stand "outside" the organization and make objective observations and assessments – they are part of the very systems they seek to influence. Therefore we become more intelligent as an organization by increasing the diversity of perspectives that are brought to bear on any situation and by including more people in decision-making processes; we "see" the organization better through increased participation, not distance and detachment. Sixth, communicative L-M-G means asking, "How could I *frame* things differently in this situation?" This question directs our attention toward how language can be used to influence certain interpretations over others. Framing is the communication practice of including or excluding certain ideas in the interpretation process, just like a photographer shapes your interpretation by foregrounding or eliminating certain aspects of the scene from the final picture. And finally, consider the value of responding with questions instead of statements in various situations, asking yourself, "What *question* could I ask as an initial response here?" If L-M-G is something we do *with* people (not *to* them), then we need to find constructive ways to invite others into the L-M-G process, and asking people questions is a great way to foster this sort of inclusion. Asking questions shows interest and builds rapport, which is what we need to create and sustain quality relationships with people we lead, manage, or direct. Responding with clarifying questions can also help diffuse tense situations and gives everyone the space needed to consider other perspectives or clarify their initial positions. But just keep in mind, we're talking about honest inquiry here, not questioning people as a form of accusation of suspicion.

To wrap up here, the practical application of communicative L-M-G means asking ourselves a series of questions in response to various circumstances. Thinking communicatively about L-M-G means understanding that the social realities of the nonprofit exist in a state of potential, and our interactions with other people continually shape the probability of the favorable outcomes we hope to achieve. Responding with best questions helps orient us to this way of thinking. Of course, this communicative approach to L-M-G can't tell you exactly what to do in any given situation, but it can give you a better way to understand what is happening, and increase the likelihood that you'll come up with better responses more often. And that is the whole point – to get out of the mindset that L-M-G is some "thing" that can be harnessed and implemented, or an algorithm that can be perfected and run, but more of a flow we participate in or a current we can ride, while also seeking to shape these forces throughout ongoing interactions. We also recognize that this could be interpreted as just another attempt to redefine L-M-G, and suggest that this way is better – just another contribution to the endless cacophony trying to stand out from the crowd, and ultimately falling into the same trap of so much of the previous work I critiqued. But that would be a mistake. I am challenging the underlying assumptions of most L-M-G work (not any particular theory or model per se): communication as transmission, organizations as machines, and L-M-G is primarily mental, individual, positional, and situational. However you practice nonprofit L-M-G, my invitation is that it would be more aligned with the alternative assumptions about communication, organizations, and human interaction that I articulated here.

3

The Marketization of Nonprofit Work

Matthew L. Sanders

Introduction

The nonprofit sector exits in a challenging space in society. It sits between government and business, acting like each in some ways, but also distinct from both as well. Operating in this contradictory space as private organizations that seek to benefit the common good poses particular challenges for the nonprofit. This chapter focuses on key questions that all nonprofits must wrestle with if they are to adequately secure funding, meet their needs, and gain and keep public support. How do nonprofits balance how they spend money on mission needs as well as overhead and salary? How do they manage their money in a way that meets the need to be financially independent while addressing causes that always require more money than they have? Conventional wisdom for many decades has been that nonprofits need to be more business-like in order to be successful. But this economic explanation raises significant concerns about the marketization of the nonprofit sector and nonprofit work. In this chapter, we will explore how communication plays a central role in managing the challenges that accompany expectations that nonprofits become more business-like. This communicative explanation will demonstrate that managing the financial imperatives of nonprofit work requires an ability to communicate about nonprofit work on its own terms and embrace the contradictions and tensions of competing needs.

***

In the days and weeks after the terrorist attacks of September 11, 2001, the American Red Cross received millions of dollars in donations to its Liberty Fund, which was set up to support victims of that tragedy. The public response was so overwhelming

Understanding Nonprofit Work: A Communication Perspective, First Edition.
Matthew A. Koschmann and Matthew L. Sanders.

and the amount of money raised was so significant, that the Red Cross decided to set aside a significant amount of the donations it had received against the possibility of future attacks or disasters in an increasingly uncertain world.

As word of this decision spread over time, many who had donated were outraged. Their donations, they said, were for the victims of the terrorist attacks, not to support organizational needs or to help with future, unidentified relief efforts. This controversy became so significant that Congress held hearings to investigate the matter and many in the media criticized the Red Cross for not using all donations in direct support of the victims and families of the terrorist attack. In the end, the CEO resigned and the Red Cross ordered external audits of the organization's finances and accounting procedures to both address and ease the public outrage.[1]

Despite the negative publicity and political nature of this controversy, this problem has not gone away for the American Red Cross. Strikingly similar events have followed it after Hurricane Katrina and Hurricane Harvey. These recurring conflicts between the Red Cross and the public highlight an inherent concern that all nonprofit organizations wrestle with: *raising and spending money for pressing, immediate needs while building organizational capacity to prepare for future needs.* The debate over how and when and where donations can be spent highlights important questions that nonprofit organizations often struggle to answer adequately. Who ultimately decides how donations should be spent? What control does a nonprofit have on deciding how to spend money? What kinds of expenses are valid, and what kinds are unethical? How should nonprofits raise funds to both help the immediate mission and prepare for the future?

In 2017, Goodwill of Omaha became the subject of an investigation by local media. Reporters scrutinized public salary information at all levels of the organization, highlighting salaries over $100 000 a year for 13 executives and managers, with the CEO receiving total compensation of over $900 000 in 2014. These high salaries were contrasted with the low wages of other employees and those working in Goodwill's job training programs, which is a central part of its mission. The *Omaha Herald* claimed that out of the millions of dollars made from selling donated goods, "the charity puts more of those dollars into pay for its leaders than it does the job programs that are the basis of its nonprofit mission and tax-exempt status."[2]

1 Henriques, D.B. and Barstow, D. (2011, Nov. 15). A Nation Challenged: The Red Cross; Red Cross Pledges Entire Fund to Sept. 11 Victims. *New York Times*, Section A Page 1; Red Cross Defends Handling of Sept. 11 Donations. *CNN*. Nov. 6 2001, Retrieved on November 12, 2019: http://edition.cnn.com/2001/US/11/06/rec.charity.hearing/index.html.

2 Cordes, H.J. Goodwill of Omaha: No culture of thrift. *Omaha World-Herald*. Retrieved November 12, 19: https://dataomaha.com/bigstory/news/goodwill-omaha-no-culture-of-thrift.

Goodwill's leadership argued that their executive and managerial salaries were warranted because they have to compete in the market for experienced executives who can successfully manage a multimillion-dollar organization and all the complexities that go with it. As evidence that this works, Goodwill pointed to the significant growth and influence of the Omaha chapter under its leadership at the time. Finding and keeping such talented leadership, they claimed, is challenging for any nonprofit organization when individuals with that level of experience can work for for-profit companies at even higher wages.

The Wounded Warrior Project, which is dedicated to helping wounded veterans rebuild their lives, faced similar criticism over wages as well as operating expenses. It came under intense criticism by both the media and former employees for lavish spending on conferences, travel, office space, and marketing. Reports found that in 2014, approximately 40% of donations – or $124 million – were spent on these and other overhead expenses. Former employees said the organization took on a for-profit feel to its use of money and resources. Leaders of the Wounded Warrior Project argued at the time that such spending was the reason that they were able to grow at such a rapid pace in a short period of time, raising hundreds of millions of dollars and helping more than 80 000 veterans. Their goal was to grow like Starbucks. They wanted to treat employees right and offer excellent services and products so they could grow their brand and expand the reach of the organization's mission.[3]

These challenges and criticisms are not unique to Goodwill of Omaha or the Wounded Warrior Project. There is plenty of debate about nonprofit compensation strategies and to what extent donations can be used for operating expenses and marketing. Many nonprofits have felt the public scrutiny of these topics, and the opposition to the practices of Goodwill of Omaha and the Wounded Warrior Project highlight an ongoing challenge in the nonprofit sector: *how to balance paying salaries and benefits, as well as the costs to run the organization, with spending funds to address a social mission*. This reality of nonprofit life raises important questions: To what extent should nonprofits use funds to improve their organization versus support their social mission? Is organizational capacity part of a nonprofit's mission? How much compensation is too much? How much money can be spent on the organization's operating expenses?

The Museum Store Association is a large and successful nonprofit organization that manages the operations and supply chains of thousands of gift shops within museums across the United States. Its size allows it to buy large quantities of merchandise at discounted rates. This expertise and purchasing power helps transform struggling museum gift shops into effective operations with significant earning power. The Museum Store Association represents many of the over 4000 museum

---

3 Phillips, D. (2016, Jan. 28). Helping Veterans Recover, Spending Lavishly on Itself. *New York Times*. Section A, Page 1.

gift shops that generate nearly $5.9 billion dollars in annual revenue and employ over 80 000 people. Some wonder, however, whether nonprofit organizations should be focusing on retail sales and question whether such significant revenue generation that isn't central to the work of a museum should be tax exempt.[4]

Others wonder about whether such retail activity is even appropriate in museums, particularly those that preserve and teach about challenging, difficult, or tragic circumstances. This was the case with the opening of the 9/11 Memorial gift shop. Those who lost family members in that tragedy have complained that selling memorabilia that stems from the circumstances connected to their grief is inappropriate. These locations, they argue, should be free from retail activities that in their mind profit on tragedy and painful memories. Those running the museum argue, however, that these keepsakes are important reminders for those visiting the museum and give them a tangible artifact that connects them to their experience in an historic place.[5]

Concerns about retail revenue generation within nonprofit organizations are not unique to museum gift shops. Any nonprofit that charges money for services or products wrestles with this same issue: *To what extent is it appropriate to engage in commercial activities to generate revenue.* This issue raises important questions about the nonprofit sector: To what extent can or should nonprofits make money from a cause? Is it ethical to make money in a nonprofit? Should that income be taxed? What should goods and services cost when delivered by a nonprofit?

All of these issues and controversies say something unique about the nonprofit. Private organizations that have such public accountability for their practices have to operate in a different environment than organizations in other sectors. If nonprofits can't get this right, there are significant consequences in public perception and financial support. So doing this well matters a great deal for a nonprofit organization's success. But how do nonprofits manage their financial landscape carefully and ethically so they don't wind up with these problems? There is an obvious expectation for public accountability because of tax exempt status. Good leadership requires watching the bottom line, paying people fairly (and even competitively), and finding a diverse set of revenue sources. Nonprofits need to be open today and tomorrow, and staying open takes money. But this is an ongoing problem that we can't adequately solve with the conventional wisdom and practice

---

4 Schneider, K. (2006, March 29). The Bottom Line: Adding Profits to the Gift Shop. *New York Times*. p. G00031. https://www.nytimes.com/2006/03/29/arts/artsspecial/adding-profits-to-the-gift-shop.html.

5 McCambridge, R. (2014, May 20). Little shop of horror? 9/11 museum's gift shop offends some. *Nonprofit Quarterly*. https://nonprofitquarterly.org/little-shop-of-horror-9-11-museum-s-gift-shop-offends-some.

of nonprofit management. Nonprofits tend to either stay overly frugal or spend too much on the organization itself. These examples point to a key underlying issue for the nonprofit: marketization. *Nonprofit marketization* refers to the effect of business logic and practices on nonprofit missions. The first step to addressing this challenge is to clearly understand the problem of nonprofit marketization in terms of its economic framing and the role a communication perspective plays in understanding it better.

Nonprofit Marketization

The stories described above illustrate a core problem that nonprofits have always faced that makes their work uniquely challenging in society. To operate, they rely on donations and grants, as well as revenue from often underpriced or underwritten products and services. As a result, nonprofits operate in a world where they can't maximize their revenues and must do a lot with less. This revenue is then used to fulfill privately unprofitable, but socially beneficial missions.[6] As they spend these funds in pursuit of their missions, they must do it in ways that meet the expectations of those they serve as well as donors, employees, volunteers, and the public. Each of these groups feel that they have a say – or at least an opinion – in how funds and resources should be used and allocated. This creates an unwritten fine line that exists between excess and frugality, between overhead and charity, between addressing immediate needs and long-term growth. This is a challenging, unclear, and complex fiscal landscape to say the least.

In short, nonprofits must live and operate within a market economy while serving the public good. When you think about nonprofit work this way, it puts this challenge in perspective. Businesses function privately and have the ability to earn and spend as they see fit without undue public scrutiny. Governments are responsible to the public for their expenditures, but demand revenue from taxes and fees that keep them going. Nonprofits function as private, independent entities that must secure their own resources while being publicly responsible for how they spend that money to address complex social needs. They have the core identity of both business (private, independent) and government (serves the public good) without the mechanisms that make each work (profit seeking and taxation). This is the unique role that the nonprofit has been designed to fill.[7]

6 Weisbrod, B.A. (1998). The nonprofit mission and its financing: growing links between nonprofits and the rest of the economy. In: *To Profit Or Not to Profit: The Commercial Transformation of the Nonprofit Sector* (ed. B.A. Weisbrod), 1–24. New York: Cambridge University Press.

7 Frumkin, P. (2002). *On Being Nonprofit: A Conceptual and Policy Primer*. Cambridge, MA: Harvard University Press.

The dramatic rise in the number of nonprofit organizations over the past several decades has made this challenge more acute. This growth, of course, is positive because it means more people are organizing to address pressing and important needs. But overall government support has fallen over this same period of time, even as funding has fluctuated with political circumstance. As a result, competition for limited resources has become more intense. In addition, the growth in the number of nonprofit organizations increases competition for philanthropic support and corporate giving. As a result, these appeals begin to saturate society making it harder to capture people's attention. Therefore, nonprofits must work even harder to find and keep support and have even more pressure to use their money and resources carefully to maximize impact.

So how can nonprofit organizations solve difficult, complex social problems on limited resources while having to independently function within a market economy? How can nonprofit organizations collectively address problems that require a seemingly unending and ever-increasing amount of resources while relying on donations, grants, and fees for services that are delivered below market prices? How do nonprofit organizations sustain privately unprofitable, but socially beneficial missions? How can they operate in ways that meet their current and future needs when donors and the public often don't want them to build organizational capacity or pay market wages?

Despite the criticism and even scandal that come from not being frugal enough with money and resources, the clear call for several decades to solve this problem has been for nonprofit organizations to become more business-like in the how they manage resources and people.[8] Being business-like is often touted as a natural means of increasing accountability, more carefully using resources, and generating new and sustainable revenue streams. Since we live in a global market economy this makes sense on the surface. Businesses make money and grow the economy. Businesses set the standards for professionalization. Capitalism and the market drive our thinking about organizations. So if nonprofits could just be more like a business, the more careful they will be with their resources and the more effectively they will be able to pursue their missions. This logic is used by those who critique the nonprofit sector as well as those within the nonprofit sector itself.

While this has been a growing sentiment, it hasn't come without its share of criticism about the potential problems that arise when nonprofits behave in more business-like ways. Indeed, the illustrations we shared at the beginning of this chapter demonstrate this business-like thinking and operating in action. As this

---

8 Bush, R. (1992). Survival of the nonprofit spirit in a for-profit world. *Nonprofit and Voluntary Sector Quarterly* 21: 391–410. doi: 10.1177/089976409202100406 Dart, R. (2004). Being "business-like" in a nonprofit organization: a grounded and inductive typology. *Nonprofit and Voluntary Sector Quarterly* 33: 290–310. doi: 10.1177/0899764004263522.

expectation to become more business-like among nonprofits has grown, and as more business-like practices emerge in nonprofit work like professionalization, competitive salaries, and for-profit revenue streams, there has been significant concern that nonprofit organizations are becoming marketized. Nonprofit scholar Angela Eikenberry has written extensively about the idea of nonprofit marketization and its impact on the nonprofit's ability to effectively fulfill its role in society.[9] Her work points to specific problems that can arise when nonprofits talk and act like businesses. She argues that market ideology and practices, though potentially beneficial for revenue streams, are incompatible with the democratic ideals of fairness, justice, and the common good that undergird nonprofit work. Becoming more business-like, therefore, runs the risk of eroding the very values that justify the existence of the nonprofit in the first place.

While the democratic ideals of justice, fairness, equality, and the common good are not unique to nonprofits, they are the core tenets of the nonprofit sector that drive the pursuit of a social mission.[10] Businesses can hold these values as well, but they are subordinate to profit maximization and self-interest that function to benefit investors and owners rather than the public. Those are the motives that have ultimately driven business in every society. Nonprofits, on the other hand, must function as value guardians in society and exist to build social capital and advocate for the disadvantaged who don't have investment or ownership in anything. Nonprofits exist, in fact, to help those that the market shuts out and leaves behind. As a result, marketization can cause nonprofits to lose sight of their social mission as they seek revenue, drift from core values to more expedient ones, or avoid the most difficult and expensive problems in favor of less expensive and more profitable ones. Marketization can also lead to a focus on short-term gains in revenue, commercial activities, and appeasing donors over a long-term outlook.[11] The stories at the beginning of this chapter point to the sensitivity that the public has toward this problem, even though people don't describe it in these exact terms.

In addition to the public seeing this problem, nonprofit researchers have also identified the potential erosion of core nonprofit ideals that arise as a result of nonprofit marketization. Museums, for example, have long struggled with balancing commercial activities to increase revenues with their mission to preserve culture and history. One case study of a museum found that their concern with

9 Eikenberry, A.M. (2009). Refusing the market: A democratic discourse for nonprofit and voluntary organizations. *Nonprofit and Voluntary Sector Quarterly* 38: 582–596. doi: 10.1177/0899764009333686.

10 O'Connell, B. (1988). Values underlying the nonprofit endeavor. In: *Educating Managers of Nonprofit Organizations* (eds. M. O'Neill and D.R. Young), 156–161. New York: Praeger.

11 Eikenberry, A.M., and Kluver, J.D. (2004). The marketization of the nonprofit sector: civil society at risk? *Public Administration Review* 64 (2): 132–140. doi: 10.1111/j.1540-6210.2004.00355.x.

generating revenue from merchandise led to a significant shift in the focus of its leadership. Over time, business planning and merchandising became the primary driver and focus of their work, leaving their mission of cultural preservation as a secondary and less important concern.[12] Another example is the partnerships that nonprofits create with businesses who donate part of their profits to support their missions. While this can be a helpful relationship for nonprofits, it can also have significant unintended consequences. Promoting the consumption of products as the means of solving significant social problems reinforces market ideals as the best way to participate in charitable giving. While this does raise money, consumerism and the significant consumption of goods by those with disposable income is a primary cause of many of the global economic inequalities that nonprofits are trying address. In the end, the primary beneficiaries of consuming products to help a cause are the businesses whose profits increase with purchases driven by social motivations.[13]

While nonprofit marketization and its effects are very real, we can't just throw off any and all business practices and pretend that nonprofits can exist outside of a market economy. That would be naïve and unhelpful. Business practices and market ideology are the larger, external environment within which nonprofits must operate. The market is the language of social calculation in society. Still, the market's focus on individual gain and self-interest stands in stark contrast to the nonprofit sector's goal to build civil society and improve the conditions of the vulnerable and voiceless. And this exposes a significant problem with the accepted logic that nonprofits should just be more like a business and everything will be fine. It's quite ironic that we don't want nonprofits to spend and earn like businesses, but in order for them to thrive and be more effective we ask them to be more business-like.

So, what are nonprofit organizations to do? To what extent can, or should, a nonprofit organization adopt business-like practices to manage people and find more adequate and sustainable sources of funding? At what point does nonprofit marketization endanger the integrity of a social mission? These are complicated questions that as of yet, nonprofit scholars have been unable to adequately answer. As a result, it seems that the nonprofit is in a somewhat impossible spot. If a nonprofit runs on a shoestring budget to maximize financial resources toward mission goals, it can be seen as unorganized, undisciplined, and ineffective because there aren't enough employees to do the work or enough resources to effectively organize its people. If a nonprofit uses more resources to increase the organization's

---

12 Oakes, L.S., Townley, B., and Cooper, D.J. (1998). Business planning as pedagogy: language and control in a changing institutional field. *Administrative Science Quarterly* 43: 257–292.
13 Nickel, P.M., and Eikenberry, A.M. (2009). A critique of the discourse of marketized philanthropy. *American Behavioral Scientist* 52 (7): 974–989. doi: 10.1177/0002764208327670.

capacity and pay competitive wages, it can be seen as self-interested and neglecting its mission. These problems are highlighted in the media and in research, but most writers offer critiques without enough solutions. We aren't any closer to an answer about how to manage this well than we were decades ago when this problem began to be identified. But the call to be business-like is still accepted as common sense. Why is this? Because the way in which we typically understand nonprofit marketization doesn't allow us to see past an economic explanation.

Economic Understandings of Nonprofit Marketization

You can't solve a problem if you cannot clearly define it. Part of the reason we struggle with the stickiness of nonprofit marketization is that we understand it in a way that makes the problem the solution as well. There is no question about the good that can come from being focused on the ideas and practices of fiscal responsibility that stem from the market such as efficiency, innovation, and accountability to funding sources. But expectations to be more business-like are also fraught with complications because nonprofits are legally defined and publicly understood as organizations without the core tenet of business – self-interest and profit motive.[14] Being self-interested and motivated by revenue in the nonprofit sector is what creates legal troubles and public scandals. Therefore, the expectation that all nonprofits should be more like businesses is an expectation that nonprofits should be like something that they cannot be. We can unpack this economic perspective in several ways.

To begin, being business-like in the nonprofit sector is primarily understood as adopting a set of managerial and financial practices. If nonprofits want to make money stretch further and be used more carefully, then they need to adopt the practices that all businesses do. Doing so, then, inevitably leads to better results and improved mission-related outcomes. These practices consist of basic financial management like conducting cost–benefit analyses, adopting standard accounting procedures, and using human resources guidelines. These practices also include those focused on financial maximization and competition, for example pricing formulas, market analyses, and board and executive leadership by business people. These practices can also be more commercially focused, such as selling merchandise in gift shops, partnering with for-profit organizations, and creating associated for-profit businesses that financially support the organization.

From an economic perspective, these practices are assumed to have direct cause-and-effect outcomes on an organization when they are used. As a result,

---

14 Frumkin, P. (2002). *On Being Nonprofit: A Conceptual and Policy Primer*. Cambridge, MA: Harvard University Press.

they are beneficial because nonprofits are assumed to be prone to disorganization because they lack the motivations that naturally come from profit motive and shareholder accountability.[15] Thus, being business-like is pretty simple. It means operating like any other business would in making decisions and engaging clients or the public. It means foregrounding finances and watching your bottom line. From this perspective, nonprofits really aren't different than any business. All organizations have to operate in these ways, and doing so increases legitimacy, trust, and ultimately revenue.

Because of this assumption, the debate over whether or not nonprofits should be business-like and use market logic is framed as an either/or debate. We've briefly described this above, but it is important to review here. This argument is simple: the nonprofit either should or shouldn't be like businesses in the market economy. Those that say nonprofits should be more business-like assume that business-like practices have some unidirectional, unavoidable influence on nonprofit work and mission. For example, some hail being business-like as necessary and inevitable as the nonprofit sector matures and evolves in the global economy; every nonprofit organization must become more like a business if it wants to survive and thrive in society and enjoy long-term viability. From this perspective, nonprofits who refuse to operate in a business-like fashion will suffer from a lack of organization, accountability, and legitimacy.

Those who argue that nonprofits should stay away from market logic and practice offer dire warnings, arguing that adopting business-like philosophies and practices will compromise or fundamentally change the nonprofit endeavor, leading to mission drift and the abandonment of the most vexing and complicated social problems for easier, more profitable ones. Therefore, nonprofit organizations must remove themselves from being business-like or eventually we won't be able to tell the difference between nonprofit and for-profit organizations. And this would then put the entire nonprofit endeavor at risk by eroding core values and decreasing the capacity to create social capital for others.

However, this perspective of nonprofit marketization has significant flaws and limitations that keep the debate spinning without any real solutions to the problem. First, this perspective assumes that nonprofit organizations are inherently flawed; that they can't function properly unless they operate like something they are not. This assumption isn't surprising; nonprofits are defined legally and in name by what they are not (for-profit businesses) rather than by what they are – organizations dedicated to the common good. Nonprofits are also understood as existing to fill in needs that the market and the state cannot. This "negative theory" framing has done little to help nonprofit practitioners or scholars clearly

15 Herzlinger, R.E. (1996, March–April). Can public trust in nonprofits and governments be restored? *Harvard Business Review*, pp. 97–107.

articulate an affirmative view of what it means to be a nonprofit organization. Even theories that articulate why nonprofit profits exist and what their role in society is argue that the nonprofit only fills in the gaps for what businesses and governments cannot do. These "failure" theories can't articulate clearly what a nonprofit is on its own terms.[16] Because of this, we cannot even talk about what financial management in the nonprofit is like.

Second, this perspective assumes that business is the gold standard of organizational life; that the ideas of accountability to others, fiscal responsibility, careful decision-making, effective management, etc. are all at their core business concepts. While these ideas are taught in schools of business and promoted by business consultants, the logic that these are primarily business ideas is flawed. Most small businesses fail and many businesses are unorganized and even dysfunctional despite operating with self-interest and profit motive. And a staggering number of corporate scandals that include corruption, fraud, and waste continually plague both private and publicly traded businesses. Businesses are accountable to shareholders and have significant reason to grow their market share, yet they spend lavishly, waste money, and often create mediocre products and services. Indeed, we can easily argue that businesses are highly prone to all kinds of problems because of their core tenets of self-interest and profit motive. These realities make it hard to believe that business *has* to be the answer.

Therefore, assuming that being business-like and using market assumptions has a monolithic, unidirectional influence on nonprofit work seems odd. Business practice is assumed to have a very specific impact on nonprofit work, but it is important that we distinguish business practices that are focused on profit and self-interest and those that are simply the practices of fiscal responsibility. All organizations in a market economy have to be fiscally responsible. From an economic perspective, what it means to be like a business encompasses everything about organizational life, when businesses, governments, nonprofits, and even families all have to manage themselves in a fiscally responsible way. Thus, it's hard to see business practice as the gold standard of organizational life or an independent actor on nonprofit work.

Taken together, an economic perspective and its assumptions provide a limited perspective in which nonprofit marketization can be understood. This perspective doesn't allow us to question or challenge the primacy of business logic or frame the debate as something other than an either/or problem that we must either embrace or reject. This economic explanation also hasn't moved us forward toward a better way of nonprofits engaging the realities of the market while trying to fulfill their missions. Rather, it keeps the nonprofit sector stuck. Therefore,

---

16 Lohmann, R.A. (1989). And lettuce is nonanimal: toward a positive economics of voluntary action. *Nonprofit and Voluntary Sector Quarterly* 18: 367–383.

scholars and practitioners have had little ability to understand nonprofit marketization in a productive way or use this phenomenon to explore what it means to be a nonprofit organization.

A Communicative Explanation of Nonprofit Marketization

Our explanation and critique of an economic perspective of nonprofit marketization also illustrates that it is grounded in a functional, transmission model of communication. Business-like practices are seen as having fixed meanings that are understood the same way by everyone. And those fixed meanings therefore, have a direct effect on nonprofit organizations. As we explained in Chapter 1, thinking of communication as transmission doesn't allow us to see how work gets its meaning or how people in organizations see their work practices differently. Too often we focus so much on what we think some aspect of organizational life is or should be, that we fail to recognize that what animates an organization's work is the meaning that people give to what they do. This meaning is what informs everyday practice. With nonprofits being told that they need to be like something they legally cannot be, a transmission perspective doesn't allow us to understand how nonprofits translate business logic and practice to nonprofit work or what it means to them in everyday organizational life.

So what would it look like to apply a communication perspective to the issue of nonprofit marketization? What can a communicative explanation of nonprofit marketization and being business-like in nonprofit work help us see differently? What insights can we gain from communication research that could help nonprofits engage their work more effectively? Understanding communication as the social construction of our organizational realities allows us to recognize that the meaning-making of human interaction in nonprofit organizations themselves defines what it means to function within a market economy while pursuing a social mission. This is important because while scholars and practitioners debate about what nonprofit marketization is and what its impact might be on the pursuit of a social mission, those working in the nonprofit sector simply deal with it every day. Perhaps they don't think about it in these terms, but they live this reality. From a communication perspective, then, being business-like in a nonprofit organization and the influence of nonprofit marketization can be seen and engaged very differently.

Communication research has revealed three important features of nonprofit marketization and how it is understood and addressed by nonprofit practitioners themselves. This knowledge helps us understand what it means to be nonprofit in more detailed and complex ways. First, nonprofit organizations exist in a contested, contradictory space in our society. That space isn't simply a set of organizational and societal structures, but rather a communication environment that practitioners have to respond to and navigate. And this navigation requires accepting this contradictory space as a normal condition of the nonprofit. Second, within this contested and contradictory space, nonprofits experience an ongoing tension between mission and market concerns. This mission–market tension, however, isn't simply the existence of a conflict or the draw of competing needs, but rather is an inherent and productive feature of the nonprofit. It is part of what it means to be nonprofit. Third, being business-like in a nonprofit organization is not the adoption of a set of market-focused practices. Though these practices exist, being business-like in the nonprofit sector is a way of talking about nonprofit work that gives altered meaning to market practices. Below we develop each of these features much more extensively.

A Contested and Contradictory Sector

Scholars and practitioners have long recognized the push and pull in nonprofit work as the influence of government and business informs the wider world of nonprofit organizational life. The demands of government regulations and funding along with the pull of market logic and solutions have always, in one form or another, been at play in nonprofit work. Nonprofit scholar Peter Frumkin has offered the most compelling and descriptive explanation of this reality in the nonprofit sector. What makes his work so compelling is that rather than framing the nonprofit (as most scholars have) as simply filling some third space between the market and the state that addresses issues and concerns that business and government cannot, he defines the nonprofit sector itself in its own terms and in a way that embraces this tension. He calls the nonprofit sector a mass of contradictions and claims that it exists as a contested arena between the state and the market.[17]

From this perspective, nonprofits exist in a contradictory space between the market and the state. They must live and act as independent entities that cannot coerce participation and rely on the goodwill of others for donations or the choice of individuals to use their services. In this regard, they function like all businesses; they invite and seek to persuade but they cannot force participation and are not public organizations. At the same time, nonprofit organizations are tax exempt and therefore have unclear lines of ownership and accountability. They must meet a public good and be accountable to the public for how, where, and when they use their money despite being private organizations. In this regard, they

17 Frumkin, P. (2002). *On Being Nonprofit: A Conceptual and Policy Primer*. Cambridge, MA: Harvard University Press.

function like government organizations that serve the public good and have greater public accountability. This contested nature, therefore, is central to understanding how to successfully engage in nonprofit work – a perspective that is especially important because it highlights the unique realities of a sector that must meet two contradictory aims. This organizational reality simply doesn't exist for businesses and governments.

This contested, contradictory environment, however, is not a flaw in nonprofit organizations. It doesn't mean that the nonprofit is somehow deficient or broken. It does mean that the nonprofit operates in a more complex environment that requires us to think about nonprofit work differently. Traditional theories of management and organizations, however, cannot adequately embrace the idea of contradiction. Business logic has always supposed that rationality in organizations requires resolving any tension or contradiction so that all can move toward a common goal. But communication research, grounded in a social construction approach, helps us see the contested and contradictory nature of the nonprofit as something more than just a difficult, confusing, and complex environment that needs to be fixed. For example, communication scholar Sarah Tracy has done extensive research in different types of organizations and argues that contradiction and tension are normal parts of every kind of work. This contradiction-centered approach recognizes that it is impossible to think that any complex organization can operate without having to wrestle with and manage competing or even contradictory needs. Recognizing and accepting the tensions and contradictions in work are the only way for people to cope with those organizational realities and do their work successfully. And that work is grounded in communication practices. Tracy explains that it isn't the contradiction or tension that is "productive or unproductive, good or bad, liberating or paralyzing, but rather, that employees can react to contradiction in various ways, and that their framing of workplace tensions can have various personal and organizational effects."[18] In other words, it's not the contradiction or tension that is the problem; it's an organization's reaction to it that makes is enabling or constraining.

Therefore, instead of viewing contradiction and tension in organizational life as challenges that must be overcome as we move toward rational and objective decisions and outcomes, a communicative explanation argues that contradiction is normal and even useful. Competing needs, goals, priorities, and influences, therefore, are an inherent part of organizing processes and organizational life, and a normal result of coordinating action among constituents in a complex environment. Embracing contradiction and tension leads us to be more responsive to

18 Tracy, S.J. (2004). Dialectic, contradiction, or double bind? Analyzing and theorizing employee reactions to organizational tension. *Journal of Applied Communication Research* 32: 119–146, p. 120. doi: 10.1080/0090988042000210025.

organizational realities, and focusing on this complexity helps develop practices that mirror the everyday realities of work.[19]

My coauthor Matthew Koschmann's own research with his colleague Nicole Laster demonstrates that tensions between competing views, needs, and goals in a neighborhood association in Austin, Texas actually helped foster greater participation and involvement which enabled that community to organize.[20] One example of a productive tension was the use of prayer to open association meetings. Members had very different views on prayer and religion, but respecting the need for some to pray as an act of unity and making the practice of prayer broad enough to include varying views of its role and purpose allowed members to engage in a community practice even though individually there was disagreement on its need or value. Another example of a productive tension was the association's understanding of diversity, which was an important topic as the neighborhood was wrestling with gentrification and changing demographics. Different members of the association defined diversity differently. For some it was based on race and ethnicity. Others include age and social class as the central components of diversity. These different views, however, allowed the group to focus on diversity in their own ways which allowed the group to address the issue more effectively. These examples illustrate that embracing contradiction and tension, and living with it, allow for effective organizing. It's not hard to image the dysfunction that could have arisen in this neighborhood association if prayers had to be understood, accepted, and enacted the same way for everyone, of if they insisted on one specific definition of diversity.

A communicative approach to contradiction, therefore, tells us that the nonprofit environment is not simply a set of fixed legal and societal structures. Instead, seeing organizations and organizational sectors as systems of human interaction that are created, maintained, and transformed through communication practices allows us to embrace this contested, contradictory context as a system of competing meanings that nonprofits must make sense of and negotiate on an ongoing basis. It is a communication environment that practitioners make sense of in everyday interactions. It doesn't go away, and is the process that gives meaning to nonprofit work. Such sense-making and negotiation of conflicting meaning isn't easy or automatic, and the efforts made by practitioners to figure out what their organization is and how their work should be done has a great impact on their success.

---

19 Trethewey, A. and Ashcraft, K.L. (2004). Practicing disorganization: the development of applied perspectives on living with tension. *Journal of Applied Communication Research* 32: 81–88. doi: 10.1080/0090988042000210007.

20 Koschmann, M. and Laster, N.M. (2011). Communicative tensions of community organizing: the case of a local neighborhood association. *Western Journal of Communication* 75: 28–51. doi: 10.1080/10570314.2010.536965.

An Inherent Mission–Market Tension

With the acceptance of the contested, contradictory nature of the nonprofit as a significant and central feature of nonprofit work, we can identify and better understand the second feature of a communication explanation of nonprofit marketization. The push and pull of mission and market demands makes nonprofit work feel like a balancing act between opposing needs. Too often, though, this is seen as a challenge rather than an explanation of nonprofit work. However, what we know from research on contradiction and tension in organizations, as we've described above, demonstrates that the tension between pursuing a social mission and meeting the demands of operating in a market economy is an inherent part of nonprofit work.

This is a very different way of seeing the nonprofit. Past research and theoretical frameworks have not seen these competing concerns as existing in a normal and useful way. Understanding how these competing concerns play out has been the focus of my own research. As I have studied how nonprofit employees and leaders make sense of the competing demands they face in their work, I began to recognize that they weren't trying to resolve the tension between business and mission needs. For those working in the nonprofit it isn't a problem to be solved or something to fix. It is an organizational reality that was understood and managed. Therefore, the mission–market tension is at the core of what it means to be nonprofit; an inherent part of nonprofit work that is both an unchangeable and productive feature of the nonprofit. In other words, all work in the nonprofit sector is guided and informed by an *organizing mission–market tension* that enables all organizations seeking to strengthen civil society within a market economy to successfully do their work. The mission–market tension is inescapable and attempting to resolve it compromises the integrity of an organization's mission or violates the financial responsibility to donors and clients.[21] Accepting the unresolvable nature of this tension and realizing its importance to nonprofit work enables practitioners to recognize and understand the mutual importance of these needs even though they can, at times, appear to contradict each other. Managing this tension is a matter of everyday communication practice. And how it is understood and managed will determine whether it will hinder a nonprofit or enable it to thrive.

In research that I conducted at the National Sports Center for the Disabled, I saw how communication practices and the meaning given to the mission–market tension enabled that organization to be successful. Indeed, its ability to fulfill its mission to empower people with disabilities rested on the ways in which leaders kept mission

21 Sanders, M.L. (2012). Theorizing nonprofit organizations and contradictory enterprises: understanding the inherent tensions of nonprofit marketization. *Management Communication Quarterly* 26: 179–185. doi: 10.1177/0893318911423761.

and market needs alive in conversations and decision-making processes. For example, this organization had one office that was dedicated to nearly all of its outdoor programming at a ski resort that was approximately 70 miles from its main office that served nearly all the executive, marketing, and fundraising functions. This was necessary because marketing and fundraising doesn't work well in a tiny ski town and outdoor mountain activities can't happen in a downtown urban center. But separating nearly all business and mission functions could potentially lead to conflict. Not seeing each other and being surrounded by those with similar work tasks could lead to one office thinking that their work is more important than the other.

Interestingly, executives and staff described working through decisions about using resources for mission goals or marketing and staff as "fighting like cats and dogs" or having "battles." However, these metaphors weren't expressed as destructive conflict, but rather emphasized the competing nature of those needs and the importance each holds. They recognized the importance of having these hard conversations so they could make better decisions. The give and take in these conversations was "absolutely" important.[22]

At times mission needs won out, like purchasing equipment to accommodate paraplegic rock climbers when they only served a few each year, or when a donated condominium at a ski resort was used for an employee social during the holidays instead of being rented to the highest bidder. At other times, financial considerations won the day as soccer camps in distant cities were canceled because past attendance was too low to justify the cost, or when volunteers had to be told that they couldn't give needy clients ski gear such as coats and hats because they had to be used by participants all winter.[23] In this sense, it didn't matter which interests won out in a particular moment on a particular issue because they knew that all interests would be considered and have their turn. That was the meaning ascribed to these battles; they represented a process where mission and financial interests were considered equally. Nobody described these decisions or the process of making them as easy. They were always hard because they were choosing between important, though competing, needs. Therefore, it is in letting these needs be heard, compete, and be fairly considered that successful navigation of the mission–market tension occurs.

Communication scholar Gary Ruud studied organizational conflict in a metropolitan symphony and showed the dysfunction that occurs when the productive

---

22 Sanders, M.L. (2015). Being nonprofit-like in a market economy: understanding the mission-market tension in nonprofit organizing. *Nonprofit and Voluntary Sector Quarterly* 44: 205–222. doi: 10.1177/0899764013508606.

23 Sanders, M.L. and McClellan, J.G. (2014). Being business-like while pursuing a social mission: acknowledging the inherent tensions in US nonprofit organizing. *Organization* 21: 68–89. doi: 10.1177/1350508412464894.

tension between mission and market needs is not recognized and embraced, and where mission and market needs are seen an incompatible.[24] Recognizing that communication creates the meanings that guide our decisions in organizations, this study highlighted two ways of talking about the symphony and its work. Executive leadership infused their conversations with business logic that placed increasing revenue streams as the primary goal of the symphony. To do this, they decided that the musicians would have to play more popular music in order to bring in more people and consequently more revenue. They talked about the symphony as a sales organization and treated music as a product. Leaders made decisions based solely on economics. Audience approval, rather than artistic standards, became the metric for choosing what music to play. Musicians, on the other hand, spoke about artistic quality, the preservation of more traditional music, and the need to be challenged as artists with the kinds of complex music that all symphonies play. Their mission was to promote and preserve classical music rather than fill all the seats. Knowledgeable audiences would appreciate that, which would drive support.

Rather than embracing the realities of the market (for example, that they needed to fill seats and grow revenue) as well as the importance of their mission (for example, to promote and perform classical music), each group's way of talking about the symphony competed for supremacy. They did not embrace this conflict as a normal part of nonprofit work. Management wouldn't budge, insisting that the musicians must only play music to draw large crowds. The musicians could go and work in fast food if they didn't like being in the symphony. The organization needed more revenue and popular music was the path they saw to get it. The artists wouldn't consider those needs. They went on strike, and then they were locked out. Their conflict played out in the media and delayed the symphony's season opening. Their reputation in the city suffered.

Ruud's study demonstrates that trying to resolve the mission–market tension by choosing one side or the other contradicts the nature of nonprofit work. Forcing a choice requires neglecting half (financial responsibility or social mission) of what is required to be an effective nonprofit. Even in compromise, if the tension is not embraced, results will lead to dysfunction if both needs aren't seen as valid and necessary. Thus, holding competing needs in productive tension is the solution, not the problem. Each of these studies illustrates both the existence of the mission–market tension and its productive nature when understood as inherent and a productive means to guide decision-making. The contrasting outcomes for each organization reinforce that the way we talk about mission and market

24 Rudd, G. (2000). The symphony: organizational discourse and the symbolic tensions between artistic and business ideologies. *Journal of Applied Communication Research* 28: 117–143. doi: 10.1080/00909880009365559.

concerns – not the specific practices or policies themselves – influence whether or not a nonprofit can succeed. This knowledge helps prevent either/or thinking that frames discussions about mission and market needs as an intractable conflict. It also removes the need to either fully embrace or completely reject nonprofit marketization. With this understanding, let's look now at how we can change the way we think about being business-like from a set of practices with direct meaning and influence to a way of talking about nonprofit work that enables it to thrive.

Communication Practice, Not Business Practice

Being able to recognize the contradictory nature of the nonprofit sector and embrace the mission–market tension as a central and productive feature of nonprofit work allows us to better understand specific business-like practices and engage them in ways that benefit and strengthen the nonprofit. Therefore, the third, and most significant, feature of a communicative explanation of nonprofit marketization is this: Being business-like is a way of talking about nonprofit work and not a specific set of practices. Certainly, the notion of business does entail specific practices and the market logic behind them, but as they are successfully adopted in nonprofit work, a communication perspective shows us that how we talk about marketization and being business-like is significantly more meaningful and influential than specific practices themselves. We give meaning to practices through our everyday communication. And, as we outlined in the section "An Inherent Mission–Market Tension," that meaning can be drastically different depending on the people in the organization and how they understand nonprofit work and the mission–market tension. Therefore, business practices by themselves don't cause nonprofit marketization and don't necessarily threaten the integrity of the nonprofit sector. Rather, how we talk about them determines whether market structures and realities will influence nonprofit work in ways that erode a social mission or undermine what it means to be nonprofit.

This was illustrated very clearly in in-depth interviews that my students and I conducted with managers and executives in both local and national nonprofits. When we asked them about the pressure to be business-like in the nonprofit sector, each one of these nonprofit leaders quickly and emphatically claimed that nonprofits are just like any other business and that they had to operate as such. They willingly and readily embraced being like a business as part of their identity. They didn't vacillate when they answered, but clearly said things like "We are a business" or "You have to understand it's a business." Of course, as we said earlier in this chapter, such claims should not be surprising when we consider that business is the language of organizational legitimacy in a market-based society.

Yet, when we asked these same nonprofit managers and executives what it meant to be a business in the nonprofit context when they can't legally operate as businesses with profit motive and self-interest, a very different and altered definition of business in the nonprofit context came to light. In fact, their definition of business turned it inside out and removed its core meaning. They actively rejected notions of self-interest and profit motive – hallmarks of what it means to be a business – even while using terms like "bottom line," "profit," and "investors." These terms were hollowed out and infused with a mission-related focus on making a difference and long-term viability to better serve more people in need. Thus, being business-like wasn't the purpose of their work, but rather was "the vehicle to get us in a position that we can make the difference we want to in people's lives."

These nonprofit leaders then described that a key part of successfully leading a nonprofit is to be able to "speak both languages," which interestingly are the two ways of talking that those in Ruud's study of the symphony couldn't embrace. Speaking both languages allowed nonprofit leaders to communicate fiscal responsibility and mission goals to different constituents in ways that helped them understand their role in fulfilling the organization's mission. This gave them credibility and legitimacy in a world dominated by the logic of business. They wanted the community, clients, and donors to see them as responsible and credible. Being business-like, therefore, is a legitimizing framework – a way of talking about themselves – that is then filled with nonprofit values and ideals in order to work in a nonprofit context.[25] As a result, for those who are successfully running nonprofits, it isn't business logic and practice that are driving nonprofit work. Instead, it's nonprofit values and motives that are driving and altering business logic and practice. And that happens through everyday communication practices.

My research on this topic has also identified how this revised definition of business informed specific work practices.[26] At the National Sports Center for the Disabled, employees and leaders embraced this revised and transformed definition of business. When I asked them to explain how being business-like played out in their organization, they reframed these ideas in ways that brought out two ways of talking about nonprofit work that may be more helpful for nonprofits as they seek legitimacy in the marketplace and among donors. They didn't talk about their work in these specific terms; they just described it as being business-like. Yet the meaning was clear, and therefore we should take that meaning seriously.

The first way that being business-like in the nonprofit sector could be better described is through the term *stewardship*. Repeatedly, when organizational

---

25 Sanders, M.L., Harper, L., and Richardson, M. (2015). Understanding what it means to be business-like in the nonprofit sector: toward a communicative explanation. *Qualitative Research Reports in Communication* 16: 1–8. doi: 10.1080/17459435.2015.1086415.

26 Sanders, M.L and McClellan, J.G. (2014). Being business-like while pursuing a social mission: acknowledging the inherent tensions in US nonprofit organizing. *Organization* 21: 68–89. doi: 10.1177/1350508412464894.

members talked about being business-like to further their mission, they clearly articulated that the organization, the outcomes, and the resources were not theirs. Neither the organization nor its outcomes belonged to them. "It's not our profit, it's their profit" one program manager said about the purpose and goal of being business-like. Such a clear departure from self-interest highlights a foundational value of nonprofit work that remains intact while using business-terminology. Telling donors, employees, volunteers, and the public that the careful use of resources is important because the money doesn't belong to the organization, but rather is a public trust that requires careful stewardship so it is not wasted or used improperly, speaks directly to the fiscal responsibility that business talk tries to convey without creating confusion by using terms that contradict the core values of nonprofit work.

The second way that being business-like in the nonprofit sector could be better described is through the term *sustainability*. While implicitly recognizing that they were stewards of the organization and its resources, organizational members also described being business-like as the means to long-term sustainability. A program manager described the importance of volunteers not giving equipment to participants, even if they could use it after their lessons because those were needed for participants coming the next day, week, and year. Recognizing that their organization existed to benefit the public, being business-like became the means by which they could be there for people who needed them both now and in the future. Fiscal responsibility and finding donors and revenue streams, therefore, were keys to long-term viability, not for the benefit of any founder, donor, or employee. Telling donors, employees, volunteers, and the public that maintaining and increasing revenue and resources ensures long-term sustainability so future clients can benefit also speaks directly to financial management and careful allocation of resources that business terms try to convey, but without the confusion of self-interest that business terms imply.

Each of these frameworks – stewardship and sustainability – is focused on the common good and building social capital. If these are the ideals evoked when defining what it means to be business-like, then clearly nonprofit managers aren't just being businesspeople, but instead are aware of and are articulating a coherent framework of being nonprofit. But if these meanings are understood among those working in the nonprofit and their organizations are doing well, then why should we worry about it? Why can't they just continue on as they are? A communication perspective, of course, tells us that meanings aren't fixed. Meanings in organizations and social systems are negotiated and each organization can frame things differently. The various nonprofit criticisms and scandals described at the beginning of the chapter, as well as some of the research described above, clearly show how nonprofits can embrace market ideology and business practices in ways that cause mission drift and compromise the spirit of nonprofit work. Consequently, there is a significant need for better ways of talking about the nonprofit and its work.

What if we stopped trying to mask nonprofit work in business language and just talked about it terms of fiscal responsibility that connects to mission goals? What if we could use terms that embraced the spirit of nonprofit work, like stewardship and sustainability, so we didn't run the risk of market terms and logic pulling nonprofits off track? What benefit would that have on management and public perception? The research described here shows that a communication perspective provides this opportunity for the nonprofit. We can articulate nonprofit work in ways that that do not lead to an inevitable marketization of the nonprofit sector. It is the communication practices that either enable or constrain nonprofit marketization. Therefore, nonprofits can embrace this and intentionally choose more productive ways to talk about their work practices in their own terms. A communication perspective allows us to do that.

Conclusion

In this chapter we have considered some important and challenging questions that face the nonprofit: How do nonprofits balance how they spend money on mission needs as well as overhead and salary? How do they manage their money in a way that meets the need to be financially independent while addressing causes that always require more money than they have? To deal with these challenges, nonprofits have faced a growing expectation to be more business-like in their practices. But this growing expectation has led to significant concerns about the marketization of the nonprofit sector and the erosion of nonprofit mission and purpose. Yet, without a way to see this problem beyond an economic explanation, nonprofit scholars and practitioners have been unable to identify ways to effectively deal with this challenge.

A communicative explanation of nonprofit marketization, however, provides us with new and compelling answers to this problem that enables nonprofits to do their work on their own terms and as a result move forward more effectively. Recognizing the contradictory and contested nature of the nonprofit sector and embracing the mission–market tension as a central and productive feature of nonprofit work enables us to see business-like practices in the nonprofit sector as ways of talking about nonprofit work rather than the practices themselves. This allows nonprofit practitioners to engage the marketization problem and not be at its mercy. Indeed, nonprofit marketization is a vexing problem that we can influence if we see it from a communication perspective. The biggest worry with nonprofit marketization – that it will undermine the nonprofit endeavor – only happens if we talk about it in ways that forget nonprofit values and embrace for-profit ideals; it only becomes a problem when nonprofits can't hold the competing, opposing needs of social and financial outcomes together. Nonprofit marketization, then, is the result of not embracing the mission–market tension in everyday talk and organizational decision-making. It's the result of not thinking and talking like a nonprofit. It stems from trying to make nonprofits become something they are not and cannot be.

Therefore, the problem of nonprofit marketization also opens a window into what it means to be a nonprofit. Being nonprofit means being something distinct and different than business and government. When we can't talk about the nonprofit on its own terms, we can't embrace the realities of the nonprofit sector. Doing so can lead to a suppression of nonprofit values and purpose. This communicative explanation, therefore, is both empowering and hopeful. We no longer have to wonder what a business-like practice or market partnership will do to a nonprofit's mission because it's how we talk about and engage business-like practice that determines its influence. Nonprofits can therefore embrace both mission and market goals, and through communication practices hold them together and make them work toward the meaningful ends of improving the common good and building the social capital of those in need. Consequently, this communicative explanation of nonprofit marketization provides a strong basis to enable nonprofit leaders and employees stay on track and thus avoid mission drift.

4

Collabrocation

Thinking Communicatively about Collaboration

Matthew A. Koschmann

Introduction

This chapter focuses on a key organizing strategy for the nonprofit: collaboration. This includes a variety of organizational arrangements, partnerships, and alliances across sectors that vary in scope and degree of formality, and are born out of necessity and/or opportunity. Collaboration is especially relevant for the communication perspective we are developing in this book because collaborations lack many of the key features of "normal" organizations we take for granted – physical structures, clear lines of authority, contractual relationships, etc. – and thus are better understood as communicative phenomena that exist in and through specific communication practices. Accordingly, I employ the term *collabrocation* to signify and describe the inseparability of collaboration and communication – to *be* a collaboration means to communicate in certain ways, and communicating in certain ways is how we create and sustain collaboration as both a process and structure of organizing. Collaboration also magnifies key issues of authority, identity, agency, and value that I argue are best understood communicatively, which reinforces our broader project in this book of developing a communication perspective on the nonprofit and nonprofit work.

***

The conventional wisdom around organizational collaboration goes something like this: Collaboration is a hallmark of modern organizing. The complexity, uncertainty, and interdependency of contemporary work makes some form of collaborative arrangement necessary for successful outcomes across many industries and sectors, and presents unique opportunities for innovation and creative

Understanding Nonprofit Work: A Communication Perspective, First Edition.
Matthew A. Koschmann and Matthew L. Sanders.

problem-solving. This is especially true in the nonprofit sector, where the scope and severity of issues involved and the reality of scarce resources necessitates the involvement of multiple stakeholders, organizations, and sectors. Plus, the cooperative ethos that pervades the nonprofit drives more organizations toward partnership instead of competition. Much of my research as a professor focuses on nonprofit collaboration, and this is basically the opening paragraph for many of the academic articles I've written.

If you spend time with almost any nonprofit professional and ask them about their work, it won't be long before they are describing some sort of partnership or alliance they are part of – or trying to form – in order to accomplish their work more effectively. Go to the website of most nonprofit organizations and they will proudly display their various organizational partners and collaboration memberships. Collaboration is essential to the nonprofit sector, and a lot of work that nonprofit organizations do happens through a variety of collaborative arrangements. Think of any important issue in your community where nonprofits are working – poverty, education, economic development, environmental protection – and there is almost certainly a collaborative group organized around that issue. Some sort of multi-stakeholder partnership, taskforce, or alliance that brings together several organizations who realize their work will be more effective if done in collaboration with others. For many nonprofit professionals, these collaborative arrangements are critical for their work, as well as a great source of enjoyment and camaraderie with others who share their passion and concern for important community issues. Of course, it's also just as likely that you'll hear nonprofit professionals complain about aspects of their work that are related to collaboration. Collaboration can be incredibly frustrating work, and it is difficult to do well. It usually requires more time and energy than "normal" work, and it is challenging to coordinate with people who are employed by other organizations with different goals, priorities, responsibilities, cultures, and systems. In fact, one of my favorite books about organizational collaboration includes this sobering piece of advice: *don't do it unless you have to.*[1]

But the reality is that many nonprofits *do* have to collaborate, out of either necessity or opportunity. Either the problem they are addressing involves multiple parties who lay claim to some aspect of the issue and therefore must be included in the work, or there is an opportunity to make progress on an issue but it requires help from other organizations to provide sufficient resources, labor, and expertise – or both. Consider a nonprofit organization here in Boulder,

1 Huxham, C. and Vangen, S. (2013). *Managing to Collaborate: The Theory and Practice of Collaborative Advantage*. Routledge.

Colorado called BridgeHouse, which has a range of programs to help adults experiencing homelessness. The amazing staff at BridgeHouse has many great ideas for tackling the problem of homelessness in our community, but almost all of those ideas encroach on someone else's turf or require approval from another party – city and county governments, agencies in the criminal justice system, local neighborhoods, the public transit system, faith-based organizations – so oftentimes they can't even do the basics without partnering with other organizations. Additionally, when they come up with a great idea for a new program that could make a significant difference, like their Ready to Work initiative that provides one year of steady employment and stable housing for homeless people, BridgeHouse needs the support, permission, and resources of several other organizations to make it all happen. Both necessity and opportunity drive them to collaborate, so over the years BridgeHouse has partnered with a number of organizations to complete their work and improve the homelessness situation in Boulder County. Whatever the case, organizational collaboration is an essential part of the nonprofit landscape, and thus something everyone involved with the nonprofit needs to understand better.

Furthermore, when you observe organizational collaboration you quickly notice how central communication is to collaborative work. Not just the obvious fact that people in collaboration are constantly meeting and talking, negotiating and emailing, sharing information and calling each other on the phone, and making decisions and trying to resolve conflicts (all very important, of course). But if you step back and consider what collaboration entails, you'll start to realize that collaboration is *inherently communicative* – everything a collaboration "is" is wrapped up in communication practice, that there's nothing else "there" beyond all these communication practices. Collaborations almost always lack many of the visible features of "normal" organizations – like permanent buildings, articles of incorporation, and formal employment contracts – so their existence is nothing but the accumulation of their ongoing communication practices (albeit materialized in various documents, websites, memorabilia, physical locations, etc.). Another way to say this is that communication is the *mode of being* for collaboration; collaborations exist *as* communication and communication constitutes the organizational form of collaboration. Think about it: a collaboration simply *is* the arrangements among various stakeholders and organizational representatives; it's what emerges from their ongoing interactions and decisions and only continues existing to the extent this communication continues. When these particular stakeholders cease to interact in these ways, the collaboration ceases to exist (even if there's still an old website or logo somewhere out there in cyberspace). The point here is that the organizational form of collaboration is inseparable from the practice of communication. Therefore, I employ the term *collabrocation* to represent this inseparability of collaboration and communication, and to signal the importance of thinking communicatively anytime we engage in collaboration.[2] Collaborations don't merely "exist" and then we communicate within them or about them; collaboration exists in and through certain communication practices that create and sustain these organizational forms. This is what I mean by the term *collabrocation*, and my goal in this chapter is to explain how thinking communicatively about collaboration (i.e. collabrocation) can enhance our understanding and practice of this important organizational strategy for the nonprofit.

Setting the Stage

The upshot of the popularity and prevalence of organizational collaboration in the nonprofit is that collaboration has come to mean almost anything and everything, "hopelessly ambiguous" in the words of John Donahue from Harvard's Kennedy School of Government.[3] Collaboration is used to describe anything from huge, multicity initiatives across large geographic regions to a few colleagues working together on a small project – and everything in between. Furthermore, collaboration is often seen as an unquestioned good for nonprofit work, as if any good work must be collaborative and any collaborative work must be good. In this way, collaboration is somewhat of a shell term that does not merely function descriptively, but remains to be filled by those have power to give and sustain its meaning.[4] This emptiness of collaboration as a concept can be seen in the tautology that is common in discussions of nonprofit work, where collaboration is said to be necessary for effective nonprofit work, and the effectiveness of this work is assessed in terms of its collaborativeness – good nonprofit work is collaborative, and because it's collaborative we know that it's good. But this circular reasoning really doesn't tell us anything insightful. We can't have an organizational strategy that is both essential for nonprofit work yet also devoid of any substantive meaning that would prevent assessment and improvement.

However, we can overcome this circularity by incorporating the communication perspective we've been developing throughout this book. Namely, by thinking more

---

2 This term originates from a *Communication Yearbook* chapter on "collaborative interaction" written by Laurie Lewis (my PhD advisor) back in 2006. Toward the end, she states, "One colleague, after hearing about this review chapter, recommended the terms 'collabrocation' and 'collabrocating' as ways of describing how we communicate in collaborative ways" (p. 222). Lewis never did anything further with these terms in her professional writings, but gave us permission to take them up in our subsequent work.

3 Donahue, J.D. (2010). The race: can collaboration outrun rivalry between American business and government. *Public Administration Review* 70 (5): 151–152.

4 See Bartesaghi, M. (2014). Coordination: examining weather as a "matter of concern." *Communication Studies* 65 (5): 535–557 on this point.

communicatively about organizational collaboration we can develop a different understanding of what collaboration "is" that can help us "do" collaboration more effectively. That is why I use the term *collabrocation* in this chapter, to signal and reinforce the idea that organizational form and communication practice should always be understood together, that collaboration means interacting in certain ways, and that certain patters of interaction shape specific organizational forms, both of which feed back upon each other for a continual cycle of mutual existence.

I also take a pragmatic approach to collaboration. This means not being ideologically devoted to collaboration as necessarily good or bad, or something we need to commit to in principle; it's simply an organizational strategy that could be more or less useful in various situations. Sometimes collaboration is a more effective way to organize in order to accomplish certain goals or realize better outcomes, as when a number of nonprofit organizations, government agencies, and local businesses realize they have similar interests in an important community problem and each bring unique resources and abilities to bear on the issue. Other times collaboration is required to operate in a given problem domain, even if it might not be the best idea to have certain organizations partner with each other, like if a private foundation requires that all nonprofit organizations working on a similar issue collaborate with each other in order for any of them to get funding. Whatever the case, the issue here is recognizing when collaboration is called for – either for opportunity or necessity, or both – and engaging in communication practices that increase the likelihood of more successful outcomes. Or conversely, having the wisdom to recognize when collaboration should be avoided, even if there seems to be a norm or expectation that nonprofits should collaborate in principle.

I'll begin with a basic definition of organizational collaboration, just so we have a common frame of reference throughout the chapter. Then we'll move on and highlight some of the key issues and challenges for nonprofit collaboration and demonstrate how a communication perspective can enhance the way we think about this important organizational form and strategy. Things like power, existence, action, and effectiveness – all of which are relevant for any collaborative endeavor and areas where "thinking communicatively" can make a significant difference.

Defining Collaboration (Sort of)

Collaboration has become such a buzzword that it practically means anything and nothing, which obviously isn't very helpful. So what exactly do we mean when we say "collaboration?" Definitions of collaboration are as frequent and varied as collaboration itself, but a few key themes tend to cut across most perspectives in the research and practitioner literatures, and thus give us a good starting point.

Here's my best attempt to bring these key themes together into a coherent working definition: collaboration is a simultaneous process and structure that involves organizational representatives who come together in a deliberate manner to address issues that affect multiple stakeholders and are beyond the scope or capacity of any single organization or sector.[5] There's probably some fuzziness at the boundaries of this definition, but in my experience, this covers the vast majority of organizational arrangements referred to as "collaboration." I chose these words carefully, so let's unpack this definition a bit more.

As a simultaneous *process and structure*, collaboration involves both how and what, verb and noun – *how* people interact with each other and *what* results from their interactions (and consequently how the results inform subsequent interactions, which shape subsequent results, etc.). Although we can make analytic distinctions between process and structure, they are best understood as mutually constitutive, which means they always shape and implicate each other – how we interact with each other depends on structures that enable and constrain those interactions, which in turn reshape those structures that consequently shape subsequent interactions, and so on. What we often identify as "the collaboration" (noun) is really just a momentary configuring of ongoing processes (verb). Next, *organizational representatives* are people who are authorized to speak for their organization and conversely speak for the collaboration back at their "home" organizations. This also implies a separation among collaboration members such that they do not have hierarchical arrangements or formal authority over each other, though inevitable power differences are always present. Furthermore, *come together* and *deliberate manner* mean that collaboration members are intentional about and aware of their partnership – collaboration is not just a loose network of abstract nodes or the result invisible market forces. Then *address issues* involves everything from exploring and updating to arguing and deciding. Some collaborations exist merely to share information and build relationships, others exist to solve specific problems on a definite timeline, but all involve orienting towards

5 I make no claim to originality here; this is just my best attempt to synthesize definitions and ideas from many influential sources such as: Gray, B. (1989). *Collaborating: Finding Common Ground for Multiparty Problems*. San Francisco, CA: Jossey-Bass; Hardy, C., Lawrence, T.B., and Grant, D. (2005). Discourse and collaboration: the role of conversations and collective identity. *Academy of Management Review* 30 (1): 58–77; Heath, R.G. and Isbell, M.G. (2017). *Interorganizational Collaboration: Complexity, Ethics, and Communication*. Waveland Press; Huxham, C. and Vangen, S. (2013). *Managing to Collaborate: The Theory and Practice of Collaborative Advantage*. Routledge; Keyton, J., Ford, D.J., and Smith, F.L. (2008). A mesolevel communicative model of collaboration. *Communication Theory* 18 (3): 376–406; Lewis, L.K. (2006). Collaborative interaction: review of communication scholarship and a research agenda. *Annals of the International Communication Association*, vol. 30 (1): 197–247. doi: https://doi.org/10.1080/23808985.2006.11679058.

some particular issue that warrants attention and engagement. *Multiple stakeholders* means that several parties are affected by – and/or can affect – the issues involved and the work of the collaboration. Sometimes these stakeholders are outside of the collaboration because they do not have the capacity to represent themselves, such as children or disadvantaged populations (in fact, that's often why collaborations form in the first place – the realization that important work needs to be done on behalf of others). Finally, *beyond the scope or capacity* of any single organization or sector means that the issue(s) the collaboration is working on cannot be addressed or resolved without involvement from several organizations – either because the work is too big or because it cuts across jurisdictions, often resulting in problems that are both everyone's and no one's.

This definition also distinguishes collaboration from other terms like cooperation or coordination, though I acknowledge some overlap between these concepts and accept that people often use them interchangeably in common vernacular. I see "cooperation" as the most generic, overarching term involving anyone merely working together and "coordination" as the alignment of tasks towards goal accomplishment. Collaboration obviously involves cooperation and coordination – clearly, people are working together and aligning their tasks in collaboration – but these necessary components are not sufficient to rise to the level of collaboration. For that, we need a greater level of interdependency and collective action among the participants, as well as the emergence of a higher-order organizational entity that transcends the relationships among the cooperating and coordinating partners and cannot be reduced to the contributions of any single member or subset of members – a specific organizational arrangement that is more than just the aggregation of partners. It's like, *a thing*... as people often say these days.

I should also say that this definition encompasses both the ideal and the reality of nonprofit collaboration. That is, you can be part of "a collaboration" without necessarily "collaborating" at any particular moment, and you can engage in interaction that is "collaborative" but that may not (yet) result in the formation of "a collaboration." Collaboration can be an ideal we pursue and also a reality we are in. Admittedly, some of this probably sounds a bit confusing and may just come down to semantics. That is why I'm not too concerned with definitional precision here (which is virtually impossible for big concepts like this anyway). Instead, my aim is to provide a working definition that orients us toward a particular nonprofit organizational phenomenon that has enough distinctiveness to warrant specialized analysis in this chapter, while also acknowledging some overlap and imprecision that will never be resolved. And thus we can get on to the more important work of exploring the unique challenges of nonprofit collaboration and demonstrating how a communication perspective can make a difference.

Collabrocation (or "Thinking Communicatively" About Collaboration)

Now that we have all that definitional work out of the way, let's move on to the real fun stuff of this chapter. Consistent with the communication perspective we're developing in this book, we don't just want to look *at* communication that appears to happen *in* collaboration, coming up with a list of communication do's and don'ts for collaboration: listen carefully to all of the stakeholders, build trust, appreciate multiple perspectives, use several channels to reinforce your message, be clear and concise, keep the lines of communication open, be willing to negotiate and compromise when necessary, and so on. This is all good stuff, but not what we want to focus on here. Not only is there already plenty of advice like this already out there,[6] but more importantly, this misses a key gap in our contemporary understanding of collaboration that needs more attention. You see, most of the research and writing and consulting about organizational collaboration approaches collaboration from a systems perspective with a focus on resource dependencies, transaction cost efficiencies, and the macro-level characteristics of individual organizations and interorganizational domains. Though useful, these systems approaches privilege the antecedent conditions, subsequent outcomes, and organizational properties of collaboration but tend to overlook the important social processes that compose the actual work of collaboration, essentially "black-boxing" human interaction in favor of more abstract structural explanations. The problem is that resource dependency and macro-economic theories tend to conflate structure and process, which results in a sterile conception of communication as a linear exchange of information – communication is just another variable to be managed, not something that has constitutive force of its own to investigate. The point is that we severely limit our range of analysis and practice if we take an existing systems arrangement as given and only look at how people send and receive messages within the system. Yes, we'll write better emails, give better speeches, and maybe even have more conversations that are constructive and diplomatic. But we'll always be limited by the unexamined conditions and practices that enable and constrain those interactions in the first place. Instead, we want to look at the broader phenomenon of collaboration and the key issues that collaboration entails for the nonprofit. Then we want to explore what it means to understand these issues communicatively, putting human interaction at the center of our explanatory framework (not just the thing that needs to be explained). When we understand collaboration *as* communication (i.e. collabrocation) we open up new possibilities for improved practice and constructive intervention.

6 And a lot of it is really good, like Dumlao's, R. (2018) *A Guide to Collaborative Communication for Service Learning and Community Engagement*. Stylus Publishing.

Even though every collaboration is different and exists for different purposes, some underlying issues are intrinsic to the phenomenon of collaboration itself and are relevant for all aspects of collaborative work. I'll focus on what I think are four of the most important because they encompass the full range of collaborative work: authority (power), identity (existence), agency (action), and value (effectiveness). I'll explain more in the sections below, but briefly, *authority* has to do with the ability to exercise power, control, or influence among collaboration members; *identity* is the emergence of a higher-order entity that is acknowledged as "the collaboration"; *agency* entails the ability of a collaboration to take substantive action as a collaboration in a given problem domain; and *value* involves the overall worth and effectiveness of a collaboration to accomplish its goal(s). That is, effective collaboration (value) is the ability to exert influence among members and stakeholders (authority) in such a way that leads to the existence of a social entity (identity) that has the capacity to act and make a difference (agency) in a specific realm of nonprofit work. All of these issues are interdependent and should be understood in relation to each other, while also pointing toward communication practices that increase the likelihood of more favorable outcomes more often. And as I explain all of this below, I'll introduce a practical example from my research and weave it through all four concepts of this communicative framework (authority, identity, agency, and value) in order to illustrate *collabrocation* in action. I'll start with the concept of authority, because this is the big one that shapes our subsequent understanding of identity, agency, and value.

Collabrocation Framework Part 1: Authority

One of the biggest challenges facing any collaborative endeavor is the ability to exercise some form of authority to get things done. We often – and rightly – contrast collaboration with a certain conception of authority that is more relevant for "normal" organizations that function through hierarchical mechanisms of control. Collaboration, however, is supposed to be more about equal players at the table who cooperate with each other to induce voluntary action. If only it were that simple.

I've been to several meetings that gather relevant stakeholders to discuss various issues that are important to a given community. People are usually excited to see so many people from different areas of society who all care about the issue and seem committed to do something about it. Information is shared, relationships are formed, ideas are hatched, and there is a general optimism that we might actually be able to make some real progress on this issue. But then something inevitable often happens: all the representatives go back to their home organizations and the endless demands of their "real" jobs, and all the excitement of the collaborative possibilities quickly falls to the bottom of everyone's to-do lists; perhaps to be rekindled at the next monthly or quarterly gathering of stakeholders, but also likely never to emerge again in any substantive way.

This reminds me of a collaborative group I followed here in Boulder County a few years ago that organized around the issue of community reentry for people who are released from jail or prison. This was an incredible group of competent, well-intended people doing yeoman's work on behalf of a marginalized population, trying to address the critical issue of recidivism in our community. They represented areas of law enforcement, the justice system, probation case managers, and nonprofit organizations, just to name a few. Although the meetings were informative and the relationships seemed valuable, after nearly two years of work this group never really accomplished anything of substance and eventually disbanded. Some of my contacts in the group confided that one of the biggest difficulties with their collaborative group is that no one had any real power to hold people accountable or follow through on commitments.

Here's the problem: The quality and effectiveness of collaboration depends on people's willingness to work together voluntarily, to share resources, and to take action in the absence of hierarchical control or market incentives. Without this level of cooperation, a collaboration can derail into a host of free-rider problems, deferred responsibility, minimal contributions, and overall inaction. But despite a noble cooperative ethos that is common in collaboration, any organizational arrangement still requires *some* system of authority to coordinate collective action. Generally speaking, authority is what makes organizations *organizations* and not other kinds of associations. In addition, most collaborations are trying to achieve a certain level of "organizationality" and thus need some kind of authority mechanism to ensure a measure of accountability and task accomplishment. Collaboration brings together people and organizations that generally do not have authority over each other, and it blurs the boundaries between groups and gives rise to ambiguous authority relations that can be tricky to resolve. This can make it difficult to accomplish collaborative goals because there is no formal authority to mediate between competing interests or induce action toward certain priorities. The sheer diversity of ideas and perspective of multiple stakeholders invites a lot of conflict about how the collaboration should proceed, and there has to be some way to reconcile various knowledge differences, power imbalances, and other "jurisdictional conflicts" that are sure to arise in any collaborative endeavor.[7]

7 These challenges and complications of collaboration and authority are explained more extensively in a number of important research publications, such as Kahn, W.A. and Kram, K.E. (1994). Authority at work: internal models and their organizational consequences. *Academy of Management Review* 19 (1): 17–50; Kellogg, K.C., Orlikowski, W.J., and Yates, J.A. (2006). Life in the trading zone: structuring coordination across boundaries in postbureaucratic organizations. *Organization Science* 17 (1): 22–44; Okhuysen, G.A. and Bechky, B.A. (2009). Coordination in organizations: an integrative perspective. *The Academy of Management Annals* 3 (1): 463–502.

Thus, the challenge for collaboration is to establish a system of authority capable of coordinating the diverse interests of multiple stakeholders, yet apart from hierarchical mechanisms of control. But in order to do this we need to think differently about the notion of authority, and a communication perspective helps us do this.

Traditionally, organizational authority has been understood as an objective feature of hierarchical relationships that is exercised through administrative power and control. This is what scholars call a "rational-legal" or "legitimate" form of authority because it derives from one's position in a bureaucracy. Thus, authority is something you have by virtue of your place within an institutional structure. This approach is most relevant for hierarchical and bureaucratic organizations that function based on power vested in specific departments and offices. But of course, this isn't quite how collaboration works. Instead, the complexity of collaborative work makes it really difficult to predict or control who is accountable for various responsibilities, and collaboration tends to obscure the boundaries among collaborators, which creates ambiguous authority relations that are difficult to reconcile. Yet when we talk about authority or power in collaboration we often still have this traditional approach in mind (especially since many people in collaborations are coming from home organizations where traditional approaches to authority and power are still quite relevant). Accordingly, an important question for collaborative work is how to develop a sufficient authority system to coordinate the diverse interests and knowledge domains of multiple stakeholders, yet apart from hierarchical or bureaucratic mechanisms of control.

To answer this question, we need to shift from the conventional thinking about authority in favor of an alternative approach that better accounts for the unique dynamics of collaboration. Overall, this will entail an understanding of authority as a distributed phenomenon that is negotiated among collaboration stakeholders, and emphasizes more emergent forms of influence and accountability that transcend boundaries and hierarchies. The key point is that authority is worked out in practice as people interact with each other and make decisions about the scope of their work and power they have (or not) over each other and their tasks in collaboration. Yet this raises further questions about how small-scale interactions can actually create the authority needed to coordinate and manage collaborative work across domains of knowledge and expertise. So we've got some further explaining to do before we can offer an alternative understanding of collaboration authority. Thankfully, a wealth of intellectual resources exists to help us do this. Scholars in the field of organizational communication have been especially interested in this question, and current research offers important insights to enhance our understanding of authority.[8]

To begin, we have to return to an idea we introduced in the opening chapter (and have developed in various ways throughout the book): the communicative constitution of organizations, or the idea that organizations exist *as* communication. This communicative existence involves two aspects or "modalities" as scholars like to say: the conversation modality and the textual modality. Basically, organizations exist communicatively through an ongoing dialectic of conversations and texts – organizations simply *are* the ongoing interactions of relevant stakeholders and the representations of those interactions, which shape subsequent interactions and further representations, and so on. For our purposes here, we are going to focus mainly on the textual modality (i.e. existence) of organizations like a collaboration. When we talk about the textual existence of an organization, we are referring to the interrelated networks of meaning that are "read" in certain ways that enable or constrain coordinated action.[9] These texts could be concrete (like a mission statement or bylaws) or figurative (like unspoken norms or informal practices). Figurative texts are especially relevant here because they help explain why people often refer to organizing or coordinating as "being on the same page," while not referring to any formal documents per se.

Now, stay with me here because this is the key point: whether concrete or figurative, texts themselves can develop authority through the processes by which they are authored (if you are starting to see the connection between *author*ity and *author*ing you are very perceptive!). Here's how it works. Smaller, localized interactions (like a staff meeting or planning session) can sometimes scale up and gain distance from their immediate circumstances, resulting in not just a loose connection of texts, but rather a distinct, abstract representation of the collective

8 This issue of authority and collaboration has been a key subject in many of my research articles: Koschmann, M., Kopczynski, J., Opdyke, A., and Javernick-Will, A. (2017). Constructing authority in disaster relief coordination. *Electronic Journal of Communication* 27 (3 & 4); Koschmann, M. and Burk, N. (2016). Accomplishing authority in collaborative work. *Western Journal of Communication* 80 (4): 393–413; Koschmann, M. (2013). The communicative constitution of collective identity in interorganizational collaboration. *Management Communication Quarterly* 27 (1): 61–89; Koschmann, M., Kuhn, T., and Pfarrer, M. (2012). A communicative framework of value in crosssector partnerships. *Academy of Management Review* 37 (3): 332–354.

9 If you want a more scholarly treatment of these ideas, see Kärreman D. (2001). The scripted organization: dramaturgy from Burke to Baudrillard. In R. Westwood & S. Linstead (Eds.) *The Language of Organization* (pp. 89–111). Thousand Oaks, CA: Sage; Timothy Kuhn (2008). A communicative theory of the firm: Developing an alternative perspective on intra-organizational power and stakeholder relationships. *Organization Studies* 29 (8–9): 1227–1254. Westwood, R. and Linstead S. (Eds.). (2001). *The Language of Organization*. Thousand Oaks, CA: Sage; Taylor, J.R. and Van Every, E.J. (2011).*The situated organization: Case studies in the pragmatics of communication research*. New York, NY: Taylor & Francis.

taken to represent all the interactions this abstraction refers to, for example when a small group of people begin meeting informally to discuss an ongoing issue, but over time simply refer to themselves as "the committee" – a notion meant to encompass all the people and interactions that make up their group. The emergent abstraction of "the committee" is now a "thing" that exists beyond the individual members or any particular interaction (i.e. people may come and go but "the committee" continues to persist because its existence is not reducible to any single member or incident). And it is this emergent abstraction that can become a source of authority for collaboration, what scholars call an *authoritative text* – a figurative representation of the collective that is "read" in certain ways (i.e. a text) that specifies relations of power and legitimacy, while also directing attention toward certain notions of structure and responsibility (i.e. authority). It is an abstract concept that provides a dominant reading of what a collaboration *is* and thus how it should operate and what it should do.

But how does this textual abstraction of small-scale interactions become authoritative? Well, the "distancing" from the local interactions creates ambiguity because the textual outcomes of the interactions are inevitably generalized and simplified as they gain distance from their original context. The resulting abstraction tends to discard evidence of individual authorship, meaning that the intentions and contributions of specific people are excluded or ignored and the remaining *abstraction itself* becomes the focus of subsequent interactions. This is why, for example, it is more authoritative for the abstraction "The White House" to release a statement than a specific official in the administration. Texts must shed evidence of individual authorship and portray a collective accomplishment (whether intentional or not) that is seen as legitimate and commanding. It is this vanishing of individual authorship that enables abstractions to develop authority – we stop attributing actions and motives to individual people and simply refer to the abstraction itself, which in turn reifies the abstraction and gives it a life of its own. The more we do this, the more authoritative the abstraction becomes. Basically, we treat the abstraction as if it were a separate entity with its own motivations, responsibilities, and capabilities. Authority is now attributed to the *abstraction itself*, ("Sorry, *the committee* won't let you do that"), and action is taken in the name of the abstraction ("*The committee* decided to pursue this new policy"), rather than any one person or group.

Additionally, this emergent authority is further bolstered because abstractions can accommodate multiple interpretations and still maintain a consistent identity. Plus, it is increasingly difficult to challenge this authority because abstractions cannot be engaged with directly, and any individual can always defer to the abstraction when confronted ("I can't speak to that issue, you'll have to take it up with *the committee*"). And as we'll see later in this chapter, the authoritative text also provides a sense of collective identity for a collaboration, which enables the capacity for a collaboration to take substantive action *as a collaboration*, and in turn gives us a way to access the value or effectiveness of collaborative work. But before we get to that, I suspect this is starting to sound pretty academic at this point, so let us see if we can illustrate all this with a practical example from a real collaboration.

Years ago when I was a graduate student at the University of Texas at Austin my dissertation research focused on a collaboration called the Community Action Network (now called the Community Advancement Network), or simply CAN for short. This was a collaboration among nonprofits, government agencies, faith-based organizations, and private businesses working to enhance the social, health, educational, and economic well-being of Central Texas. At the time, CAN consisted of 13 subcommittees devoted to specific issue areas (e.g. literacy, poverty, aging services, criminal recidivism), as well as a larger governing board that oversaw the overall work of CAN. They had a paid, full-time executive director and a small staff of two paid employees, but the majority of this collaboration consisted of members from partner organizations who volunteered to fill various roles. Despite many years of successful work, when I connected with CAN it was in a time of transition and struggle: their longtime and beloved executive director had recently retired, the new executive director had only been on the job for a few months, and there was a lot of soul searching about the scope of their work and who they were as a collaboration. Compared to their previous decade of productive work, it was a time of relative stalemate and inaction – still regular meetings and standing committees, but not much was getting done and discussions often involved debates about responsibility, accountability, and "turf" (i.e. jurisdiction). In short, CAN suffered from an absence of authority to coordinate and organize their work. They existed on paper and online, but they were not a functioning unit that could make a substantive difference in their community.[10]

However, roughly a year later they were back on track with a newfound sense of purpose and mission, and several tangible accomplishments to illustrate their influence in many areas of society. So what happened? My research traced the development of a new authority system that served to align and coordinate their work – not a form of control that was imposed from the top down, but an emergent form of authority that arose in practice as CAN members interacted with each other in certain ways, and built upon those interactions with subsequent practices. In short, a concept called the "community dashboard" emerged as an *authoritative text*. That is, an imposing, representative, abstraction of their work – an idea that proved to be powerful enough to organize a variety of divergent

10 You can read the full study in: Koschmann, M. (2013). The communicative constitution of collective identity in interorganizational collaboration. *Management Communication Quarterly* 27 (1): 61–89.

interests, as well as provide clarity and direction for their different projects and initiatives. And if you go to CAN's website today, you'll see that this idea of a community dashboard is the dominant concept that orients its work.[11]

So how did a simple idea like a community dashboard become an authoritative text to coordinate and organize the work of this large collaboration? It began innocently enough, with what seemed to be a throwaway comment at an inconspicuous meeting on a forgettable weekday afternoon. For several months, CAN members had been involved in numerous retreats and workshops to "reimagine" their future during this time of transition and stagnation. Lots of nice-sounding and well-intended ideas and plans were drafted, but nothing that seemed to stick or have any notable impact. But then at one of these meetings someone on the executive team said:

> So maybe we could think of our [CAN's] work as sort of like keeping an eye on the dashboard of a car. You've got all these gauges ... gas, temperature, mileage, whatever, that tell you how the car is doing. But someone has to keep an eye on everything and make sure everything is working together. Maybe that's our job.

At the time this comment seemed insignificant, just another attempt to explain CAN's work that would get buried in the meeting minutes and soon forgotten.

But as I continued my research I began to notice something: people started referencing the "dashboard thing" in subsequent meetings, and CAN's executive director started incorporating the dashboard metaphor more explicitly in her presentations and comments at meetings. She and others extended the metaphor by saying things like "moving the needle" on key issues and making sure the "tank was full" and that "we aren't stuck on cruise control." Then at meetings it began to be common to hear people mention the "so-called dashboard idea" or "that dashboard thing we're using now," and the dashboard concept was showing up more and more in CAN documents (e.g. PowerPoint slides, meeting minutes, memos; etc.). As I followed up with people in several research interviews, I confirmed that this wasn't a calculated plan to implement the "dashboard strategy," but rather recognition by various people that the dashboard concept seemed to be gaining traction and was thus a good way to frame their ideas and comments at subsequent meetings. In the ensuing months of my research, I saw the formation of a "dashboard committee" and "dashboard planning meetings." This committee worked to identify 16 indicators of key issues (organized within four broader categories) that CAN would monitor to provide an overview of the social health and well-being of the city. The result was CAN's

11 http://canatx.org/dashboard.

official "community dashboard report," which is updated annually and posted on the CAN website as the central feature of their work. And as I document further in my research, this notion of a community dashboard was continually referenced and employed to justify, validate, or defend various decisions across the scope of CAN's collaborative work. The community dashboard had gone from a seemingly harmless comment in an uneventful meeting to the dominant organizing principle for this collaboration – it had developed a life of its own with an authoritative presence that was continually invoked in their collaborative work. It had become an *authoritative text.*

The key to all this was the way that the dashboard metaphor gained distance from its original conversational circumstances through subsequent textual representations, illustrating the process of "distancing" that is a key aspect of the communicative approach to authority, which is central to the collabrocation framework I'm developing in this chapter. Furthermore, it is important to note that CAN members had a variety of interpretations of where the dashboard idea came from and how it developed – it can't be pinned on one person or group, and thus dismissed as "their" idea. Instead, it became an authoritative abstraction of the collective that represented and served the whole collaboration, thus making it difficult to resist, which further bolstered its authority. Basically, "community dashboard" emerged as the authoritative text to organize and orient the work of CAN; this emergent abstraction provided a form of authority apart from hierarchical mechanisms of control that is needed for collaborative work. And it's important to note that when analyzing collaboration for an authoritative text, we're not looking for a formal document per se, but rather trying to figure out what people are "reading" as they embark on their work. What script does everyone seem to be working off? What is the dominant reading of the situation that seems to orient everyone to the work? When you figure that out, you've found a key source of authority for collaboration, and thinking communicatively helps us do this more insightfully.

The crucial point here is that all of this happens in and through communication – it is not a form of authority that can be imposed as an objective feature of the collaboration structure, but rather an abstraction that emerges from interaction and gains power through representation in practice. And as I'll explain in the remaining sections of this chapter, this idea of the community dashboard also provided a collective sense of self (identity) for CAN that enabled it to take substantive action in its community (agency) in ways that proved effective and successful (value). Thus, we have a communicative account of authority as a negotiated phenomenon, a social accomplishment that is achieved in interaction. The main idea is that authority is *relational* because it emerges from interactive circumstances and can only be understood in reference to the actions of others. This shifts the emphasis away from hierarchical positions and more toward the meanings and interpretations that are worked out among collaboration members in practice. Collaboration authority is not in a hierarchical position or people who give commands, but rather in the *process of authoring* a definitive representation of the collective. Authority is not something someone can *have*, but rather something we *do* as our interactions create (or not) figurative texts that are "read" in ways that perpetuate certain understandings of structure, direction, and relations of power. This directs our attention toward the ways in which people are interacting with each other and how those interactions enable (or constrain) the emergence of collective abstractions that develop the authority to organize and coordinate collaborative work. It can also help us understand why some collaborations fail to generate the necessary authority to accomplish their goals, and shows us how we might intervene to improve the authority dynamics in collaborative work.

We've now done the heavy lifting of the collabrocation framework by developing an alternative conception of collaboration authority based on communicative constitution. This underwrites the remaining three concepts of the collabrocation framework: identity, agency, and value. So let's go further. Another reason why collective abstractions develop authority is that they can provide a sense of shared identity for collaboration members, which is a key source of motivation for collaborative work. A shared identity is a crucial way (maybe even *the* way) to induce action and sustain commitment apart from hierarchical mechanisms of control, and thus a significant concept for our communicative framework of collaboration, that is, *collabrocation*. Next, I explain how authority and identity come together in the concept of the *authoritative text* that serves as a collective sense of self for collaborative work.

Collabrocation Framework Part 2: Identity

Identity is a tricky concept for collaboration. If you've ever been involved in collaborative work, you've probably noticed how often people talk about the different "hats" they wear. That's because people are constantly oscillating back and forth between the various groups and organizations they represent. In my research observations, I constantly hear people say things like "Speaking with my funding agency hat on..." or "I'm going to take off my director hat and just speak as a community member..." This is simply a common way to signal that our identities in collaboration are varied and complicated, and to clarify the interests and motivations that might be related to a particular statement or question. The problem for collaboration, however, is that the mere aggregation of individual identities will rarely – if ever – result in successful collective action because there is no legitimate mechanism to adjudicate between competing interests. Instead, collaboration requires more of a *collective* identity or shared sense of self that transcends individual obligations and affiliations. Collective identity refers to the "we-ness" of a group, a communal property that cannot be reduced to any particular member or organization. Collaboration always involves ongoing tensions between self and others, and balancing one's loyalty to a home organization while also committing to collective goals and responsibilities that are necessary for successful collaboration. How this happens relates to the notion of authority and authoritative texts we developed in the previous section. But before we get to that, we may need to rethink our understanding of what identity actually is in the first place.

In the study of organizations and organizing, the idea of collective identity is often grounded in conventional notions of *organizational identity*, a well-established concept in the research and practitioner literatures. Much of this work describes organizational identity as a cognitive construct, referring to the central, enduring, and distinctive qualities of an organization.[12] But if we are thinking communicatively about organizational identity and collaboration, this understanding is a bit problematic. For starters, collaborations are not necessarily known for their enduring or fixed qualities, but rather their temporality, variability, and turnover. Additionally, a growing number of scholars argue that identity should be conceptualized as a process that is produced and reproduced through communication, not a cognitively held belief in the minds of organizational members.[13] From this perspective, organizational, or collective identity exists and is made present in communication – it is the outward manifestation of identity that makes the difference, not simply a private belief or mental state. And thus, if we want to understand collective identity, we should focus more on collective constructions, not just individual cognitions. This is what a communicative approach to collaboration (i.e. collabrocation) is all about – paying more attention to the ways in which our interactions with each other constitute the organizational phenomena of collaborative work.

Let us explore this in a bit more detail, and then look at how these ideas are illustrated in the practical example of the CAN collaboration I introduced in the previous section on authority. Remember we learned how collaboration authority

---

12 See Scott, S.G. and Lane, V.R. (2000). A stakeholder approach to organizational identity. *Academy of Management Review* 25 (1): 43–62; Whetten, D.A. (2006). Albert and Whetten revisited: strengthening the concept of organizational identity. *Journal of Management Inquiry* 15 (3): 219–234.

13 See Cheney, G. and Tompkins, P.K. (1987). Coming to terms with organizational identification and commitment. *Communication Studies* 38 (1): 1–15; Hardy, C., Lawrence, T.B., and Grant, D. (2005). Discourse and collaboration: the role of conversations and collective identity. *Academy of Management Review* 30 (1): 58–77; Kuhn, T. and Nelson, N. (2000). Reengineering identity: a case study of multiplicity and duality in organizational identification. *Management Communication Quarterly* 16 (1): 5–38; Scott, C.R. (2007). Communication and social identity theory: existing and potential connections in organizational identification research. *Communication Studies* 58 (2): 123–138.

emerges as a figurative abstraction that has the power to organize and coordinate work. Not because any one person or group is in charge and can impose their will on their fellow collaborators, but rather because certain communication practices and patterns of interaction give rise to specific conceptions that develop a life of their own and become a focal point for subsequent decisions and actions. This *authoritative text* represents the dominant understanding of what a collaboration is, the underlying script that most people seem to be reading and invoking as they engage in their work. Furthermore, an authoritative text gains even more power as it develops a specific name and becomes shorthand for the whole collaboration, and thus an important *identity* marker. The point here is that the naming of an authoritative text signals the development of a collaboration's collective identity, its broader sense of self as distinct from any individual identity within the collaboration. It provides collaboration members a sense of who *we* really are – beyond just a formal title, membership list, or website description.

With all this in mind, an important factor then is the story we tell ourselves about who we are as a collaboration and how that story comes about, or what we could call the *narrative construction* of a collective identity. That's because our shared sense of self – our collective identity – maintains its very existence through the ways in which we define the collaboration and justify various decisions in relation to an authoritative abstraction of who we think we are in the first place (i.e. an authoritative text). The key point is that collective identity is not simply an individual cognition or private mental state, but rather an ongoing process of telling a story with other collaboration members and outside stakeholders about who we are and why we do the work that we do. It is the telling and retelling of the story that reinforces the power of the authoritative text as it is made present again and again in our various interactions, and as it is used "self-referencing-ly" (if that's a word) to justify and make sense of previous actions – like a feedback loop that gets stronger with every cycle of self-referencing. This simply means that every invocation of an authoritative text to justify various decisions and explain who we are as a collaboration serves to further strengthen the authoritative text as the very source of meaning and influence for the collaboration. When we stop telling our story, we lose our sense of identity.

The example of CAN I introduced above illustrates all this very nicely. CAN's difficulties and struggles can really be understood as a loss of identity, and thus a loss of authoritative influence to organize and orient their work. In the language of our collabrocation framework, the problem for CAN was its inability to facilitate the emergence of an authoritative textual abstraction of itself, a collective sense of who it was as a collaboration that was "read" in a consistent way that aligned the divergent interests and motivations of the members. Before, we saw how the notion of a community dashboard gained distance from its original circumstances and took on a life of its own as an authoritative text, a collective abstraction that became a shorthand representation for understanding the main thrust of CAN's work. Now let's go further and actually call this authoritative text CAN's collective identity. Despite the formal name of CAN or a description on its website, this collaboration really *is* the community dashboard, this is essentially who they *are* – the community dashboard is their identity.

In my case study of CAN I documented several times where collaboration members justified and explained various decisions in terms of identity and in relation to the dashboard concept. In particular, I witnessed some intense discussions about the publication of an annual immigration assessment report that involved a lot of comments about "who CAN is" and "what we do," as well as some fascinating meetings about a new annual award for collaboration members that sought to recognize CAN partners that best exemplified "what CAN was all about." The community dashboard idea was strong enough to serve as a shared identity for this collaboration because it emerged as an authoritative abstraction of the collective that transcended the contributions of any one member or subgroup of CAN, and because it gained distance from its original circumstances and took on a life of its own through ongoing interaction across the collaboration. It was not something that was imposed by leadership or enforced through formal documentation. Instead, its meaning and authority were created and sustained (and potentially lost) in and through the communication practices of CAN members.

Now that we've developed a communicative approach to collaboration authority and explained how this relates to collective identity, let's move on to the third component of the collabrocation framework. This involves the ability of a collaboration to take meaningful action and make a tangible difference *as a collaboration*.

Collabrocation Framework Part 3: Agency

The third component of the collabrocation framework involves another key issue that is inherently problematic for collaborative work, something that every collaboration has to figure out in order to be successful. This is the issue of taking action as a collective in order to have a meaningful impact in a given problem domain (like poverty, education, environmental protection, etc.). After all, the whole reason for collaboration is to come together as a collection of stakeholders because people recognize that they cannot have a meaningful impact as individuals. So what's the point if the collaboration cannot make a difference *as a collaboration* beyond what individual organizations or representatives could do on their own? This is the issue of *agency*, and it is absolutely critical for anyone involved in collaboration to have a basic understanding of what agency is and how it works. And right on cue, the communication perspective we're developing throughout this book can provide this understanding. Let's explore a communicative approach to collaboration action (i.e. agency), and then see how this plays out in the continued practical example of CAN and its collaborative work.

Agency is the capacity to take action or make a difference in a particular situation. To be an agent is to be a cause or instrument for action. It doesn't mean being in complete control, but it does entail being a key impetus in bringing about specific outcomes. We often talk about people who are *agents* for change, which simply means they played a key role in producing some end result that is different from the way things used to be; they exhibited agency. Obviously, nonprofit collaborations exist to make some sort of difference in their communities, and thus a key issue is how collaborations constitute themselves as legitimate and capable actors in a given problem domain, as agents with a capacity for action. This is what we're trying to do in this third component of our collabrocation framework – develop a communicative approach to collaboration agency. However, the challenge we have is to walk a tightrope between two insufficient and mistaken explanations of collaboration agency, two tempting alternatives for understanding collaboration action that could take us off track.

The first I'll call the *reductionist* mistake, where all collaboration actions are eventually reduced to the actions of certain individuals. In this regard, a collaboration has no real existence as a collective actor, it's just a metaphor or "useful fiction" for the aggregation of individuals. From this perspective, when we say that the collaboration acted or did something of course what we really mean is that individual people did this; there's nothing else "there" except individual collaboration members taking action on their own. Yet upon further examination this reductionist approach is inadequate and unsatisfying. Yes, of course collaboration always involves the actions and activities of various people, but collaborations also cannot be reduced to mere individuals. We know this intuitively because we constantly refer to collaborations as if they have some sort of separate existence from their individual members, and we constantly attribute actions and intentions to collaborations. This isn't just a matter of sloppy vernacular; it reveals something about the existence and character of collaborations, which we know are distinct organizational forms that transcend any one member or stakeholder group. So we have to preserve the idea that collaborations actually exist and thus can act in ways that cannot be completely reduced to individual members.

On the other hand, we also have to be careful not to portray the distinct organizational forms of collaboration as if they have a separate essence or existence that is completely independent from their individual members. This is the *essentialist* mistake, which involves swinging the pendulum too far away from the reductionist mistake, as if collaborations just "exist" out there and act on their own, and we don't have to worry about how individuals and their interactions affect this existence and action. If the reductionist mistake doesn't give enough recognition to a collaboration's distinct existence, the essentialist mistake gives it too much.

It presumes that collaborations somehow have a prior existence apart from their members and can act upon and through them, but without accounting for how the collaboration came into existence in the first place or how a collaboration independent of individual actions could actually make a difference on its own. But we know this can't be the case either. Obviously, collaboration action is tied to the actions of its members, and sustained collaborative action is no guarantee if we don't keep up certain communication practices and interactions. Therefore, we know we can't go too far down the essentialist path, but we also don't want to revert back to the reductionist mistake either. So how do we explain collaboration agency without reducing it to the actions of individual members, but also without "essentializing" collaboration as a completely independent thing that can act on its own apart from its members?

To answer this question, we have to reconcile two aspects of collaboration that we know to be true but also appear to be in contradiction with each other: (i) that collaborations obviously are collections of individual people, yet (ii) collaborations also seem to have a unique existence that cannot be reduced to the mere aggregation of individuals. In other words, collaborations cannot act apart from individuals, but their actions also cannot be reduced to that of mere individuals. This is the paradox of agency. So how do we square this circle? This is where our communication perspective comes in. What plagues both of these mistaken approaches – reductionism and essentialism – is an instrumentalist approach toward communication as a relatively neutral conduit of human intentionality (i.e. the transmission approach to communication we talked about in Chapter 1), but without any constitutive power of its own. That is, either agency is reduced to the actions and intentions of individual collaboration members, or agency is a "thing" that a nebulous and independent collaboration simply "has" and can exercise. But if we want to reconcile the tension between reductionism and essentialism to develop a more sophisticated understanding of collaboration agency, we have to start from the position that our interactions with other people do not just "carry" meanings and intentions; they actually have the capacity to create and sustain social realities (the constitutive or social constructionist approach to communication we also talked about in Chapter 1). As I'll explain, a collaboration develops and exercises agency by constituting itself as legitimate actor in a given problem domain, and this happens by making present or bringing forth an *authoritative text* through the *appropriation* and *attribution* of collaborative action – all of which involve distinct communication practices. Now, that's a lot of scholarly language to digest, so let's break this down a bit more and then apply it to the practical example of the CAN collaboration.

We said from the beginning that all four components of the collabrocation framework (authority, identity, agency, and value) are related and interdependent. Furthermore, everything hangs on our initial conception of authority, the emergent textual abstraction that also serves as a collaboration's collective identity – an authoritative text. Now we build upon this with the idea that collaborations take action *as a collaboration* (collaborative agency) when people bring forth the authoritative text as the focal point and justification of action. This enables the collaboration to take or absorb the actions and intentions of their members (appropriation) as these actions and intentions are credited back to the collaboration itself (attribution), and thus a collaboration possesses the aggregate actions of its members as a constitutive feature of its being. That is, this ongoing appropriation and attribution of action is what creates and sustains a collaboration's existence and agency. The point here is that collaborations develop the capacity to act as we continually attribute agency to the collaboration itself and allow its authoritative text (i.e. its collective identity) to further appropriate the actions and intentions of its members, like when we say "the collaboration" accomplished something rather than pointing out the individual people who did the work, or when we allow the collective to claim our individual actions as their own instead of demanding individual credit. This isn't a one-time thing, but an ongoing feedback loop that continually scales up until we have robust social construction (i.e. a recognizable collaboration with a distinct identity as an authoritative text) that most people recognize and accept as the source of action and intentionality.[14]

Before we get back to our practical example of CAN, I bet a few people are thinking, "Wait, so you're saying that this is really just a big game of pretend? That if we just play along with the idea that the collaboration actually exists and has agency and keep talking like this, somehow it makes it all true?" Well, sort of. I don't think it's just a silly game of make-believe. But at some level, this is how social constructions and social realities work. We all agree that they are real, and in turn, these ongoing beliefs in practice make them real and consequential in our lives. Think about the example of money. Money has no intrinsic value; it only has value to the extent we all continue to believe it does and act accordingly (just think how quickly a currency can fail or devalue based on mere perceptions of worthlessness). And if you think about it, money is only real to the extent that we all agree to keep playing the game. But no one would say that the concept of money isn't real just because it's a social construction that depends on our consent. Yes, it's a different kind of reality than the brute physical reality of rocks and trees and rivers, but still real nonetheless.[15] And that's how collaboration agency works too. If we continue to attribute action and intentionality to the collaboration itself (and particularly to its

---

14 If you want to learn more about the conceptual foundations of these ideas of appropriation and attribution, I highly recommend the work of Bencherki, N. and François, C. (2011). Having to be: the possessive constitution of organization. *Human Relations* 64 (12): 1579–1607.
15 See John Searle's work on social reality for a much more detailed philosophical account of this phenomenon: Searle, J.R. (1995). *The Construction of Social Reality*. Simon and Schuster.

collective identity of an authoritative text), and continue to allow the collective to appropriate the actions of individuals, the collaboration will become and continue to exist as a legitimate and capable actor in a given problem domain. Conversely, if we stop doing this process of attribution and appropriation, collaboration agency will diminish and eventually disappear. Therefore, the key implication is that if we want to act and make a difference as a collaboration, we have to communicate in ways that enable, preserve, and expand this cycle of making the authoritative text present through attribution and appropriation.

All of this points towards an alternative approach to agency that does not take for granted the apparent independence of a collaboration (essentialism), nor does it reduce agency to the actions and intentions of collaboration members (reductionism), thus avoiding the two mistakes I described above. What we now have is a *communicative* approach to agency that keeps collaboration action tethered to the *terra firma* of human interaction, but also recognizes that our interactions can scale up to emergent social constructions that are "real" and have the capacity to act as a collective entity with a distinct identity. This approach to agency claims that collaborations exist and take action in and through all the things that act or speak on behalf of the collaboration (and more specifically, its collective identity as an authoritative text). This obviously includes people, but it also includes material objects and artifacts – like websites, logos, equipment – that bring forth the authoritative text and make it present in various situations. Thus we can also think of this communicative approach to agency as *hybrid* and *relational* because it recognizes that agency isn't really a singular "thing" a collaboration has, but rather a chain of associations among several entities that interact in ways to enable collaborations to emerge as collective actors. In other words, collaborations can develop and exhibit agency by assuming the actions of others who credit the collaboration (and particularly its collective identity) as the source of this action.

Let's return to the example of CAN to see what this looks like in practice. In order for CAN to take action and have a meaningful impact in its community, the people involved have to constitute themselves as a collective actor with a distinct identity; and furthermore, this identity (recognized as an authoritative text) has to be the site of attribution and appropriation for the actions of the collaboration. If this process is kept up through ongoing communication practices, we can say that CAN is indeed acting and making a difference *as a collaboration*. CAN acts *as CAN* to the extent that people and other material artifacts make present the authoritative text of "community dashboard" in their attributions and appropriations of action and intentionality. Consider a couple of examples from my research with CAN.

Part of my work with CAN took place during the economic recession of 2007–2009. One of CAN's big successes during that time was convening a major summit on employment and workforce issues affecting Austin, Texas, and the surrounding communities. This summit brought together many key players (businesses, non-profits, government agencies) that hadn't always worked well together in the past, and resulted in several tangible outcomes that had a notable impact in the community, such as job training programs, new partnerships around childcare and indigent healthcare, and foreclosure assistance. Overall, this summit was seen as a success by most of the people involved. However, the interesting thing for our purposes here is the way in which the notion of "community dashboard" showed up in how people talked about CAN and its work. Obviously, individual people did the work of convening the key stakeholders and taking action on a variety of important issues. But CAN *as a collaboration* was actually credited with the work, and people in CAN spoke of their efforts as if the community dashboard was doing the work, not them as individuals. "These people had not been brought together for years, so this was a big accomplishment. A lot of good decisions and actions came out of that summit and CAN was the main driver. I really think the dashboard idea played a big role in that," someone who was involved told me. Another summit participant discussed how the community dashboard concept was, "*Very present* ... in ways that seemed kind of *powerful* ... and it was like the dashboard idea *imposed itself* on how we talked and made decisions" (emphasis added). The point here is that CAN was credited as accomplishing something substantive *as a collaboration*. CAN's distinct identity as the community dashboard was brought forth as an authoritative presence in multiple interactions, and people saw this idea of a community dashboard itself as the main impetus for action.

A second example involved the allocation of money that the city of Austin received from the federal stimulus package to combat the effects of the recession. As you might imagine, this was a complicated process that was sure to end up in conflicts about how best to spend these funds. The result certainly wasn't perfect (is there any way for a city to spend millions of dollars where everyone would agree?), but the process and outcomes were generally seen as successful, and CAN was largely credited for leading the effort. As one interviewee told me:

> The stimulus thing was huge. That could have been real ugly, with so much money being thrown around and so much need. But CAN took the lead on that and everyone kind of looked at them for direction. I remember the dashboard report playing a big role because they could show they knew what was going on in all these areas. Only CAN could have done that.

Again, its identity as community dashboard was what enabled CAN to be a legitimate and influential actor in this space. The point here is that CAN was able to act and make a difference (i.e. exhibit agency) as a collaboration because its collective identity was an authoritative presence in the deliberations about the stimulus money. The community dashboard idea is what motivated people and influenced their decisions, and thus lead people to talk about CAN itself taking action (vs. any individual CAN member or subgroup). CAN has been influential in its community because its collective identity is consistently made present as an authoritative motivation and explanation for its work. And its agency as a collaboration is continually bolstered each time "community dashboard" is invoked as the source of action and intentionality, thus further reinforcing CAN as a legitimate and capable actor in their community.

The key implication of all this is that collaborations cannot act and make a difference (i.e. exhibit agency) *as collaborations* if they are reduced to the actions of their individual members, or if they are perceived as merely vague abstractions divorced from human interaction. In both cases collaborations are left impotent and without agency. Collaborations cannot take meaningful action as collaborations without a robust collective identity that is seen as authoritative and is made present in ways that continually reinforce this authority. However, a communicative approach to agency helps us understand how multiple interactions can eventually scale up to authoritative abstractions that can give collaborations a collective identity – an authoritative text that is "read" in ways that portray a collaboration as a recognizable agent. Furthermore, if this identity is invoked as the site of action and intentionality through ongoing attribution and appropriation, then we can indeed say that a collaboration has agency and can make a substantive difference in a given problem domain. And all this gives us a way to assess the overall value and worth of a collaboration, which is the final part of the collabrocation framework.

Collabrocation Framework Part 4: Value

For anyone involved in collaboration, some notion of value or overall "effectiveness" looms large. Collaborations often involve extra work beyond the demands and responsibilities of one's home organization, so there is added pressure for collaboration to be successful – otherwise, why bother wasting our time with this new endeavor if we are not accomplishing anything of value? Additionally, many collaborations are initiated and supported by outside funders (government agencies, private foundations, or even member contributions) who want to ensure their money is being spent wisely and expect collaborations to achieve something worthwhile. Plus, many collaborations are formed because they are thought to be a *more* effective form of organizing than the status quo of individual groups and organizations working separately. Therefore it's important to assess collaboration value and effectiveness at the partnership level, not just the success of individual entities within the collaboration. This involves evaluating collaborations as organizational forms that are conceptually distinct from their member organizations.

However, the unfortunate reality is research and practical experience continue to show that many collaborative efforts are largely ineffective and fail to make a substantial difference on the issues and areas in which they work. Anyone who has been involved in collaboration knows that it can be incredibly frustrating and problematic: unproductive meetings, endless discussions, political maneuvering, free riders who do not do their fair share, hoarding of information, and lowest common denominator "agreements" that no one really likes. That's because the complexity that makes collaboration necessary – the interdependence and the diversity of stakeholders – also makes collaboration very difficult. And research consistently shows that collaborations often produce limited results, involve members with contrasting goals and motivations that are difficult to manage, are prone to gridlock and fragmentation, often do not produce intended outcomes, and can even exacerbate the problems they are trying to solve. Furthermore, research also demonstrates that many collaborations do not create innovative solutions or balance stakeholder interests, and some collaborations fail to generate any collective action at all.[16] This is especially puzzling because many collaborative efforts are motivated by good intentions to be effective and follow much of the advice and best practices from the extant literature. Overall, there is a notable discrepancy between the positive connotations of collaboration throughout society and the difficulties and disappointments of actual collaboration practice. Thus, my goal in this final section of the collabrocation framework is to explain how a communication approach can help us better understand the value of collaboration and assess its effectiveness more insightfully.

The complications I described above are rooted mainly in the messiness of vague concepts like "value" and "effectiveness," which often mean different things to different people in a variety of situations. In fact, most people recognize that there are several ways that a collaboration could be successful. Success certainly involves solving a problem or resolving a difficult issue. But it could also include building trust among the key players in the community, developing a new understanding of the relevant issues, forming new structures and networks among stakeholders, or even creating alternative ways for participation and power sharing.[17] Depending on the issue and community involved, any of these outcomes could be used to assess a collaboration as "effective." But if we think about

16 See Hardy, C., Lawrence, T.B., and Grant, D. 2005. Discourse and collaboration: the role of conversations and collective identity. *Academy of Management Review* 30 (1): 58–77; Koschmann, M.A., Kuhn, T.R., and Pfarrer, M.D. (2012). A communicative framework of value in cross-sector partnerships. *Academy of Management Review* 37 (3): 332–354.

17 Gray, B. (2000). Assessing inter-organizational collaboration: multiple conceptions and multiple methods. *Cooperative Strategy: Economic, Business, and Organizational Issues*:Oxford University Press. 243–260.

collaborations *as* communication, as our collabrocation frameworks suggests, we'll see that we can develop an approach to collaboration value and effectiveness that cuts across all these criteria. This helps us do two key things: (i) assess collaborations as distinct organizational forms, and (ii) assess the actual interactions and communication practices that constitute collaboration; both of which are crucial for an improved understanding of collaboration value and effectiveness.

First, collaborations should be assessed as organizational forms that are conceptually distinct from their member organizations or the individuals involved. Yes, individual people or groups who happen to be members of a collaboration may do valuable things in their community, but the real measure of a collaboration should be its ability to make a meaningful difference *as* a collaboration. Often we think of collaboration value much too narrowly, just in terms of the success of the member organizations involved – whether or not they met their organizational goals as a result of being part of the collaboration. Of course, the success of member organizations is important, but it really doesn't tell us much about the notion of collaboration as an organizing strategy, and it takes us back to that reductionist position we already know we need to avoid.

Recall that we defined collaboration as an emergent entity that transcends the relationships among the cooperating and coordinating partners and cannot be reduced to the contributions of any single member or group. Accordingly, assessments of value or effectiveness should focus on whether or not a distinct organizational form has indeed emerged, *and* whether or not this emergent entity has developed the capacity to act and take meaningful action within a given problem domain. Mere existence is not enough, nor is simply connecting interested parties or getting people to the table, as important as these may be. Collaboration value is about the ability to take meaningful action as a collaboration. That is, we can say a collaboration is valuable or effective to the extent that stakeholder interactions result in the creation of a recognizable and legitimate collective actor that has the ability to make a difference in its community. Conversely, if we don't have a recognizable organizational form with a distinct identity, and this "thing" can't or hasn't done anything to make a difference in the community, then I think it's fair to say this collaboration isn't valuable or effective.

In the example above, CAN was an effective collaboration because the people involved interacted with each other in ways that enabled them to constitute themselves into a distinct organizational entity with a clear identity and an authoritative presence in their community. And what makes this approach to collaboration value *communicative* is that it emphasizes communication practices and patterns of interaction as the focal point for assessing collaboration effectiveness. It is also communicative in that collaboration effectiveness will show up in how people talk about the value of a particular collaboration. This involves accounts people give to home organizations and external constituents about the value of the collaboration, as well as the way its identity (as an authoritative text) is portrayed as shaping perceptions around various issues – like the way CAN was described in public and the media as being an effective collaboration, and the way its identity as community dashboard was credited for influencing key outcomes. But we can go further. Near the beginning of this chapter we defined collaboration as a simultaneous process and structure, involving both *how* people interact with each other and *what* results. We just explained assessing the value of the *what*, so now let's look at assessing the value of the *how*.

The second key thing the collabrocation framework helps us do here is evaluate the actual interactions and communication practices that constitute collaboration. Now, we don't want to nitpick every little comment or conversation; that won't be very productive. After all, communication always happens in the realm of probability – there is no periodic table of communication elements that allows us to come up with a perfect formula that applies equally for all people in all situations. But we can look at patterns and trends to assess what trajectory we're on if we communicate in certain ways. Rather than coming up with a simple list of things to say or not say, we focus instead on things that characterize the broader conversation or discussion. In that regard, let's consider a number of contrasting communication practices that shape the eventual outcomes of our interactions.[18]

First is a contrast between *aggregation and emergence*. Given the variety of perspectives involved in collaboration, it is tempting to merely aggregate everyone's ideas and take a sum-of-the-parts approach to collaboration. This may give a measure of voice to everyone's perspectives, but won't help us reach the ultimate goal of constituting a distinct organizational form with its own identity that can take action as a collaboration. Instead, our communication should move us toward generative knowledge and a shared identity; our interactions should be driven by a logic of emergence versus aggregation. That is, our communication should give rise to new and novel outcomes, not just combining what we already know. Next, is a contrast between *representation* and *exploration*. Similar to the logic of aggregation we just explained, another common impulse of collaboration is to have all the stakeholders represented at the table. Of course we do need broad representation, but if we overemphasize representation it means our conversations are likely to focus mainly on advancing individual interests and protecting one's turf. Instead, exploration involves a willingness to consider ideas and solutions beyond one's narrow interests, a willingness to inquire and not just advocate. Exploration is communicating in ways that look for something new, not that just rearrange existing positions. A final contrast is between *expression* and *engagement*.

18 These contrasting communication practices are developed more fully in one of my previous research studies: Koschmann, M.A. (2016). The communicative accomplishment of collaboration failure. *Journal of Communication* 66 (3): 409–432.

Given the emphasis on aggregation and representation that is common for collaboration, a focus on expressing one's perspective naturally follows – being heard and getting your ideas on the record. But often this comes at the expense of actually engaging with other people to explore differences and develop new ideas. If collaboration is merely a forum for expressing ideas but does not involve actual engagement among participants (however messy that might be), it won't have the interactions that are necessary for a distinct organizational form and collective identity to emerge, there will be nothing authoritative about the collaboration, and it won't have the capacity for legitimate and substantive action. Thus, from a communication perspective, we can understand ineffective collaboration in terms of communication practices characterized primarily by aggregation, representation, and expression. This doesn't mean anything good can't come from this work, it just means that this is unlikely to result in the constitution of distinct organizational forms that have the capacity to take meaningful action *as a collaboration*. Instead, successful collaborations that make a tangible difference in their communities are marked by communication practices that foreground emergence, exploration, and engagement. We can't guarantee this will always lead to effective collaboration – there are too many unique factors involved. But we can increase the probability of more favorable outcomes more often; we can get on a path that leads to more valuable and effective collaboration.

Putting It All Together

So that's it, the collabrocation framework consisting of four key concepts: authority, identity, agency, and value. I call this *collabrocation* because it signifies the inseparability of collaboration and communication, and that the main aspects of becoming a functional collaboration (power, existence, action, and effectiveness) are fundamentally communicative. It's all about how we interact with each other in our collaborative work, and how the outcomes of those interactions give rise to organizational forms that influence our subsequent interactions, which in turn shape new outcomes, and so on. This distinctively communicative approach allows us to explain effective collaboration (value) as the ability to exert influence among organizational representatives (authority) in such a way that leads to the existence of a social entity (identity) that has the capacity to act and make a difference (agency) in a specific domain of nonprofit work. Thus, to think "collabrocatively" means focusing on the communicative constitution of distinct organizational forms that have the capacity to take meaningful action, and communicating in ways that are characterized by emergence, exploration, and engagement (in contrast to aggregation, representation, and expression).

Collaboration is a critical organizational strategy for much of the nonprofit, but collaboration also presents many difficult challenges, especially in terms of exercising authority, developing a shared identity, taking meaningful action, and achieving a sufficient level of effectiveness. We'll never be able to perfect collaboration, but we can practice it more constructively more often and in more situations. A key part of doing this well is recognizing that collaboration is fundamentally communicative, and that communication should be front and center in all our attempts to understand, explain, and engage in collaboration – what we can call *collabrocation*.

5

Meaningful Work and the Nonprofit

Matthew L. Sanders

Introduction

How can the nonprofit sector foster organizational environments that imbue work with meaning that (i) draws people to participate in their mission and (ii) motivates them to stay, contribute, and make a difference? How can nonprofits do this when they cannot entice employees with high salaries or benefits and require a significant amount of volunteer work on some of the most challenging problems in society? This chapter focuses on a key feature (and opportunity) of the nonprofit: connecting people to the meaningfulness of work within a social mission in order to make nonprofit work worthwhile for employees and volunteers. This is an inherently communicative process that can improve how nonprofits recruit and retain the help they need. In this chapter I do not view meaningful work as individual preferences for specific tasks or occupations. Nor do I see it as sets of organizational practices and policies to make work more enjoyable and rewarding. Instead, I view meaningful work as a way of talking and interacting that helps employees and volunteers make sense of the often challenging and underpaid work they do, infuse it with meaning, and justify its value and importance in society. This communicative explanation of meaningful work enables us to connect people to what matters most to them, helping them recognize the value of their work.

***

In the 1990s, John Wood was working as a successful executive at Microsoft. He was living abroad in Australia and China, earning high wages, and working for one of the biggest and fastest growing companies in the world. And he wasn't yet 40 years

Understanding Nonprofit Work: A Communication Perspective, First Edition.
Matthew A. Koschmann and Matthew L. Sanders.

old. But a trek in Nepal for a much-needed vacation led him to an impoverished school with a library that had no books for the children to read. As he took in this scene, the headmaster said, "Perhaps, Sir, someday you will return with books."[1] That experience changed him. A voracious reader as a child and as an adult, John Wood couldn't image what life would be like without books. He had felt somewhat restless in his work at Microsoft, and this experience motivated him to do something to help. So, he organized a book drive and to his surprise collected 3000 books.

With the help of a Nepali friend, he returned and delivered the books to multiple schools. Children lined the streets welcoming him and were in awe of the books. Most of the children had never held a book or seen pictures of animals or planets. Nor had they seen illustrations of people and places. Work in the world of software development and marketing quickly lost its meaning and John Wood walked away from a lucrative career to start a nonprofit organization called Room to Read. His goal: become the Andrew Carnegie of the developing world. Now, with millions of books delivered and thousands of libraries established, Room to Read is making a significant difference in eradicating intergenerational poverty by bringing education to those for whom it would otherwise be limited or unavailable.

Wendy Kopp was a student at Princeton University in the late 1980s. Coming from the wealthy suburbs of Dallas, she found college to be exciting and invigorating and looked forward to the opportunities it would afford. The most transformative part of her experience, however, wasn't her course work; it was becoming close friends with a roommate who had grown up in very difficult economic and social circumstances. This made her reflect on the unfairness that socioeconomic differences can create in a person's life. Her educational experience wasn't as hard as her roommate's because she had been given opportunities and experiences in her education that prepared her for success at an elite college.[2]

This weighed so deeply on her mind that she decided that she did not want the Wall Street banking and consulting jobs that most of her classmates were seeking as they approached graduation. Instead, she turned her senior thesis into a proposal for a nonprofit called Teach for America. Without experience or expertise, she raised $2.5 million and recruited dozens of the nation's top college students to teach in public schools in the nation's poorest and most challenging districts. Though extremely challenging to start, her efforts have created a space for thousands of college graduates across the country to make a difference where it is needed the most. Over time, Teach for America has become one of the United States' largest service programs for graduating college students.

---

1 Wood, J. (2006). *Leaving Microsoft to Change the World: An Entrepreneur's Odyssey to Educate the World's Children*, 10. New York: HarperCollins.

2 Kopp, W. (2003). *One Day, All Children: The Unlikely Triumph of Teach for America and What I Learned Along the Way*. New York: PublicAffairs.

The stories of John Wood and Wendy Kopp are remarkable. They are the kind of tales that can inspire others to make a difference. Both are driven and successful social entrepreneurs who have made a significant difference in the world. And their impact continues. We know their stories because they have been celebrated in the media and published in successful autobiographies. But, their stories also represent the stories of the many, many people around the world who make similar choices when they choose nonprofit careers or spend significant time and effort volunteering for causes that they care about.

Though the stories of most people working and volunteering in the nonprofit sector aren't as dramatic or remarkable in scope and impact, they are the same story at their core. Accountants and marketers who choose to work for nonprofits because they want to work for a cause rather than focusing on making a profit. College graduates who take lesser paying jobs working on social issues they feel compelled to address. Volunteer coordinators, event planners, and human resource specialists who decide that nonprofit work will better meet their personal goals and address problems that they want to help solve. Each one isn't publicly celebrated, but their path, choices, sacrifices, and success follow the same trajectory. They make similar decisions to John Wood and Wendy Kopp; to work in the nonprofit sector and address issues that matter to them. Equally significant are the countless people in communities everywhere who give away their greatest resource on a regular basis – their time. Volunteers give their time and money to help address social needs that are bigger than themselves. They volunteer in homeless shelters, churches, museums, youth programs, and health clinics.

Indeed, while the stories of nonprofit founders like John Wood and Wendy Kopp stand out, their organizations are built on the volunteer efforts, donations, and employment of hundreds and thousands of others who – in both large and small ways – make their organization's success possible. When you think about it this way, each nonprofit organization is a web of interconnected donors, volunteers, and employees who pull off the remarkable work of their organizations. Every nonprofit organization lives this story in one way or another. It is the foundation of nonprofit work.

Because nonprofit organizations cannot force participation (as the government does with taxation) or incentivize participation with lucrative salaries (as for-profit businesses can), they require voluntary support and ask people to give their time and money. Therefore, they wrestle with challenging and important questions: How do nonprofits get people to willingly give up their time, money, or higher paying jobs to solve social problems that benefit the common good? What drives a person to choose nonprofit work when they could make higher wages in other sectors or organizations? What moves a person to donate several hours of their time each week or month when they are already busy with full-time work in addition to personal and family commitments? What motivates a person to give their money away with no financial return?

On the surface, an easy answer would be that many people care about making communities, the environment, education, etc. better – for themselves and others. Another would be that people feel connected to particular causes and therefore engage with them. Though there are varying motivations for volunteering, when it comes to a person actually giving time and resources or making personal sacrifices to pursue nonprofit employment, it cannot be that simple. Even if these easy answers are true on the surface, we all receive far more solicitations for support that we can adequately respond to, even if we may be supportive of them all. Think of your own experiences being asked to donate money or volunteer your time. What is it that draws you to some and not others? What is it that drives you to donate or volunteer for one cause but not another? What keeps you coming back? Or, what would motivate you to take a lower salary job? And it isn't just the decision-making point that matters; the bigger question is: What keeps people doing this kind of work and making sacrifices of money and time instead of making other choices?

Understanding the complexity of these motivations and decisions is important because fewer people are making these decisions at all. In a 2018 report by the Do Good Institute at the University of Maryland, an analysis of census data showed that despite recent record totals in volunteer hours and money donated, the United States has seen a significant decline in volunteer and donation *rates*. Since an all-time peak between 2003 and 2005, the national volunteer rate hit a 15-year low in 2015 at 24.9%, which equates to 9.8 million fewer people volunteering in 2015 than in 2004. The percentage of people donating money has declined similarly, dropping more than 10% between 2000 and 2014. Perhaps the most troubling part of these trends is that these declines are most prevalent in suburban and rural areas, which are also the areas that have much higher social capital and therefore ability to give and volunteer. Volunteer rates in urban areas, where the most help is needed, has remained flat.[3] We don't know if these trends will continue downward or not, but regardless, these numbers show us that nonprofits always need to be mindful and intentional about the challenge of drawing people to their causes.

It's never been easy for people to give time or money, but this significant drop in participation rates is something the nonprofit sector cannot afford and needs to address. The nonprofit sector needs more participation, not less. Nonprofits need to understand what draws people to engage in improving civil society; what gets them to come, and what compels them to stay. Good answers would provide a significant boost to finding and retaining the right people in the nonprofit sector. But if nonprofits can't compel people to participate and they can't lure people with

---

3 Grimm, R.T., Jr. and Dietz, N. (2018, October). *Where are America's volunteers? A look at America's widespread decline in volunteering in cities and states*. (Research Brief: Do Good Institute, University of Maryland).

salary and benefits, then there is something else we need to draw upon to make this happen that we can't explain through economics or psychology alone. There is something more than crafting carefully framed persuasive requests. There is something more than incentives like food, t-shirts, or other gifts for volunteering at events. The choices that John Wood and Wendy Kopp made and the things they were able to do can't be understood economically and not fully understood psychologically. There is something deeper about meaning and connection that motivates such work.

One answer to these important questions is found in the meaning of work, what constitutes meaningful work for people, and how those meanings are created and sustained with others. Meaningful work is a central feature of the nonprofit, and is defined as work and activities that people freely engage in that, for them, draws on their values, makes a difference in the world, connects them to others, values their contributions, and serves a purpose greater than themselves.[4] Meaningful work creates a deep connection between people and what they do. The meaning of work facilitates the process of making commitments to various nonprofit causes and keeps people engaged in the work that they do. But meaningful work isn't just a set of practices or policies. It isn't specific kinds of work. Nor is it something that we can simply tell people about. Meaningful work is a way of talking about and connecting with people and organizations that *gives* meaning and purpose to the work being done that can be taken up and shared with others. With volunteer and donation rates declining and the number of nonprofits and social needs increasing, nonprofits have a great need to understand, support, and promote meaningful work in a way that allows more people to contribute and helps them more effectively promote their causes by fostering within and among donors, volunteers, and employees the meaning they seek. The question is, what does this look like and how does it work? As we'll see, a communication approach to these questions will provide compelling and useful answers, but to begin, we first need to review the history of work and how its meaning has changed over time.

A Brief History of Work

When you consider a brief history of the evolution of work in society over the past 200 years, it's easy to understand it as a progression and development of organizational forms and functions; as an ongoing evolution of processes and practices

4 Cheney, G., Zorn T.E., Jr, Planalp, S., and Lair, D.J. (2008). Meaningful work and personal/social well-being: organizational communication engages the meanings of work. *Annals of the International Communication Association* 32: 137–185. doi: 10.1080/23808985.2008.11679077.

that help people organize to accomplish goals. But I want you to look at it differently and consider it as an evolution of the meanings and meaningfulness of the work people do. When considered this way, we can see the various changes over time as a process of organizations (meaning those who start and lead them) trying to make work more meaningful in order to improve outcomes.

The industrial revolution changed the experience of work for the vast majority of people. Prior to the technological advancements that led to assembly lines, mass production, and large, powerful organizations, the world of work was largely agricultural and community centered. Most people did not live in urban centers; large cities were still relatively small. Towns and villages with local trades like blacksmiths and retail stores supported agricultural work that was at the center of most people's lives. Work was often a family effort as everyone played a role in making a living and supporting immediate and extended families. The meaning of work was grounded in family, community, and self-sufficiency in all areas of life. Work itself was done throughout most of the day and changed with the seasons.

With the development of mass production and large factories, including large-scale agricultural production, vast numbers of people moved from rural communities to urban centers in large cities to find work in this new world of employment. Work was much different in a factory than it was on a farm, and cities were very different from small towns. Assembly lines led to the scientific management of workers and a deskilling that forced people to perform routine tasks over and over again.[5] Rather than experiencing work as an integrated part of family and community life, the industrial revolution moved the meaning of work away from expertise and self-sufficiency and brought about the notion of a fair day's work for a fair day's pay. Though laborers in all eras probably lived by this idea, the deskilling of work made this the logic of the employment exchange. Consequently, the meaning in doing routine and monotonous work that was separate from family and community life logically moved to pure economic exchange. Time and labor were exchanged for money, and work was done in a place distinct and separate from other spheres of life. As a result, the meaning of work changed in dramatic ways. The inherent meaning that came from work's connection to family, community, and self-sufficiency was lost as workers became alienated from both the processes and outcomes of the work that they did. Work began to take on a meaninglessness for many as hard, simple labor was traded for wages.

As the processes, practices, and understanding of work and employment evolved in each decade of the twentieth century, conditions improved significantly and the meaning of work began to change as well. Organizations moved from the time and motion studies of scientific management with its assumptions

5 Taylor, F.W. (1911). *The Principles of Scientific Management.* New York: Harper & Brothers.

that workers were unintelligent and unmotivated to a human relations focus that recognized that social conditions and attention to workers would help productivity.[6] Though workers were not seen as assets or able to contribute to how work should be done, the shift to focusing on the human needs of workers was significant. Over time, this focus on workers led to a human resources perspective of management in organizations where workers were seen as assets to an organization instead of as cogs in a machine.[7] Employee recognition and involvement became, and continue to be, central characteristics of making work matter to employees. But throughout all of these developments, the bottom line of exchanging labor for money as the primary driver of work has continued. And it will always be a central feature for why nearly all people work and what motivates them to do it.

As a result of these many developments, much of our thinking about meaningful work has been driven by understandings of for-profit employment rooted in the traditions of twentieth-century management. This has led to three dominant views of meaningful work. First, meaningful work has been understood from an economic perspective. Rewards, compensation, and perks have long been used as ways to make work meaningful. In other words, the higher the wage the more prestigious and meaningful the work. Or, the more benefits you have, the more meaningful your work is. Second, meaningful work is characterized from a managerial approach, using flexible schedules, innovative or playful work environments, and other policies that give employees more control and freedom to work as they need to in connection with their lives. Managing in a way where people feel like they have choice, flexibility, and work-life balance can be used as a way to give meaningfulness to work. Third, a psychological understanding of meaningful work suggests that it is connected to values within individuals. Making the right match between a person and the type work they will do helps identify connections that are inherently meaningful on an individual level. These perspectives of meaningful work explain the various ways that organizations have tried to make work meaningful for people.

Overall, this approach has always been focused on organizations trying to make what is less meaningful – the economic exchange of labor – more meaningful and fulfilling. This process has been characterized by improving incentives, wages, policies, and structures. And in doing this, mindsets and beliefs about workers and their value have also evolved to the point where people matter in their organizations. But if that is all that makes work meaningful, then we should have figured out meaningful work in organizations by now. But we haven't. Survey

---

6 Schwartzman, H.B. (1993). *Ethnography in Organizations*. Newbury Park, CA: Sage.
7 Harris, T.E. and Nelson, M.D. (2008). *Applied Organizational Communication: Theory and Practice in a Global Environment*, 3e. New York: Lawrence Earlbaum Associates.

research shows that despite improvements over the years, more than half of workers do not feel engaged in and connected to their work.[8] This ongoing search for more meaning in work continues, and it's currently making another significant shift that reflects values that are more closely aligned with the nonprofit.

Rather than finally identifying what structures or processes or policies make work meaningful, the first two decades of the twenty-first century have turned our search for meaningful work toward a deeper, more personal and relational end. In addition to contributing knowledge to improve processes and products, feeling heard and valued by the organization, having flexible work environments and schedules, and more equitable compensation, people (especially younger workers) want meaning and fulfillment. Certainly, this claim can sound like so many that argue that younger workers require work to be different than it was in the past; that younger workers want to make an impact and work for organizations that make a difference. And it is true that more and more younger workers want their work to matter to themselves and others. But that is only one part of the story. The rise of cause marketing, corporate social responsibility, sustainability efforts, etc. shows that people want more out of their work. In addition, people want the organizations they patronize to care about social causes and the common good. All of this is leading to a growing sense that social purpose can be compatible with profitability. This has been best illustrated by the rise of *B Corporations*, which write social goals that benefit the public into their articles of incorporation and explicitly state that a fair return on investment, rather than profit maximization, is the goal for their business. However, this trend is not confined to a unique type of business; social trends in work and consumption are moving all organizations toward a greater merger of purpose and meaning with capitalism.[9]

Indeed, people increasingly want their work to be conscious of social needs and injustices and speak to societal concerns beyond their organizations. In short, many people are looking for more personally meaningful work. And while this doesn't mean people are less concerned with the economic exchange for labor, it does mean that more and more people want more meaningfulness to accompany it. Despite all the improvements to organizations over time, there is still something missing.

For those of us focused on the nonprofit, it is very interesting that this specific turn to meaningfulness looks beyond structures, practices, and policies and demands purpose and impact. This "new" focus is really an old one. Meaning grounded in purpose and impact is what the nonprofit sector has always experienced. These seemingly new and emerging corporate models for purpose-driven

---

8 Harter, J. (2018). Employee engagement on the rise in the US. https://news.gallup.com/poll/241649/employee-engagement-rise.aspx.

9 Wood, J. and McGibbon, A. (2017). *Purpose, Incorporated: Turning Cause into Your Competitive Advantage*. Big Purpose Press.

meaningful work are simply the organizational realities that the nonprofit sector has always experienced and had to address with its employees and volunteers. Indeed, meaningful work has always been the underlying motivator for every kind of nonprofit organization.

The nonprofit sector began with the rise of democracy in the United States, when people were first allowed to legally organize and associate to address their common problems and develop and improve civil society. In its earliest stages, nonprofit work was primarily centered on clergy, medicine, and private education.[10] Overtime, the need to address social problems has led to nonprofit work in every facet of society. All of these efforts stand upon the underlying values of commitment beyond self, worth and dignity of the individual, and freedom.[11] These values give meaning to the challenges and joys of nonprofit work. Every nonprofit effort is focused on impact and making a difference. Those working in the nonprofit sector have had to organize, manage, and solve problems with purpose, rather than profit, as the primary goal. As a result, all nonprofit work is driven by the meaningfulness associated with it.

Thus, the business world's long effort to make work more meaningful has led it to a point of needing to embrace a nonprofit mindset. This development is exciting but also points to a potential problem. The nonprofit has long been defined by what it is not, rather than what it is. Such a negative framing has resulted in business practice becoming the logic by which nonprofits are expected to be successful. But as we've outlined above, those assumptions and practices of meaningful work don't make work fully meaningful. Indeed, for-profit enterprises have sought for meaningful work for decades but can't quite get there because business – for good and ill – will always be fundamentally motivated by self-interest. Therefore, if the nonprofit sector is going to address the shrinking number of volunteers and donors, provide better employment for those who pursue careers in the sector, and meet growing demands by expanding its reach, then the nonprofit needs to more fully connect to its roots and core values. Nonprofits need to double down on what they are and why they exist to fully make work have the meaning that is necessary for successfully pursuing a social mission.

But if we can't fully rely on economic, managerial, and psychological explanations of meaningful work, what do we do? How can we tap into the core of nonprofit work and let those values infuse it with the meaning it inherently has?

---

10 Hammack, D.C. (2002). Nonprofit organizations in American history: research opportunities and sources. *American Behavioral Scientist* 45: 1638–1674. doi: 10.1177/0002764202045011004; Hall, P.D. (1987). A historical overview of the private nonprofit sector. In: *The Nonprofit Sector: A Research Handbook* (ed. W.W. Powell), 3–21. New Haven, CT: Yale University Press.

11 O'Connell, B. (1988). Values underlying the nonprofit endeavor. In: *Educating Managers of Nonprofit Organizations* (ed. M. O'Neill and D.R. Young), 156–161. New York: Praeger.

How do we surface the purpose inherent in nonprofit work and foster it among volunteers or employees? A communicative explanation of meaningful work allows us to see how this takes place. For the nonprofit, the question isn't, "How do we make our work more meaningful?" That's already a given. By definition and legal classification, nonprofit work is purpose-driven toward the benefit of the common good. The important questions from a communication perspective are how do we give our work meaning? What are the communication practices and processes that give meaning to our work and connect others to it? How do we foster those practices to help those who work with us experience the meaning they are seeking? Next we'll discuss a communicative explanation of meaningful work, which emphasizes the notion of *discourse*, or how our ways of talking about work constitute deeper systems of meaning that in turn shape our subsequent interactions.

Communicative Explanation of Meaningful Work

A communicative explanation of meaningful work, grounded in the core values of the nonprofit, offers a different way to understand and foster meaningful work that will help employees and volunteers thrive in their roles and better serve the social causes in which they have chosen to participate. From this perspective, we are primarily concerned with what work *means*, not simply what it *is*. As we explained in Chapter 1, communication is the social process that creates and sustains our organizational realities and gives them meaning. These social realities – the norms, values, beliefs, interpretations, and understandings of what we do – are created with others in communication. Therefore, understanding communication as the process of social construction allows us to see the meanings that arise from the complexities of people interacting with their environment and making sense of what they are doing. That is the process that gives work meaning, not just the work itself.

In this way, we can see why other explanations of meaningful work have failed to move our understanding of work to a place that ultimately connects to purpose. Economic, managerial, and psychological explanations have assumed that the meaning of work is a cognitive puzzle that we have to figure out. Therefore, we see communication as simply the transmission of practices, policies, and incentives and their pre-established meanings that others have created and expect to be understood. But seeing communication as transmission cannot tell us the meaning that a specific practice or incentive has been given by employees or volunteers. It also cannot tell us why a similar policy might have different meanings for different groups and why one set of meaning becomes more influential than others. And seeing communication as transmission cannot tell us why someone chooses to do the work in the first place, what meaning they bring to it, or how they retrospectively make sense of their work after the fact. All it can do is tell us what we think it is or should be. That assumes that the organization creates the connection between purpose and work that people accept or reject.

So, if we want to understand meaningful work in a way that connects people and purpose, we need to understand the communication and interaction that surround and construct it. We need to know what meaning those doing the work give it, not what we think that meaning is. Consider this simple illustration. A couple of undergraduate students in one of my classes volunteered at a local food pantry as part of a class project. They chose to volunteer at the food panty because they felt connected to its mission. They wanted to help those in need and be part of feeding the hungry. When they reported to volunteer, however, the supervisor treated them with indifference and gave them their tasks. As they worked, they quickly realized that most of the other volunteers were there on a court mandate as part of a criminal conviction. They were not necessarily interested in the work and didn't find great meaning in it. As a result, the conversations and interactions during their work were quite different than you would expect. This kind of unsupportive and unenthusiastic interaction changed the whole dynamic. Even more, when they finished the shift, the supervisor asked them if they needed their documents signed to prove they had completed their volunteer hours. He was surprised that they were there voluntarily. After a semester of this kind of interaction, these students felt very different about the food pantry and the work they did there. What started as meaningful felt somewhat meaningless at the end. The actual work didn't change. The mission of the organization didn't change. But the interactions and meanings that were created about the work through communication, however, robbed it of meaning for these students who were not interested in continuing their volunteer work. The key point here is that the exact same work can mean very different things to different people, and the meaning of work can even change for the same people – all depending on how people interact with each other and make sense of their experiences. Thus meaningful (or not) work is constituted communicatively, and subject to change based on our communication with other people; the meaningfulness of work is not some objective property of the work itself. This simple example illustrates how a communicative explanation of meaningful work, at its core, tells us that meaningful work is created and sustained in how we talk about and make sense of work with other people. Therefore, meaningful work functions primarily as a *discourse*, rather than as only a set of organizational practices or policies.

Discourse is a term that scholars use to describe everyday language and understandings that people readily draw upon and share in order to talk about their social worlds and what they mean. Discourse is both a way of talking about something and the deeper systems of meaning that shape how we talk about things in the first place. And of course both of these aspects of discourse influence each other – how we talk about things sets the tone for how those things are supposed to be talked about in future interactions. Let's look at a quick example from another context to help clarify this idea. If you've paid attention to recent debates about college athletes and whether or not they should be paid, you'll notice there is a certain way that people tend to talk about these issues, as well as a broader framework of meaning that shapes how we have the discussion and what is even on the table to discuss. In particular, there is a discourse of *amateurism* that pervades discussions about paying college athletes – a way of talking about athletics that guides our thinking about who participates, what is at stake, and the end goal of athletic competition. When someone is an amateur athlete, we know they aren't profiting from their sport and are less skilled and experienced. Of course, the discourse of amateurism has also prevented us from seeing or addressing problems in amateur sports that keep athletes from sharing in revenue or focusing on academics. And once you appreciate this perspective you'll see that most of what we discuss in our society is shaped by the discourses of those topics. The discourse of parenting, the discourse of immigration, the discourse of space exploration, the discourse of healthcare, the discourse of criminal justice reform, and so on. There is a particular way of talking about these topics, plus a broader framework of meaning that shape how we have these discussions and what is even possible to discuss. Taking a communication perspective here means paying attention to both of these dynamics. So as a discourse, meaningful work is a way of *perceiving* and then *talking* about work that infuses work practices and policies with meaning and value. This doesn't mean that practices and policies, as well as personal preferences and dispositions, can't help make work meaningful, but without thinking communicatively about meaningful work, we miss how such practices get imbued with meaning in the first place and how that meaning then gets taken up and shared by others in ways that develop organizational and professional cultures.

Communicative practices of meaningful work, therefore, are (i) the events that put people, processes, and participants together in relationship to each other, and (ii) the words and meanings that people use to describe what they do and why they do it. When this happens, work becomes seen as meaningful or not meaningful, impactful or unimpactful, depending on the ways in which people think, experience, and talk about it with others.[12]

---

12 Kuhn, T., Golden, A.G., Jorgenson, J. et al. (2008). Cultural discourses and discursive resources for meaning/ful work: constructing and disrupting identities in contemporary capitalism. *Management Communication Quarterly* 22: 162–171. doi: 10.1177/0893318908318262.

Therefore, meaningful work isn't the work itself; it is the means (i.e. communication processes and practices) by which people imbue their work with meaning. This is an important communicative explanation because people find meaning in all kinds of work and activities that others would find less meaningful, unpleasant, challenging, or even meaningless. We are all drawn to different kinds of work and different kinds of causes and different kinds of social missions. In addition, in order for anyone to find any kind of work meaningful, they have to hear that value from others and then communicate and enact that meaning themselves. In other words, someone may be drawn to a specific kind of nonprofit work because it is meaningful to them, but they also need that meaning to be accepted and reinforced by others as it is collectively taken up in everyday conversations and activities. That is why work that is deemed meaningful by some can lose its meaning when they start to think and talk about it differently. It is the discourses that surround us that affect how we think and feel about our work and the work of others. Again, this is where economic, managerial, and psychological explanations cannot fully explain meaningful work and how it creates more connection between people and their work. These perspectives assume that meaning is a property of the work itself instead of existing in the discourses about the work, that meaning is in the job itself rather than the communication about the job that make it connect or disconnect with those who do it.

Granted, some work has been talked about the same way by most people for very long periods of time. As a result, the discourse has become so stable that we take it for granted as a property of the work itself. But this doesn't change the fact that we still can't fully understand the meaning of work apart from these interactions. This also doesn't account for how quickly and extensively the meaning of work can change if people just start talking about it differently (for example, how the meaning of journalism has changed so rapidly in such a short amount of time in our modern era of digital media). When changes in the meaning of work happen quickly and extensively, it exposes how meaning was never in the work itself, but rather in our collective understanding and talk about it (i.e. the *discourse* of the work).

For the nonprofit, meaningful work is the cornerstone in a sector that seeks to improve the common good for all, give advantage to those without it, make a difference in people's lives, improve communities, and protect both individual rights and the natural world. Without meaningful work operating as a discourse that people draw upon to bring out the purpose and impact of a social mission that animates the nonprofit endeavor, the difficult and challenging work that is required to make this kind of work possible would be too much to ask for many people, especially in a sustained and dedicated way. It is these discourses of meaningful work that support and sustain and motivate us when we give our time for social causes and give meaning to the challenging and underfunded work that we often do.

To make these ideas more concrete, I describe below two specific ways in which a communicative explanation of meaningful work helps us better understand nonprofit work and how to enable employees and volunteers to connect with and engage their work so they feel motivated and justified in their efforts. First, a discourse of meaningful work serves as a way to legitimize nonprofit work and careers. Second, a discourse of meaningful work enables people to see the work itself as a form of compensation.

Meaningful Work as a Legitimizing Discourse

Because the nonprofit sector's legal tax standing doesn't allow it to distribute revenue or earnings (profit in business terms) to any member of the organization, it has to fund itself through donations, grants, government support, and charging fees for services. And because nonprofits often work on pressing problems for those who are disadvantaged or for issues that are beneficial but unprofitable, the fees they can charge are typically below market value. All of this means that those working in the nonprofit sector typically make less than those in for-profit organizations while working on equally complex challenges. Of course, large nonprofit hospitals and private universities are some exceptions to this, but on the whole, most nonprofit work is done using fewer resources than needed. These limited resources often restrict the kinds of salaries and benefits that can be paid to employees. This leads to an important question: Why do nonprofit employees and volunteers stay and do such challenging work without adequate (or any) compensation?

Discourses of meaningful work function as a way of justifying and legitimizing nonprofit careers in the face of cultural discourses that make lower-wage work seem less meaningful. Salary is typically the primary means by which society tends to judge the value of work and wealth tends to measure a person's success. Indeed, notions of "good work" and "real jobs" typically place for-profit work with personal gain as the standard for work and leave much nonprofit work in need of some kind of justification for doing it. This creates a struggle that high-profile nonprofit founders, everyday nonprofit employees, and volunteers must deal with: Why would they walk away from better wages or more benefits to work in the nonprofit sector? Meaningful work serves as a tool to address this.

Research on nonprofit careers has uncovered specific ways in which nonprofit professionals talk about their work that evokes its meaningfulness in ways that help them legitimize their work in a world that measures the value of work by income. Communication scholar Jennifer Mize Smith has been studying nonprofit careers and her research offers important insights to understand how nonprofit employees working in the arts justify doing this work for lower than average wages. Using in-depth interviews across a number of organizations, she brings out specific ways of talking about the meaningfulness of nonprofit work that keep people connected to their purpose and mission. One way people did this was by framing their work as a calling. This way of talking about meaningful work insists that contributing to some purpose greater than the self has deep meaning and significant value for themselves and others. It's the kind of work that people describe as choosing them rather than them choosing that work. People are drawn to it and feel that it is something that they must do. This way of talking about nonprofit careers is evidenced in statements like, "I kind of had this feeling that this is where I was supposed to be, what I should be doing." And "I could never conceive of doing anything else. It wouldn't occur to me, wouldn't appeal to me. It's like saying, 'Why do you breathe?' It's a part of who I am."[13] This kind of framing helps people understand the intense caring that they have for a cause and the feeling of being drawn toward it, giving meaning to their choice of career in nonprofit work.

Another way nonprofit employees in the arts talked about their work in order to make sense of it compared to more lucrative work is through a discourse of meaningful work as an act of service. This is a community and other-focused way of talking about nonprofit work that connects an individual's personal ideals to a higher purpose that requires individual sacrifices for the greater good. Mize Smith's research brings out this way of talking with responses like these: "The most fulfilling thing is when somebody calls and we're able to connect them to what they need to be connected to. I still get that thrill every day."; "I know I'm touching lives with what I'm doing ... even though I felt 18 different defeats earlier in the week, those times really keep me motivated. Knowing that if no one's fighting for it, it's definitely not going to happen."; and "You're not just in it for yourself or for your board; you're in it for the community."[14] Drawing on a discourse of service functions as a way for nonprofit employees to communicate the reasons why they do nonprofit work and the value it holds for others. Thus, work becomes meaningful and has important impact beyond compensation or perceptions of the type of work.

---

13 Mize Smith, J., Arendt, C., Lahman, J.B. et al. (2006) Framing the work of art: spirituality and career discourse in the nonprofit arts sector. *Communication Studies* 57: 25–46. (p. 33). doi: 10.1080/10510970500481672.

14 Mize Smith, J., Arendt, C., Lahman, J.B. et al. (2006). Framing the work of art: spirituality and career discourse in the nonprofit arts sector. *Communication Studies* 57: 25–46. (pp. 34–35). doi: 10.1080/10510970500481672.

As you can see, discourses of meaningful work that highlight the ideas of calling and service allows nonprofit employees to frame their work according to their own values and personal goals instead of by other extrinsic measures that cannot adequately explain why they do this kind of work. What makes this work feel like a calling or an act of service, however, isn't something in the work itself, but that meaning has been constructed through these ongoing communication practices that imbue them as such. In seeing these discourses of meaningful work in this way, it shows us that this justification process isn't just a state of mind, but something that is talked about and worked out with others. It's a specific and purposeful way of talking with others that enables them to legitimize their work, enabling themselves and others to draw upon the meaningfulness of the missions they serve.

Meaningful Work as a Form of Compensation

Discourses of meaningful work also serve as a way to make the work itself the end goal and therefore a form of compensation that makes the work worthwhile even though it may pay less and be more challenging than other types of work. Pay, therefore, is talked about as part of the reward and compensation that nonprofit work provides. This way of talking about work connects it to some gain outside of the individual doing the work and connects the employee to something much bigger. Discourses of meaningful work in for-profit enterprises can become hollow when labor serves as the means of enriching others and seeking personal gain, especially when some of the work being done is simple or routine. In the nonprofit sector, personal gain is typically less significant and therefore the work itself must function as an end itself, instead of a means to an end.

Again, Jennifer Mize Smith and her colleagues have identified different ways that nonprofit employees communicate about their work in order to give it this meaning. For example, many nonprofit employees in the arts evoke the idea of sacrifice in relation to financial compensation. Talking about nonprofit work in this way is important because a discourse of sacrifice argues that giving up something valuable or desirable (in this case salary) for something more important is inherently rewarding and noble. Responses from in-depth interviews show how people intentionally frame their work as meaningful because of the sacrifice they make: "I work probably five times as much here [as my corporate job] and get paid half ... but I wouldn't trade it for the world."; "I think a lot of people who work in nonprofits don't make a lot of money and that's pretty much a given. You don't go into a job like that with the understanding that you're going to become rich. I think a lot of people who are in it depend on another source of income, a spouse or some other source, to make a living wage. And you know, there are tradeoffs with all of that. I have to decide what I want. Do I want to enjoy what I'm doing, or do I want to make a lot of money?"[15] Recognizing the sacrifices that come with nonprofit work and then showing why such sacrifices are worthwhile enables nonprofit work to be taken up as meaningful in ways that enable people to work more happily and with greater purpose.

Those who work in the nonprofit sector also see personal rewards in doing this kind of work and place those kinds of rewards as more important or more worthwhile than financial gain. Responses from Mize Smith's work clearly illustrate this way of talking about nonprofit work as well: "Here they give me a lot of creative freedom, and they put a lot of responsibility on my shoulders, and they have a lot of faith in me."; "Things you are doing affect the community in a positive way."; "I'm doing something worthwhile."; and "Just being involved in a not-for-profit, you learn so much about yourself and the organizations and especially this community."[16] Such rewards are clearly communicated and taken up as part of the overall compensation of nonprofit work. Therefore, nonprofit employees can recognize and accept the reality of lower wages but see greater benefits to themselves and to the causes their organizations serve.

Therefore, discourses of meaningful work that highlight the meaning people infuse into their work allows nonprofit employees to embrace their work and connect to the purpose and impact of the mission they are serving. Without these ways of evoking calling, service, sacrifice, and personal rewards, it would be much more difficult to accept the wage realities of nonprofit work because there would be no way to highlight their value in conversation with others. The fact that these ways of communicating come out in interviews tells us that these are readily used and persuasive. It is likely that in any conversation, nonprofit employees will draw upon these meanings to tell others why their work matters and why they keep doing it. Doing so allows them to see the full value of what they do and communicate it to others. When these kinds of conversations are taken up in organizations and among volunteer groups, you can see the impact it could have on supporting and retaining good people in the nonprofit sector. Now that we've seen how work can be understood and engaged as meaningful through discourses of legitimization and compensation, let's look at a few specific communication practices that support and sustain these discourses.

15 Mize Smith, J., Arendt, C., Lahman, J.B. et al. (2006). Framing the work of art: spirituality and career discourse in the nonprofit arts sector. *Communication Studies* 57: 25–46. (p. 35). doi: 10.1080/10510970500481672.

16 Mize Smith, J., Arendt, C., Lahman, J.B. et al. (2006). Framing the work of art: spirituality and career discourse in the nonprofit arts sector. *Communication Studies* 57: 25–46. (p. 36). doi: 10.1080/10510970500481672.

Communicative Practices of Meaningful Work

Because meaningful work is a way of thinking and talking about various practices, nonprofit organizations should carefully focus on how they can foster discourses of meaningful work through specific communicative practices. Though described below as discrete practices, each exists as a part of everyday conversations that foreground the inherent meaningfulness of nonprofit work and allow it to be taken up and used as part of daily interactions that socially construct our organizational environments as supportive of and connected to the social missions of the nonprofit. Fostering discourses of meaningful work in nonprofits develops a greater sense of mission and purpose across the organization and helps employees and volunteers realize the purposes for which they choose to do their work. It also helps motivate them when work becomes challenging and complicated. While discourses of meaningful work help people legitimize their paid or volunteer work and help them see benefits beyond financial compensation, nonprofits should not expect that this will just happen naturally and automatically, but rather should seek to actively foster the conversations and interactions that support such meanings. Below I describe three specific communicative practices that nonprofits can use to foster connections to meaningful work for employees and volunteers.

Memorable Messages

Volunteers serve in nonprofit organizations for various reasons. Though we typically think of volunteers feeling strong connection to a nonprofit's mission, they also come because of the relationships they have with other volunteers, special expertise that is specifically needed, or because they see personal benefit to their volunteer work.[17] Regardless of the reason a volunteer comes, that reason is meaningful to them. And given that nonprofits typically have very little leverage to keep a volunteer (as opposed to pay for employees), how they are connected to and experience the meaningfulness of their work matters. As is the case in many nonprofits, volunteers experience an interesting tension: they feel like members of the organization, as they should, but because of their contingent role, they often receive less training and experience less connection than employees. Therefore, how nonprofits communicate the value and impact of their work matters a great deal.

One important way to overcome this challenge and help volunteers feel connected and valued is through memorable messages. Many times volunteers are

17 Wilson, J. (2000). Volunteering. *Annual Review of Sociology* 26: 215–240.

oriented with a quick review of procedures, rules, and guidelines. It is not uncommon for volunteers to show up to help and be rushed through an explanation of the work to be done and how to do it. Nonprofits are often underfunded and pressed for time, so such an orientation process is understandable. But these kinds of procedural messages are ineffective in helping volunteers feel like they are part of the organization. Volunteers simply don't feel connected to the meaningfulness of their work through communication about rules and procedures, even though that information is important and wanted. Instead, messages about the significance of their work is the key for volunteers to feel connected to a nonprofit, regardless of their reasons for donating their time and energy.

The research of communication scholar Sarah Steimel on how nonprofits can better connect with volunteers helps us see what these messages can look like and how they work.[18] She identifies three specific memorable messages that are worth considering in connection to meaningful work. First, messages of *significance*. These messages communicate the importance, value, and impact of volunteers' work in fulfilling the mission of the organization. For example: "You're work today has made a significant difference to the children in this school." Or, "Without your help, we would not have been able to complete this project." These messages are especially important when the volunteer work being done isn't glamorous or immediately connected with the mission. Messages of significance help make work more meaningful by reaffirming the value of the work.

Second, messages of *gratitude*. The most valuable resource anyone can give a nonprofit is time. Money and resources are also important contributions, but time is equal to everyone. Therefore, communicating sincere gratitude for what a volunteer does is a significant way to make work meaningful. Such messages of gratitude for donations of time and resources are easily connected to messages of significance and can be done together. For example, "Thank you so much for giving us part of your weekend. We know your time is valuable. You're work today has made a significant difference to the children in this school." Or, "Thank you for your continued donations to our organization. Without your help, we would not have been able to complete this project." It is also important to note that communicating such messages individually – face-to-face and one-on-one – is important for making them meaningful.

Third, messages that *praise a person's competence and expertise*. Nonprofits require all kinds of expertise from volunteers in order fulfill their missions. Some of this expertise, particularly that given by board members who have legal,

18 Steimel, S. (2013). Connecting with volunteers: memorable messages and volunteer identification. *Communication Research Reports* 30: 12–21. doi: 10.1080/08824096.2012.746220.

financial, administrative, and technical backgrounds, is expensive but given freely. Taking the time to offer support for a person's expertise frames that particular work or activity as meaningful because of its connection to a social mission. For example, accounting work or administrative expertise doesn't always feel inherently meaningful, but when connected to the mission, it has great meaning. And that meaning is primarily enacted through communication. For example, "We greatly appreciate all the legal advice you help us with on our board. Your expertise is essential to our success." And "It is so important to have good accounting advice in our board meetings. Your expertise is a big help to our cause."

We understand that these kinds of messages seem simple and obvious, and they are. But because of that, they are often overlooked or forgotten in the hectic pace of work and activities. Yet they take very little time and effort per person and can easily be done with sincerity. And these kinds of interpersonal messages are essential in helping retain volunteers by reinforcing and supporting their work as meaningful. Without these kinds of messages in our interactions with volunteers, it is much harder for them to experience the meaningfulness of their work in connection with the organization's mission. As we communicate these kinds of memorable messages, an additional step we can take to promote meaningful work is to connect people to the purpose and impact of the nonprofit by connecting a volunteer or employee's personal identity to the identity of the organization. Though this connection may exist internally for many, it is essential to create an environment where identities can be expressed and reinforced.

Connecting Organizational and Personal Identity

While paid employment in nonprofits is motivated by compensation and benefits (as in all sectors of work), it is not the primary motivator for most people who pursue careers in the nonprofit sector. Successfully recruiting and retaining employees depends on their connection to the work and the extent to which they see it as meaningful and impactful. Since meaningful work is rooted in notions of service, sacrifice, making a difference in the lives of others, and finding personal fulfillment, it is important that those ways of thinking about nonprofit work are reinforced within the organization through everyday communication. In this way, discourses of meaningful work can be fostered and strengthened for the benefit of employees who often do challenging work for below-market wages. To do this, nonprofits can focus on connecting their organizational identity to the individual identities of those in their organizations.

Organizational identity is the set of characteristics and meanings that an organization communicates to the public. It encompasses the meaning of the organization and its work. Organizational identity is contained in mission statements and messages about the organization's vision and purpose. It is this identity that captures the attention and support of the public and individual donors and volunteers.[19] An organization's identity also has a significant impact on how prospective employees see the organization and it influences how they anticipate their work and its role in the organization's mission. Employees, therefore, come to nonprofits with expectations for how they will connect to the meaningful work of fulfilling a social mission.

Of course, most people are drawn to work with which they can personally identify in one way or another. Whether that identification is steeped in a person's experience, abilities, or relationships, that connection is vital to enabling people to successfully do their work. It is important to remember, however, that personal identity is something that people both feel they are *and* want to become. It is something that people enact in everyday interaction with others, and in doing so, people seek reinforcement that they are who they are trying to become. Therefore, nonprofit work needs to reinforce organizational and individual identity so that employees can talk about and feel connected to the greater meaning in their work.

When this doesn't happen, it fosters a disconnection from work that an employee wanted to be meaningful. For example, I worked with an undergraduate student who had great ambitions to work in the nonprofit sector. She was thrilled to get a summer internship at a large, national nonprofit that focused on helping children. This was the kind of cause that she cared about and the type of organization that she wanted to be part of after graduation. She left campus with high expectations for the work she would be doing, even though she knew it would be internship level tasks. When she returned in the fall and visited with me, I excitedly asked her how her internship had gone. "It was really disappointing," she said. "I wanted to help children but I spent the summer by myself in a cubicle stuffing envelopes. I didn't even see a kid the entire time." She didn't expect that her summer internship would be glamorous or that she would have some significant impact on the organization's mission, but as an individual, her identity had strongly connected to the organization's identity. And she had no way to talk about or connect them. No conversations about why she was there, how her work mattered, or how her goals of making a difference aligned with the organization. She simply did her work every day feeling isolated from the mission. Her expectations were not met because the organization did not engage with her to find that connection or help foster it. And she left with no desire to work there or support their mission. She could find other nonprofits to work for and support.

Therefore, organizational identity, when connected to individual identity through communication and interaction is important because it keeps people

19 Albert, S. and Whetten, D.A. (1985). Organizational identity. *Research in Organizational Behavior* 7: 263–295.

connected to the nonprofit and its mission. This is important for nonprofit employees who invest significant time into an organization as well as for the recruitment and retention of volunteers. Again, these kinds of conversations are simple. They don't require extensive time. They simply require a focus on understanding another person and engaging with them to reinforce the meaning that they are already looking for. And over time, these conversations can become so commonplace that they happen without much effort at all. Another way to make the connection between individual and organization identity more explicit is connecting the role of work practices to the organization's mission.

Connecting Work Practices to Organizational Mission

Meaningful work for an individual in the nonprofit sector is nearly always rooted in the mission as a whole. Whether it's education, poverty, health, the environment, etc., framing work as meaningful means understanding and embracing the organizational mission as a whole. However, many nonprofit employees and volunteers don't work on the "whole" mission; not all organizational tasks and volunteer roles are directly and immediately connected to the people or places that the mission serves. Managerial tasks, administrative functions, accounting, marketing, grant writing, etc. are activities that help fulfill a mission but are often done behind the scenes. The nature of work segments responsibilities and no one participates in everything or sees all the outcomes. Therefore, helping nonprofit employees and volunteers see how their work fits into the overall mission is essential in supporting and fostering work as meaningful. This sense of belonging and purpose is central to helping organizational members flourish.

Research that I have conducted with nonprofit employees working in administrative, marketing, and financial roles showed specific ways to of talking about this type of work that helps connect people to the meaningfulness of their work in nonprofit organizations, allowing them to do the everyday, and sometimes even mundane, types of work necessary in any organization. In-depth interviews brought to light an interconnected way of talking about various work practices so that each is seen as necessary to the social mission. The first was characterized by talking about the *organization as a puzzle*. This constructed an organizational reality for employees where each function mattered for the whole to be meaningful. For example, marketers and event planners raise money. Without them, volunteers and staff members could not do their work with clients. Without administrative support and volunteer coordination, those interactions could not take place. And without financial and executive management, the whole organization could not function long term. This understanding is represented in the following comment by a participant in that study: "Everyone kind of fits together in the puzzle. It's pretty interesting. I've got to do my job so everybody else can do their job too. There's a lot of back and forth. If I can't provide on my end, then it makes it difficult for everyone else to do the fundraising or teach the lessons."[20] Puzzles are not complete if pieces are missing. Talking in this way enables people to see the contribution of their role. Nonprofits can and should explicitly frame conversations about roles and assignments that lead each person to know how they fit in the pursuit of the mission.

The second communicative practice identified in this research was a *circular framing of all organizational functions*. Similar to seeing the organization as a puzzle, a circular framing enables each position to feed into others. Donors, grant writers, and fundraisers provide financing, which enables volunteers to do the work, which is supported by administrative staff who make sure events and services are successful. However, the ability to maintain this circular framing requires more than simply talking about it. Part of fostering productive communication is putting others into conversation and interaction with various parts of the organization and the people it serves. Without this connection, a circular framing can become abstract and less meaningful. Therefore, all members of the organization who are not regularly and directly in contact with mission-focused activities need on occasion to have interactions that put them in contact with the mission itself. Whether it is being with people or working in places where they see the value of their work, having experiences that can be taken up in everyday conversations over time will greatly facilitate the meaningfulness of all organizational processes and practices.

This is illustrated by a marketing director who spent nearly every work day in her office working on marketing plans and organizing fundraising events. But her organization had a policy that allowed and strongly encouraged the staff to volunteer in their various programs as part of their work schedule. The hectic pace of her work only allowed this to happen occasionally, but these interactions were extremely meaningful to her. When asked how she felt connected to the mission of her organization, she said, "I know that those kids are up there skiing because we raised the money."[21]

Like the practices of memorable messages and connecting personal and organizational identity, connecting work practices to organizational mission isn't complicated. These practices are about focusing conversations in specific ways so employees and volunteers can talk about and express the meaningfulness of their

20 Sanders, M.L. (2015). Being nonprofit-like in a market economy: understanding the mission–market tension in nonprofit organizing. *Nonprofit and Voluntary Sector Quarterly* 44: 205–222. (p. 216). doi: 10.1177/0899764013508606.

21 Sanders, M.L. (2015). Being nonprofit-like in a market economy: understanding the mission–market tension in nonprofit organizing. *Nonprofit and Voluntary Sector Quarterly* 44: 205–222. (p. 217). doi: 10.1177/0899764013508606.

work; a simple way of creating an organizational environment that connects people to purpose. But as with all communication practices, we need to make sure they are used ethically. We turn our attention to this question in the final section of this chapter.

Ethical Understandings of Meaningful Work

Discourses of meaningful work are positive and highlight the inherent value of work and its connection to improving the common good and fulfilling social missions. Meaningful work evokes positive affect in people and the various ways to foster it described above are very effective ways of understanding and leveraging discourses of meaningful work in order to help further social missions and foster positive change. However, like all communication, the way we talk about something can be used to benefit individuals and organizations or to intentionally or unknowingly exploit them. To this point, we've talked about how to use discourses of meaningful work in ways that are productive and helpful for organizations, employees, and volunteers. This is based on a view of ethical communication that seeks to create the conditions under which people can make self-determined decisions and flourish in what they choose to do.[22] Now we will explore ways that these discourses can be used to justify practices and expectations that are unhelpful, unhealthy, and unrealistic.

We began this chapter with the stories of John Wood and Wendy Kopp. Both have inspiring tales of nonprofit success. Their stories demonstrate what is possible in the nonprofit sector. They show what happens when people are able to connect what they do with the meaningfulness of a social mission. But these stories can also be read another way that raises cautions that those nonprofit leaders should consider. In a study of autobiographies of social entrepreneurs that I conducted with my colleague Sarah Dempsey from the University of North Carolina, we discovered that these autobiographical hero narratives also evoke ways of thinking and talking about meaningful work that are not helpful. We did this research because of an interesting phenomenon in the nonprofit classes we were teaching. We assigned these books to inspire our students because we had been inspired by them. But for a good number of our students, because they were new to thinking about the nonprofit sector, they had strong negative reactions to the stories. For these students, the tales of hard work and success posed unrealistic

---

22 Lyon, A. and Mirivel, J.C. (2011). Reconstructing Merck's practical theory of communication: the ethics of pharmaceutical sales representative–physician encounters. *Communication Monographs* 78: 53–72. doi: 10.1080/03637751.2010.542578.

barriers to nonprofit work. They couldn't see themselves doing nonprofit work because they weren't like these social entrepreneurs. Our analysis of these stories found that while these "hero tales" do celebrate the role of meaningful work in personal fulfillment and making a difference in the world, they also offer a detailed narrative that can promote unpaid and underpaid labor as a key component of their success and frame extreme self-sacrifice as the price for personal fulfillment in nonprofit work.[23]

For example, John Wood and his early partners spent the first years of Room to Read with little to no pay or benefits. He describes using much of his personal savings and watching his bank accounts quickly drain. Wendy Kopp used an egalitarian salary structure of very low pay that also required extremely long hours and weeks with little or no break in order to keep their doors open. This unpaid and underpaid labor was also accompanied by significant self-sacrifice. Wood was told by his board of directors that they were worried about him burning out from his relentless work schedule. And Wood expressed that his schedule kept him from seeing family and made developing new relationships nearly impossible, admitting in his book that he came to a point where his life was a mess. Kopp describes finally agreeing with her employees that staff meetings would no longer go past midnight. And her story describes long periods of time working and living in significant financial insecurity as she tried to find resources to pay her employees and keep the doors open.

Certainly, the work of John Wood and Wendy Kopp deserves to be celebrated. Their achievements are remarkable. But since these are the public narratives of these organizations, it is possible that they can be taken as a normal way of doing nonprofit work. This could lead to expectations of long hours, low pay, distressed relationships, and extreme stress as a normal part of nonprofit work. That may be what some social entrepreneurs have to do in order to achieve significant results in a short amount of time as they start new organizations, but that is not a realistic expectation for nonprofit employees and volunteers and certainly not the story of every nonprofit founder. Meaningful work is important to most everyone, but we cannot expect everyone working in nonprofits to sacrifice and take risks in the same ways as founders or others who are extraordinarily dedicated to their work. We don't want discourses of meaningful work to be used – intentionally or unintentionally – to coerce or guilt others into working too many hours, sacrificing too much time, or taking other risks that would lead to diminished happiness and personal well-being.

---

23 Dempsey, S.E. and Sanders, M.L. (2010). Meaningful work? Marketization and work/life imbalance in popular autobiographies of social entrepreneurship. *Organization* 17: 437–459. doi: 10.1177/1350508410364198.

Therefore, nonprofit organizations must be mindful of the discourses of meaningful work that are used so they foster connection, meaning, and contributions without expecting or coercing ways of working that are unhealthy or unethical. For those who want their work to be the purpose of their life and their sole source of meaning, that is great. Everyone should be able to put in as much time, energy, focus, and devotion as they want to. But for those who don't (because of all sorts of other important demands and needs in their lives) they should not be made to feel guilty for not engaging in a social mission the same way as a founder. We certainly do not do that for those who don't want to put their heart and soul into a corporate job. And we should not do it for nonprofit employees and volunteers either. They are not founders, and for that reason have very different motivations and needs regardless of how much they believe in and care about the mission.

In addition, it is important that we make sure we don't use discourses of meaningful work – for example sacrifice, service, compensation, or calling – to justify low-wage and unpaid work when other alternatives could be considered. Though nonprofit work will probably always exist in a space where it can't pay full market wages, that doesn't mean that nonprofit work has to be done on the cheap. Nonprofits should pay the best wages possible and offer reasonable benefits to attract more people and better talent. Boards and executive directors should organize in ways that enable better pay and organizational support. In addition, we should not use discourses of meaningful work as a means of shaming those who make competitive wages in the nonprofit sector. Just because work is focused on a social mission doesn't mean that those working toward those goals cannot make a decent living doing it. And for volunteers who are already giving free labor and financial resources, they too must be able to have discourses of meaningful work support them and not coerce or guilt them into doing more. Volunteers are already balancing many competing demands and using the meaningfulness of work to coerce them will ultimately diminish the importance of a social mission in their eyes. And that reputation oftentimes moves on through a community. Therefore, discourses of meaningful work should be used to maximize the potential of individuals to do their best work and connect to the mission and impact they want to have. Furthermore, we also need to pay careful attention to what discourses seem to be emerging around work and think critically about how we might intervene or alter those discourses. In other words, discourses have a way of "using" us and requiring our constructive responses, just as much as we try to use those discourses in strategic ways. Thinking communicatively about meaningful work requires an understanding of both of these dynamics in order to foster the mutual success and growth of people and organizations.

Conclusion

The meaningfulness of nonprofit work is always there. It's inherent in the nonprofit and the reason that this sector exists. But whether or not specific organizations and organizational environments foster these meanings and imbue them in relationships and work is another story. We can ignore these meanings or assume that they are understood, but this leaves the outcome completely out of our control. Or, we can continuously evoke the meaningfulness of work in our interactions and communication so that it is always explicit and part of how we talk about and engage our work. This communicative explanation pushes us to see beyond economic, managerial, and psychological explanations and recognize that because organizational realities are socially constructed by those who do the work, we need to be intentional in the practices that we use so that we foster and not shut out the discourses of meaningful work.

Doing this can help us answer the important questions I posed at the beginning of this chapter. How can the nonprofit sector foster organizational environments that imbue work with meaning that (i) draws people to participate in their mission and (ii) motivates them to stay, contribute, and make a difference? How can nonprofits do this when they cannot entice employees with high salaries or benefits and require a significant amount of volunteer work on some of the most challenging problems in society? When, from a communicative perspective of meaningful work, we understand why people do the really hard work of nonprofit causes and are willing to sacrifice time and money and when we identify what kind of communicative practices connects them to different and varied causes, we are better able to intentionally attract and keep committed employees and volunteers. And that enables those in the nonprofit to better fulfill their important social missions.

6

International Nonprofit Work

Matthew A. Koschmann

Introduction

This chapter focuses on distinct issues of organizational communication for international nonprofit work. Of course, the term "international" is relative and depends on one's initial point of reference; and so is what constitutes an "issue" (things that are difficult for international workers may not be problematic for locals). So in this chapter we're talking about nonprofit work outside of the United States being done by people who are not from the countries where the work is taking place. Additionally, I'll concentrate on nonprofit work in so-called developing nations[1], which I think is what most Westerners have in mind when we consider international nonprofit work, and is the kind of work that most readers of this book are more likely to engage in. Admittedly, a fair amount of nonprofit work is similar across geographic locations: fundraising, volunteer work, civic engagement, and helping vulnerable populations – to name just a few – are prevalent everywhere. But when we look at nonprofit work in other developing

1 I use the term "developing nations" in this chapter as a socioeconomic designation, following the United Nations Development Programme and their Human Development Index. I recognize that any classification of other countries–especially by Westerners–is fraught with complications and will always be subject to criticism. The term "developing nations" likely won't be used in the future, just like we don't say "third-world countries" anymore (recently, the World Bank eliminated the term "developing country" from its data vocabulary). But for now, "developing nations" is the most widely-accepted – yet still contested – term for describing a number of countries that face significant challenges in terms of economics, governance, health, education, etc. and where a number of nonprofit organizations are providing assistance. Other terms such as "global south" or "advanced vs. emerging economies" or "low and middle-income countries" seem to be gaining tracktion these days, but it's still unclear if there will ever be term that isn't controversial or critically accepted. National Public Radio (NPR) did a story on this a few years ago you might find informative: https://www.npr.org/sections/goatsandsoda/2015/01/04/372684438/if-you-shouldnt-call-it-the-third-world-what-should-you-call-it.

Understanding Nonprofit Work: A Communication Perspective, First Edition.
Matthew A. Koschmann and Matthew L. Sanders.

countries, we also see a number of features that are either unique or magnified in these international contexts. Things like language and terminology, knowledge and knowing, religion, and financial arrangements. Therefore, my goal in this chapter is to explore these features and see how a communication perspective can influence how we think about these aspects of international nonprofit work.

***

If international nonprofit work had a social media profile, its relationship status would undoubtedly be "it's complicated." Nonprofit work here in the United States is hard enough, but outside our shores things can be even more problematic, where some routine issues are much more difficult, and many new complications arise. In fact, I am writing this chapter from Metro Manila in the Philippines, where I am working as a visiting Fulbright scholar at Ateneo de Manila University in Quezon City, here to learn more about how the nonprofit sector works in this island nation. I am amazed at the social, political, and economic differences that shape the nonprofit sector in the Philippines compared to what I am used to back in the United States. The nonprofit sector here is tightly connected to the People's Power Revolution of 1986 that ousted the dictatorship of Ferdinand Marcos. That history looms large in the way Filipino nonprofits are organized and operate, and you'll never fully understand how things work around here without a deep appreciation for the particular character of nonprofit organizing that emerged during the transition from martial law to re-democratization – a context that really does not have a parallel back home in the United States.

Meanwhile, on the other side of the world in the mountains outside of Tegucigalpa, Honduras, Holly Tompkins, a nurse practitioner from Colorado, labors tirelessly to provide medical care to villagers from the surrounding area. She works for a religious nonprofit organization based in the United States that operates a medical clinic and orphanage called La Casa de Esperanza (House of Hope) and a children's home called Rancho Ebenezer. The rampant inflation in Honduras means they have to develop a new financial strategy to maintain current operations. Relatedly, the medical clinic relies on a steady stream of American volunteers on short-term mission trips. Holly is responsible for coordinating these visits, which requires a substantial amount of cross-cultural training to keep things running smoothly despite the influx of new workers month after month. Additionally, Holly endures countless frustrations related to cultural differences and resource deficiencies. Recently I corresponded with Holly via email and she said it can be so difficult to complete basic tasks. "Honduras is such a 'yes culture'," she reported, "where many people prefer to give wrong information rather than simply admit they do not know something – especially frustrating when asking for directions!" Plus, she told me how government offices frequently run out of basic supplies like paper and plastic lamination that are essential for the documentation they need to do their work (e.g. birth certificates and building permits).

Back in the United States, Brad Riley works out of a small office in Boulder, Colorado to coordinate projects as far off as Cambodia and Mexico City. Brad is the executive director of iEmpathize, an international arts-advocacy nonprofit that works to end child trafficking throughout the world. Over the years, Brad and his team have partnered with elders in small Cambodian villages to help them communicate the dangers of human trafficking to younger residents who go off to the big city in search of economic opportunities to help their families. At the same time, he and his team have also helped develop the media resources that supported representative Rossio Orozco's efforts to pass sweeping legislation in the Mexican congress to combat human trafficking, and which helped initiate the United Nations Blue Heart Campaign for victims of human trafficking. Efforts like this involve a number of organizational communication challenges, especially in terms of navigating cultural differences and figuring out how to get things done in other countries. A few years ago, I tagged along with Brad and his team for a week in Mexico City to see their work up close. It was a difficult adjustment for everyone involved, and I was reminded just how pervasive the impact of cultural differences on organizational communication can be. Things like planning meetings and making routine decisions that I take for granted as relatively straightforward became complex diplomatic exercises that required a much higher level of coordination and consideration than I was used to based on my American nonprofit experiences.

And these examples are just a tiny fraction of the various projects that make up international nonprofit work. Many of you reading this book will have the opportunity to work in a foreign country with a nonprofit organization, or you might work for an American nonprofit organization with global operations, or you may even work for a corporation or government agency that coordinates with nonprofit organizations in other countries. Whatever the case, it is important to understand the context of international nonprofit work for a well-rounded approach to organizational communication and the nonprofit.

So, what are the key differences and distinguishing characteristics of international nonprofit organizational communication we need to understand? Of course, anything we put on this list could simply be chalked up to "cultural differences," but that is so broad that it does not really tell us anything. It is also unhelpful to lump everything under the characteristics that define so-called developing nations in the first place. Thinks like resource scarcity, weaker institutions, limited civil society networks, various levels of government dysfunction, and/or insufficient infrastructure are what make developing nations *developing*, so merely identifying these features does not add much insight either. Instead, let's start from the premise that *by definition*, international nonprofit work involves cultural differences in underdeveloped institutional and economic contexts, and then from there figure out what more we need to explore and understand. Accordingly, in this chapter I focus on key areas where the underlying challenges are distinctly communicative. That is, areas where issues of meaning, interpretation, understanding, and interaction are especially prevalent and significant, and thus areas where "thinking communicatively" can make a big difference.

Even though every region and country and sector are going to have their own unique features and idiosyncrasies, there are some common themes that run across most international nonprofit work in developing nations. I focus on four of these themes in this chapter: language and terminology, knowledge and knowing, religion, and financial arrangements. Each of these draws our attention to processes of social construction and meaning negotiation, and thus magnifies the significance of communication. There's plenty of overlap across these themes, yet also enough differences to justify treating them as analytically separate for our purposes in this chapter. But the big idea running through all these themes is that each has a substantial impact on how people communicate while simultaneously being shaped and changed through those same communication processes, and each sets the stage for how nonprofit work is organized and practiced in other countries. Below I introduce and explain each of these themes, showing how a simplistic view of communication is insufficient and problematic for the complexities of international nonprofit work, while pointing to the need for a more nuanced understanding of communication that we have been developing throughout this book.

However, before we get started, let me mention three important qualifications for this chapter. First, one of the biggest differences between national and international nonprofit work is something we are *not* going to discuss in this chapter: the legal and tax considerations of doing nonprofit work in a foreign country. Certainly these have considerable impact on organizational communication, but legal and tax implications of nonprofit work are so specific to each country and each type of organization that it is beyond our purposes (or capacity) in this book to say anything besides "consult your legal and tax advisors." And there are lots of other books and resources that cover these issues.[2]

I should also mention that the term "nonprofit" is not as prevalent in other countries as it is in the United States. Elsewhere terms like "nongovernmental organizations" (NGOs) or "civil society organizations" are much more common. Consistent with the communication perspective we're advocating in this book, these terms signal something about the constitution of these organizations and their relation to other entities in their societies, namely the state (which may involve a more antagonistic or fragmented relationship in developing nations), the public sector (which may have a more formal status or standing in other countries), and the market (which may or may not be relevant, depending on the prevailing economic system in a given country). We'll stick with the term "nonprofit" for the remainder of this chapter to be consistent with the rest of the book; just keep in mind that my use of nonprofit is intended to encompass the broad range of related terms and organizational arrangements we find in other countries.

Finally, and perhaps most importantly, I also want to be careful here not to imply some notion of superiority as Americans and Westerners, that what we are discussing

2 For example: Norton, L. (2013). *How to Be a Global Nonprofit: Legal and Practical Guidance for International Activities*. Wiley.

in this chapter suggests that our nonprofit sector and organizations are somehow better. All we are saying here is that when we Americans and others from Western nations (who are likely the majority readership of this book) go beyond our shores and head to other areas of the world, there are important issues we need to consider as we engage in nonprofit work. A communication perspective can help us understand some of these issues more insightfully and can enable us to develop more constructive responses and practices. I certainly recognize that there are notable shortcomings of nonprofit organizations in the United States and the nonprofit sector in other Western nations; in fact, we have much to learn from our international counterparts. I am also painfully aware that many challenges of nonprofit work in developing nations come from legacies of imperialism, colonialism, and globalization that were/are imposed on these nations, not some character flaw in their people or cultures. Those realities lurk around many aspects of international nonprofit work – sometimes beneath the surface, other times more visibly – and I do not take that for granted as I proceed with the rest of this chapter.

So with those caveats in mind, let's proceed.

Language and Terminology

This is arguably the most significant – or at least most pervasive – theme we need to consider. So many issues of international nonprofit organizational communication involve the language we use to interact with each other and the terminology that is unique to particular cultures of people or sectors of international work. Of course, there are important language differences and barriers that can make international nonprofit work more complicated, and this is a big aspect of organizational communication. A substantial amount of international nonprofit work involves the practical details of hiring translators[3] to accomplish basic communication, and working with local community members to help navigate the myriad cultural differences and nuances that impact daily work. This is an obvious part of international organizational communication and should be a standard consideration for anyone involved in international nonprofit work.

But I want to go deeper in this chapter. I want to explore how international nonprofit organizational communication always involves an ongoing negotiation to develop shared meanings about the key concepts that define the work. Language does not merely refer to objective concepts that exist independently of human interaction, even if these referents seem to have a stable existence over long periods of time. Instead, language is how we actively construct the very social realities that enable and constrain our lives. For example, a "partnership" between

3 Special recognition to Darlyn Diang and Kristhyl Tunggolh, the fantastic translators we hired on a recent return trip to the Philippines for our on-going research on housing reconstruction after natural disasters.

a nonprofit organization and a government agency is not some objective feature of the world that merely exists regardless of how people communicate with each other. Instead, a partnership is a form of negotiated order that only exists in and through the patterns of interaction among the people involved. The notion of "partnership" can mean different things to different people, and those meanings can be used to accomplish or prevent various outcomes. So if we want to be more effective and constructive in international nonprofit work, we have to move beyond simplistic thinking that language merely reflects reality and all we need is to have a competent translator. Instead, we need to do the more difficult (but rewarding and fruitful) work of figuring out how various terms came to mean what they do, how certain terms are used in everyday practice, and how we can work more effectively in complicated language landscapes.

Now, all this could get pretty deep into linguistics and semiotics, but that is beyond our purposes here. Instead, my goal is to explore some key areas where language and terminology are central, and invite readers to consider how a communication perspective could make a difference in these situations. Someone who is "thinking communicatively" about international nonprofit work will always be mindful of the taken-for-granted concepts and terminology that define her work, recognizing how fragile some conceptions may be and how certain patterns of interaction are needed to sustain these terms. She understands that so many decisions and programs depend not just on what things *are*, but more importantly, what they *mean* and what they *do* for certain people in a given situation.

For example, consider one of the interesting problems I came across in my research here in the Philippines. I traveled to the small coastal town of Carigara on the island of Leyte, one of the areas hardest hit by typhoon Haiyan back in 2013. I was there to observe a collaborative project between the Peace Corps and the local disaster management office, who were working to develop new disaster response plans for the surrounding *barangays* (villages or neighborhoods) in anticipation of future storms. This began with several days of "hazard mapping" workshops where several community representatives worked with project staff to make accurate maps of their *barangays*, indicating where the vulnerable structures were located, where elderly and disabled people lived, and what areas were prone to more significant flooding. But first they had to account for everyone living in the *barangay* so that they could qualify for government assistance in the event of a disaster (one of the problems in post-disaster situations is that some people who don't live in a damaged area come in seeking financial assistance from the government and relief organizations, taking advantage of resources intended for affected communities). This involved listing everyone who was part of each household because government assistance is given to households, not individuals. Seemed easy enough – just have everyone quickly confirm who lives in each household and move on to the more important work of hazard mapping. Wrong.

Turns out the concept of "household" means something different across cultures, and it is not so simple to identify who constitutes a household in this region of Filipino culture. In much of the Visayas region of the Philippines (where Carigara and Leyte are located), "household" is a more abstract concept that signifies complex family relations, not a straightforward term referring to family members living under one roof. For people in the Carigara *barangays*, "household" could include family members living in different houses or even different villages, and might also include non-family members who may or may not live under the same roof, while some who are living under the same roof may not be considered part of the formal household. So right from the beginning this project was a lot more complicated than expected because there was not a common understanding of the basic social unit that influenced all other aspects of the hazard mapping project and the delivery of financial assistance in the event of a future natural disaster. And after I did a little more research I realized things could get even more complicated. Turns out some NGOs and relief agencies define households differently, and even some government agencies have contrasting definitions of what constitutes a household. So it's not as simple as quickly listing the members of each household and then getting on with the "real" work of hazard mapping – the whole endeavor completely depended on the nuances of language and meaning before it could even get off the ground.

For some this may seem like a nuisance, a silly language game that gets in the way of the "real work." But someone thinking *communicatively* recognizes that situations like this are often what international nonprofit work is all about. Language and terminology are not something separate from the actual stuff of international nonprofit work; complications with language and terminology are not abnormalities that disrupt how things are supposed to go. No, language constitutes the very social realities that structure the day-to-day work of international nonprofits, shaping the landscape of what is possible and what is outside the realm of possibility (at least in a given situation). And for these social landscapes to change requires a corresponding change in language and meaning – that is often what the "real" work is all about. Furthermore, there are in fact real material consequences for language and what things mean; we're not just talking about matters of perception, as some critics note. What things mean and what language is used directly affects where and how resources are allocated, whether contracts are signed, if physical structures are built, or if people are displaced and relocated.

Consider another example from the Philippines, this time in the Metro Manila area. Manila is a sprawling global mega-city composed of 16 independent municipalities with over 20 million people. Flooding is a major challenge for Metro Manila, not simply because the area is exposed to multiple tropical storms each year, but also because there are so many people living in slum or squatter communities (aka informal settlements) along the many waterways – both natural and manmade – that carve throughout the region. During major storms, many of these communities are threatened by rising water or even completely wiped out by the time a storm is over. Therefore, the national government has embarked on a major initiative to move informal settlement communities away from the "dangerous" waterways to more "safe" government housing projects. You might think that people would appreciate this intervention to protect them from danger and provide safer housing, but that assumes a shared understanding of "danger" and "safety" to underwrite this initiative – and that simply isn't the case in this situation.

Instead, many informal settlement communities (represented by various nonprofit organizations, neighborhood associations, and community leaders) vehemently denied that they were in "danger" living on the waterways or that they would be "safer" in government housing projects. Over the years these communities had develop sophisticated ways of living along the Manila waterways and managing their livelihoods during the rainy season. Although floods often damaged their material possessions (of which there were few to begin with), few lives were lost and housing structures were easily repaired or rebuilt. People I talked to saw all this as a fairly normal part of living in a metro region of a tropical nation. They did not see themselves in significant danger. Conversely, they did see the government housing projects as dangerous because they were located outside the city. Although they would be more protected from floodwaters, they would be further from so many other things essential for their survival, like employment opportunities, markets, schools, healthcare facilities, transportation networks, cell phone service, reliable drinking water, and dependable electricity. In their estimation, moving to a government housing project was much more dangerous that living in an informal settlement community along the city waterways.

I attended several meetings with nonprofit organizations who worked with informal settlement communities to negotiate and coordinate with government officials in charge of this housing program. So many of these discussions were about what constituted "danger" and "safety," who got to define these terms, and how the definitions would shape subsequent decisions and policies. What became clear was that "danger" and "safety" were not neutral terms referring to some objective, factual state of the world, but rather loaded terms that were being used to accomplish something rhetorically. From the government's perspective, "safety" became a euphemism for a metropolitan area that was cleaner and with fewer visible slum communities (i.e. safer for foreign investment and tourism). For residents, "safety" was often a euphemism for maintaining a lifestyle free from institutional responsibility (i.e. taxes, land ownership, utility bills, etc.).

In this situation, the important nonprofit work of urban development and flood mitigation was all about language and terminology, figuring out who was in "danger" and how to make them "safe," and how these terms enabled or constrained certain kinds of nonprofit work. Previous research demonstrates that a similar dynamic happens around the concept of "risk" and figuring out who should be evacuated in disaster situations.[4] What all this reveals is just how central language and terminology are to international nonprofit work. This is not some peripheral issue that gets in the way of the real work; many times this *is* the real work. That is, doing the difficult work of developing shared meanings of key concepts that shape subsequent policies and decisions – and the ongoing work of sustaining those shared meanings. A communication approach elevates language and meaning as central aspects of international nonprofit work.

Knowledge and Knowing

It might seem painfully obvious, but knowledge is a key aspect of international nonprofit work – whatever work we *do* is based on what we think we *know* about a particular situation, what we *know* about the relevant factors involved, or what we *know* are the most effective strategies that are likely to work. The problem, however is that what it means "to know" is not universal across cultures and nations. We have different standards of what constitutes "knowledge" and thus different understandings about what to do in a given situation. For example, members of an agrarian community may "know" that a recent bad harvest was caused by dissent among competing tribes, whereas foreign aid workers might "know" that the bad harvest was due to poor topsoil cultivation. Conversely, foreign developers might "know" that building housing structures in a certain region should be safe from flooding based on civil engineering assessments, while local residents "know" that houses should never be built in that area based on stories passed down from their ancestors. This means that most people who get involved in international nonprofit work are likely to experience tensions between what they know, what other people know, and what counts as "knowledge" in a given situation.

I saw this first hand here in the Philippines with the hazard mapping workshops in the town of Carigara that I mentioned above. The team I was observing ran into some discrepancies between what their GPS (global positioning system) calculations and satellite images showed was "true" about the landscape compared to what community representative "knew" about their own villages. For example, some of the flood calculations were based on the flow and volume of rivers in the area. The hazard mapping team seemed to have all the right information on these

4 See Dalisay, S.N. and De Guzman, M.T. (2016). Risk and culture: the case of typhoon Haiyan in the Philippines. *Disaster Prevention and Management: An International Journal* 25 (5): 701–714; Šakić Trogrlić, R., Wright, G.B., Adeloye, A.J. et al. (2018). Taking stock of community-based flood risk management in Malawi: different stakeholders, different perspectives. *Environmental Hazards* 17 (2): 107–127.

factors, yet could not figure out why the community representatives were questioning their assessments. Turns out that some of the rivers located close to the ocean actually flowed in the "wrong" direction for a brief time each day because of the changing tides. This was well-known throughout the community but never factored into the computer models. Both groups – the hazard mapping team and the community representatives – claimed to "know" something about the situation and justified their plans or actions based on this knowledge. Yet sometimes their knowledge was in conflict and not easily reconciled, revealing that the concept of knowledge is a bit more complicated than we might think.

This tension is often understood as a difference between local and expert knowledge, between residents who know how things work in their communities and the professionals who know what is true about a given situation. *Local knowledge* is generally understood as contextual, situated, and tacit. It involves applied wisdom or good judgment that develops in everyday life among a community of practitioners. Conversely, *expert knowledge* involves a way of knowing rooted in the scientific method, resulting in universal, objective truths that are generalized across contexts and situations. In the world of international nonprofit work, it is very common for these contrasting forms of knowledge to intersect and conflict. That is because a large portion of international nonprofit work inevitably involves outside "experts" from developed nations bringing "solutions" to developing nations and local communities that likely see and understand the world quite differently.

But what does this have to do with communication? At issue here is our conception of what knowledge is, and the role that communication plays in creating and sustaining what we know in any particular situation. The prevailing view is that knowledge should be understood as a *commodity*, an objective substance or entity that can be possessed and managed by organizational members (thus the rise of "knowledge management" as a key strategy for modern organizations). Accordingly, communication is simply the process by which people transmit knowledge to each other, with a corresponding concern about the clarity and efficiency of this transmission. The emphasis here is on *cognition*, that knowledge resides in our brains and exists independently from the events where that knowledge was formed, and communication (i.e. transmission) is how knowledge moves from brain to brain. Of course there is clearly an important cognitive aspect to knowledge – obviously we use our brains to know stuff and we couldn't know anything without them.

However, upon further examination the commodity/cognition approach to knowledge doesn't tell the full story and is too simple for the complex world of modern organizing and international nonprofit work. Scholars from a variety of disciplines have demonstrated that a substantial amount of organizational knowledge is intricately tied to *practice* – the active involvement in situated, context-specific problem-solving activities. The idea here is that we often know more than can be captured in cognition, and thus a commodity view of knowledge fails to account for so much of what we and others know about a situation, and reduces knowledge to that which can be codified objectively. But this ignores what we "know" to be true about knowledge, that there is a tacit dimension to many things we know, an informal knack or intuition we have about situations and how best to respond to the circumstances. In fact, much of what we do in our professional pursuits is not based on cognitive reflection, but instead involves our instinctual reactions as we are caught up in the flow of our work. Furthermore, the commodity/cognitive view of knowledge also fails to account for the fact that a lot of what we know is emergent and improvisational, and thus dependent upon – not independent from – the people and interactions that make up a particular activity. Thus knowledge is *in* the practice and cannot be understood apart from the situated, context-specific problem-solving activities. Consequently, communication plays a much more important role in all this because it is the fundamental social process by which knowledge is created and sustained (not a separate process of simply transmitting knowledge that exists independently from human interaction). That's what a practice view of knowledge is all about.

A great example of this comes from a fascinating research study about safety operations at a U.S. Air Force base. Organizational communication scholar Larry Browning and his colleagues at the University of Texas at Austin, Michigan, and Duke studied a successful aircraft maintenance team tasked with repairing military planes and keeping them operational.[5] What they discovered was that despite extensive safety standard rules mandated by the Air Force (i.e. objective, codified knowledge), this maintenance team actually didn't follow these rules directly, but rather adhered to the *spirit* of the rules in ways that were improvisational, creative, self-organizing, and emergent – and this is why they were so successful. They developed a complex way of interacting with each other, the pilots, and the written rules that resulted in a robust system of safety improvement that could not be fully captured or accounted for by the formal rules. The researchers were able to surface and articulate a set of tacit rules for aircraft repair that were uncodified but clearly "known" among the team. But this knowledge only emerged within the *practice* of their work and only made sense within the *flow* of their activities – it wasn't easy to codify and it wasn't transferable or generalizable to other situations, nor was it easy to understand apart from being engaged in the work itself. Yet it was also the most valuable knowledge for them to complete their work successfully. Thus the technicians developed a shared understanding of aircraft maintenance and safety that could not be reduced to a commodity or located in one person's brain.

---

5 Browning, L.D., Sitkin, S.B., Sutcliffe, K.M. et al. (2000). Keep 'em flying: The constitutive dynamics of an organizational change in the US Air Force. *Electronic Journal of Communication* 10 (1/2).

And this sort of thing happens all the time in international nonprofit work. We are consistently involved in situations where so-called expert and local knowledge appear to be in conflict. But the communicative perspective that we are developing and advocating for in this book – that communication is more than the transmission of information but instead constitutes our social realities – helps us move past this conflict. "Thinking communicatively" here means going beyond a commodity/cognition approach to knowledge toward a practice approach that foregrounds the social processes by which knowledge is created and sustained. Organizational communication scholar Timothy Kuhn puts it nicely:

> The [practice] view generally does not deny that knowledge can have a cognitive location but asserts that the cognitive view ignores substantial communicative complexity ... A practice view argues that *to know* implies competent participation in a web if relationships among people, artifacts, discourses, and (often conflicting) streams of action ... The unit of analysis shifts from individual knowers to activity processes, because the perspective holds that the doing of conjoint action is the primary site of social/organizational reality.[6]

This shift from commodity/cognition to practice means that knowledge is a *practical accomplishment* that is realized in communication. What is "known" often isn't objective or universal and thus simply needs to be transmitted to other brains. Instead, what we *know* is bound up in what we are *doing*. Accordingly, a practice-based approach entails a shift in emphasis from knowledge to knowing, focusing more on situated problem-solving than abstract generalizations.

All this can help us understand the tension between so-called expert and local knowledge: the process of commodifying knowledge tends to strip away all the practical know-how and tacit understanding that can only be known *in practice*. The key issue here is that what counts as knowledge or what it means to know something is a social process wrapped up in communication practice; it's not about simply coming in and applying what we think we already know to the situation. Furthermore, distinguishing the commodified "expert" knowledge is also problematic because what qualifies as expertise in many international settings refers to a technocratic discourse that prioritizes efficiency and scale and privileges certain ways of knowing (e.g. scientific method) while marginalizing others (e.g. tradition and intuition). The mistake is to presume that expert knowledge is "true" and simply needs to be shared and implemented, whereas

---

6 Kuhn, T.R. (2014) Knowledge and knowing in organizational communication. In: *The SAGE Handbook of Organizational Communication: Advances in Theory, Research, and Methods* (ed. L.L. Putnam and D.K. Mumby), 481–502. Thousand Oaks, CA: SAGE, p. 483.

local knowledge is better understood as beliefs or customs and really just gets in the way. At issue here is what counts as "knowledge" and how expertise gets recognized as such. A communication perspective draws our attention to the practices of knowledge production and implementation, not the objective qualities of commodified knowledge per se. Again, organizational communication scholar Timothy Kuhn (with colleague Michele Jackson): "Knowledge in a given context is simply that which enables and sustains problem solving and not necessarily that which can be independently justified as *true*" (p. 456, emphasis in the original).[7]

If you're going to be successful at international nonprofit work you have to navigate the knowledge landscape, and a communication perspective (or "thinking communicatively") can help us do this more constructively. This entails a shift beyond seeing knowledge as an objective commodity toward appreciating the tacit, improvisational, and emergent aspects of knowledge that are tied to our ongoing interactions with other people in the context of problem-solving and practical application. Yes, of course there are many aspects of international nonprofit work that involve objective, cognitive knowledge that can be commodified and transmitted to other people, even across cultures and languages. A practice-based view of knowledge does not deny this. Instead, what I (and many others) are claiming here is that the commodity/cognition approach to knowledge is insufficient for understanding the complexities of international nonprofit work or for succeeding in this context. Instead, a practice-based view is less concerned with using codified knowledge than with developing practical insights that enable continued action and problem-solving – the very things we need in international nonprofit work.

Religion

Anyone who has lived or worked in a developing nation knows that the issue of religion looms large in many aspects of professional, personal, and civic life. Throughout history and across the world, religion is often the most significant part of any culture, and understanding religion and religious practice is absolutely essential for effective international nonprofit work. Of course, this does not mean you have to be a true believer or religious scholar, but you do have to realize that religion is a major factor that cannot (and should not) be dismissed or overlooked. Those of us from developed nations in the more secularized West do not always

7 Kuhn, T.R. and Jackson, M.H. (2008) Accomplishing knowledge: a framework for investigating knowing in organizations. *Management Communication Quarterly* 21 (4). 454–485.

appreciate just how fully integrated religion is in the day-to-day life of many other countries – and how common and normal this is.

For example, recently I had some meetings with the mayor and other government officials from the city of Taytay, a midsized municipality of Rizal Province in the Philippines, just outside of Metro Manila. We met at Taytay city hall, an impressive structure just off the main street from the bustling garment center and public market. I walked through the main entrance and was surprised to see a full Catholic chapel right in the middle of city hall, surrounded by all the government offices, and a clear reminder of what was central in this island nation. After my meetings, I talked with some of my contacts about this, asking if they thought it was odd that there was a place of religious worship so prominently placed in the main government building. I was met with confused looks, as if the only unusual thing here was someone questioning the place of religion in their municipal work.

The Philippines has a long history with Catholicism, and the Catholic Church is the most important institutional actor in the country – there is no substantive societal change without Church support. Additionally, an independent pseudo-Christian church movement called *Iglesia ni Cristo*, wields significant power throughout the Philippines, with its elaborate temples prominently displayed throughout major cities and rural provinces alike.[8] During election seasons politicians openly court *Iglesia ni Cristo* leaders, whose endorsements are as common (and legal) as yard signs in the United States. During my time here in Manila I have seen how inseparable religious belief and religious practice are from "normal" life and work – it's futile to try and carve out some distinct realm for each and understand them separately. That's just not how things work here, and similar dynamics are at work in many other nations throughout the world.

Obviously none of us will ever become experts on all the world religions. But it would be beneficial if we thought differently about religion and nonprofit organizing, and a communication perspective can help us do that. Conventional wisdom sees religion as a descriptive variable to classify organizations and people: whether an aid organization is Islamic or Christian or whether a community is Buddhist or Hindu, for example. Much of the previous research on religion and organizing shares this assumption, identifying the religious affiliation of humanitarian organizations, or developing various classifications and typologies for religious nonprofits. Although this certainly can be helpful, it also reveals a key shortcoming: overemphasizing description and classification ignores the dynamic and situated aspects of religious practice. Religious faith is not necessarily a stable attribute that can easily be attached to an organization and/or its members. Like all concepts, religious faith has its existence in the ongoing negotiations and symbolic representations that are

8 See: Cornelio, J. S. (2017). Religion and civic engagement: the case of Iglesia ni Cristo in the Philippines. Religion, State & Society, 45(1), 23–38.

manifested in a variety of social contexts. Thus for many people religion isn't just a descriptive characteristic, but rather an overarching framework for constructing the social realities they enact throughout their daily lives. Rather than simply asking what religion someone or some organization is, it is better to ask how religious belief is manifest in practice, and how those practices are sustained through various patterns of interactions and communication processes.

Even if a nonprofit organization has a particular religious designation, or a community has a specific religious identity, how people actually practice and experience their religious faith can vary substantially. Therefore, if we want to better understand the role of religion and nonprofit work, we need to look beyond typologies and classifications. We need to explore the micro- and meso-level interactions that constitute the actual work of international nonprofits, we need to look at how religious faith is actually practiced in specific situations, and we need to consider how religious beliefs and practices actually make a difference in nonprofit work. Communication scholars are well-positioned for this kind of work, and a growing body of communication research related to religion and organizing provides a helpful starting point.

Two of the main (and related) themes that cut across a wide variety of research about religion and organizational communication are the notions of *tension* and *paradox*. Regarding *tension*, we must remember that religious faith is never practiced in a vacuum, but rather always involves institutional and cultural constraints that force religious believers to reconcile the ideals of their faith with the practical realities of various organizational and institutional realities. For example, tensions are bound to exist between the ideals of mercy and forgiveness espoused by many religions, and the merit-based policies of many professional work environments; between ideals of cooperation and modesty on one hand and the aggressive ethos of neoliberal market competition and profit maximization on the other. The point here is that for many people religion involves the ongoing practice of working out their faith in relation to the competing demands of our contemporary world. But the key insight from communication scholars is that these tensions are never resolved or eliminated; instead they are managed communicatively through a variety of discursive and rhetorical strategies, making *tension* a way of being for religious identity and practice.

I saw this firsthand in Mexico when I followed nonprofit members working to combat human trafficking in the streets of Mexico City and the halls of congress, as I mentioned at the beginning of this chapter. Many of these nonprofit workers were Christian believers whose work was motivated by their religious faith, but they wrestled with how to incorporate these religious motivations with their work that also involved coordinating with many people who did not share their religious convictions, as well as government policies that restricted the explicit involvement of religion. I observed how they figured out how to conduct and discuss their work in ways that balanced the competing tensions of their religious beliefs and the organizational constraints of religious expression. What I concluded in my research was that their religious faith actually existed in and through these communication practices, which in turn constituted their nonprofit work. Religion was not simply a static variable I could attribute to them or their organization that somehow existed separately from their work. This insight helped me understand their work better, and enabled us to collaborate to develop new strategies to improve their work.[9]

Relatedly, the notion of *paradox* is central to understanding religion and organizational communication. By paradox, I simply mean an apparent contradiction that can be worked out through further examination, or that can be held in tension with no perceived need (or possibility) for reconciliation. I'm no scholar of religion, but I think it's safe to say that most all religions are complicated mixtures of sacred texts, historical events, and cultural practices that are not entirely consistent – at least at face value to the outside observer. In fact, much of what constitutes actual religious practice is the ongoing reconciliation or mere acceptance of apparent contradictions (i.e. paradoxes) that permeate our understanding of religious doctrines in relation to our modern lived experiences. To *be* a Christian, for example, *is* to wrestle with the paradox of God as both fully human and fully divine, to understand God as both perfectly just and perfectly merciful. These beliefs don't exist separately and then people go about living their Christian lives. No, religious practice in this context is all about the means by which people work out these paradoxes throughout their daily lives in dozens of practical and mundane ways. And the practical realities of modern life often create the paradoxes that religious adherents must reconcile or come to terms with.

I was reminded of this as I learned about a popular anecdote in Filipino culture. When you arrive at the main terminal of Manila's Ninoy Aquino International Airport you used to be greeted by a large sign saying "Welcome to the Philippines, the most Christian country in Asia." And just beneath it a smaller sign saying "Beware of pickpockets."[10] A clear paradox if I ever heard one! The point here is that to be a practicing Christian in the Philippines means working out one's religious convictions within the context of global capitalism, neoliberal economic policies, and the petty crime associated with high poverty rates – all of which seem necessary to accept if one is to survive daily life in this nation. Religious practice in this setting is constituted by all the ways in which people respond to the political, economic, cultural, and institutional paradoxes they confront on a daily basis. Practically speaking, this happens in and through communication – how people interact with each other, make

9 You can learn more about this project in the following research article: Koschmann, M. (2013). Integrating religious faith in human rights collaboration. *Journal of Communication and Religion* 36 (2): 1–27.
10 This popular anecdote is recounted in Syjuco, M. (2010) *Illustrado: A Novel*. New York: Farrar, Straus and Giroux.

sense of their experiences, and justify their actions – and therefore this is what we should pay attention to if we want to fully understand the role of religion in international nonprofit work.

The value of a communication perspective is that it helps us move beyond seeing religion as merely a structural property of a nonprofit organization or a point on a continuum to categorize nonprofit programs or initiatives. Instead, religion is seen as a framework for constructing social realities that we enact in our daily interactions. This perspective helps us see religious faith as created and sustained though our communication practices, and enables us to understand how people recreate notions of self and religiosity as they continually position themselves in relation to their nonprofit work and the tensions they have to manage. Religion influences how people make and justify decisions, how they resolve conflict, how they make sense of their circumstances, and how they interact with multiple stakeholders. But we miss the point if we don't see how all of this exists in and through communication practice.

All of this is more pronounced in other nations where religion is more intricately woven into the fabric of cultural and political life. We certainly cannot anticipate all the ways in which religion will influence international nonprofit work, but we can navigate this territory more constructively if we think more communicatively about religion and international nonprofit work. Religion is a major factor in much international nonprofit work that we must pay close attention to, but not just in terms of description and classification. Instead, when we think communicatively about religion and international nonprofit work we redirect our attention toward seeing religion as a situated communication practice that is continually worked out in our interactions with other people. Regardless of the beliefs or convictions of any particular religion, the claim here is that the meaning and practice of those beliefs exist within continual efforts to develop practical communicative responses to the tensions and paradoxes that inevitably arise between religion and modern life.

Financial Arrangements

A final aspect of international nonprofit work that significantly affects – and is affected by – organizational communication involves the financial arrangements that make this work possible in the first place. The financial management aspect of nonprofit work is a huge topic, covered extensively elsewhere and not directly relevant to our purposes in this book.[11] So what do financial

11 See: Batts, M.E. (2017). *Nonprofit Financial Oversight: The Complete and Concise Guide for Boards and Finance Committees*. CreateSpace Publishing; McCarthy, J.H., Shelmon, N.E., and Mattie, J.A. (2012). *Financial and Accounting Guide for Not-for-Profit Organizations*, vol. 6. Wiley.

arrangements have to do with organizational communication? Obviously, international nonprofit work involves raising money, balancing budgets, funding various projects and initiatives, and communicating this financial information to relevant stakeholders. That is all very important, but it is not what I am focusing on here. Instead, I want to draw your attention to the relational context of financial arrangements that inevitably creates a problem of "serving multiple masters," leading to substantial challenges for how people organize and communicate to accomplish their work. This happens when the majority of the operating revenue comes from outside the country where that work takes place, which is a common feature of international nonprofit work because of the resource scarcity that is prevalent in many developing nations. This means there is a substantial gap between the work being done and the provision of resources to support that work, which can result in tensions between responding to the wishes of donors (both public and private) and responding to local conditions on the ground. Of course, this disconnect between service provision and service receipt is common for all charitable work, but things are magnified and more complicated for international nonprofit work.

As just one example, consider the work of Compassion International, a child sponsorship nonprofit organization based in the United States that operates in over 25 countries across the world. Compassion International partners with local organizations to run child development programs – which include education, nutrition, hygiene, and medical care – in a variety of rural and urban settings. The work is conducted by local staff and overseen by regional offices in host countries, but it is funded almost exclusively by donors from North America and Europe, either through individual child sponsorship or through larger donations given to fund various programs and initiatives. This results in a very decentralized funding network where thousands of individual donors across the world are contributing financially to even more thousands of children and communities in dozens of locations throughout the world. In the middle of all this are Compassion International staff, trying to communicate the financial needs of local programs to (mainly) Western donors who have a limited understanding of local conditions, but who are also likely to have strong opinions (however uninformed and inaccurate) about the politics and economics of poverty and humanitarian aid. Sometimes what is most attractive to donors is not the most effective on the ground, and vice versa. Thus international nonprofit work is complicated by the need to secure funding from sources that are vastly different from where those funds will be spent – but still having to please both sides of the equation.

This dynamic of serving multiple masters is also relevant in the context of humanitarian aid in response to natural disasters and health crises. Nonprofit organizations are very important for the implementation of humanitarian aid at the local level, but they depend heavily on outside donors for their funding and resources. The problem is when the desires of donors are at odds with conditions on the ground, or when donors put restrictions on their funding that prevent nonprofit organizations from using the money where it is most needed – even if these discrepancies are well-intended or resulting from mere ignorance. We saw this issue firsthand in the Philippines for our research on housing reconstruction after Typhoon Haiyan.[12] For example, in the northern Santa Fe region on the island of Cebu, the new houses built for the community of Poblacion did not have individual bathrooms because of restrictions on funding. Donors had specified that their money only be used for certain kinds of projects and direct aid to the people, and latrines did not make the list. This is often the case – essential items like sewage, plumbing, sanitation, or even administrative support are just not very attractive to many donors. Thankfully, the relief organization we studied for this case was able to come up with a creative solution involving communal bathrooms in conjunction with the newly built community center. But even this was a stretch, and lack of ongoing support meant that the bathrooms were rarely maintained and were under-used. All this stemmed from the tension between donor specifications and local conditions

This is a dilemma for international nonprofit work: communicate specific needs on the ground to potential donors, but risk getting limited funding because people and agencies do not want to fund certain projects; or adapt your funding requests to what potential donors want to support, but then face obstacles when trying to spend the money or end up providing services and facilities that local communities really do not want or need. In fact, the trend of donor-restricted funding, or "donor choice" as it often is called, is only increasing, which is understandable, especially given recent high-profile scandals – or at least public relations faux pas – where funds were misused or used differently than donors expected (recall the public outrage at the Red Cross over the handling of their 9/11 emergency fund). In response, many watchdog groups have encouraged donors to specify how they want their money to be used, which then increases the demand for more specialized funding opportunities, which in turn leads more nonprofit organizations to offer niche funding programs (consider the donation catalogs for organizations like Heifer International or World Vision, or donation websites that allow donors to target their funding rather than simply giving to the overall organization), and so the cycle continues. Relatedly, donations to general funds like the United Way have been in decline lately.

12 National Science Foundation: *Resilient and Sustainable Infrastructure Systems: Post-Disaster Reconstruction Processes and Stakeholder Networks* (award #1434791), Division of Civil, Mechanical & Manufacturing Innovation (Co-Pi with Amy Javernick-Will): https://www.nsf.gov/awardsearch/showAward?AWD_ID=1434791.

Similarly, foundations and large philanthropic organizations take a very active role in setting agendas for humanitarian aid and international nonprofit work, as do government agencies like the United States Agency for International Development (USAID). They have considerable resources and much international nonprofit work is completely dependent on their support – if they do not fund a project, it does not happen. Now, this is not at all to suggest that these organizations do not know what they are doing and are simply imposing their ignorant will on developing nations with large donations. Quite the opposite, in fact. Organizations like the Gates Foundation, the Ford Foundation, and the Rockefeller Foundation, to name just a few, have knowledgeable experts on their staff and spend a considerable amount of time coordinating with international nonprofit workers and local communities (and of course are nonprofit organizations themselves). Likewise, government aid agencies are full of people with substantial work experience in the field. Nevertheless, foundation funding will always be contingent on strategic imperatives that are often decided in conference rooms far from affected communities, and government aid agencies will always be subject to the prevailing political currents shaping public policy. This means that international nonprofit work always involves an ongoing negotiation between donor/funder priorities and local conditions.

The communication challenge here is twofold: international nonprofit managers must simultaneously convince donors that local projects fit within their funding priorities, while also convincing local communities that these initiatives are beneficial for them and align with their values. This is no small task, and it certainly involves much more than simply transmitting the right information between senders and receivers. Instead, it involves a complex process of negotiation, co-construction, and shared understanding. This is what thinking communicatively in this context is all about: figuring out how to frame/create social realities for multiple audiences in ways that align with their interests and principles, getting involved in processes where these social realities are being constructed, and inviting more people to participate in these processes in meaningful ways.

Too often international nonprofit workers express frustration that donors "just don't get it" when it comes to the work they are doing; and similarly, donors are concerned that local workers do not understand or appreciate their strategic initiatives and worry that their money is not being spent properly. The communication mistake in these situations is to presume that "funding priorities" or "local needs" simply exist as "things" in the first place and merely need to be described to relevant parties through effective message transmission, and the numbers will speak for themselves. By now, we know that communication is much more nuanced than that. Instead, what constitutes a funding priority or a local need emerges from complex interaction processes involving multiple stakeholders, interests, and values – and whatever emerges only continues to exist through certain patterns of interaction and communication practices. Plus, the numbers rarely speak for themselves; someone is usually speaking for the numbers. Sound financial management for international nonprofit work is about more than just revenue and expenses; it also involves understanding and appreciating the social processes that create and sustain funding relationships, which will always involve serving multiple masters. A communication approach draws our attention to this important dynamic and provides conceptual resources for navigating the territory.

Conclusion

International work is an important part of the nonprofit – so much of the charitable work of the nonprofit is desperately needed throughout the world. But how this work is conducted and whether or not it is successful depends on our understanding of the key issues involved and how we approach international nonprofit work. What I have done in this chapter is identify a handful of key issues for international nonprofit work where "thinking communicatively" can make a big difference and where this kind of thinking is especially important. These include language and terminology, knowledge and knowing, religion, and financial arrangements. Each of these, as we noted in this chapter's introduction, draws our attention to processes of social construction and meaning negotiation, and thus magnifies the significance of communication. The big idea running through all these themes is that each has a substantial impact on how people communicate while simultaneously being shaped and changed through those same communication processes, and each sets the stage for how nonprofit work is organized and practiced in other countries. Of course, there is plenty of overlap between these topics, and there are other important topics for international nonprofit work that I did not include in this chapter. But my goal was not to provide an exhaustive list; instead I am trying to demonstrate the value of thinking communicatively about important issues of international nonprofit work and show what it could look like to do this – in ways that are applicable for many other issues.

If you work for or with a nonprofit organization in another country, you will immediately be confronted by a host of complications and challenges related to organizational communication. How you understand communication in these situations could make all the difference – what it is you think you're doing when you communicate and what you think communication is accomplishing will have direct impacts on the success of your projects and the quality of your relationships. And this is what international nonprofit work is all about, making a difference in a world that desperately needs support and assistance to overcome difficult challenges to thrive in our modern society. Organizational communication is central to these endeavors and it matters how we approach our task. "Thinking communicatively" is the mindset we need as we approach the variety of issues that make up international nonprofit work. We certainly cannot anticipate all the situations that we might find ourselves in when working with or for international nonprofit organizations, but we can work in this environment more constructively if we think communicatively about the nature of this important work.

Conclusion

Understanding What it Means to be Nonprofit

Matthew A. Koschmann and Matthew L. Sanders

Our purpose in this closing chapter is to synthesize what we developed throughout the book and further explore the implications of a communication perceptive on the nonprofit. We also want to step back from the specific contents of the chapters and consider how communicative thinking enhances our understanding of what it means to be nonprofit and do nonprofit work. Too often the nonprofit is defined based on what it isn't, or is understood as subordinate to other sectors (i.e. business and government). But as we'll see, a communication perspective on the nonprofit can help us understand the nonprofit on its own terms, and reclaim an affirmative position of the nonprofit for this admittedly conflicted term.

We began in Chapter 1 by introducing the idea of a *communication perspective* and explaining why this is a much-needed approach to enhance our understanding of the nonprofit, and to improve much of the work we do across the nonprofit sector. A communication perspective is all about elevating communication to a mode of explanation; communication isn't just a specific *thing to be explained* but rather a novel *way of explaining other things*. It involves how we see the world, a lens by which we view all social phenomena in terms of human interaction and the communication practices that constitute our social worlds. This does not exclude other perspectives, but it does expose some of the shortcomings of alternative approaches, while also expanding our explanatory resources for a more extensive and sophisticated understanding of the nonprofit.

A communication perspective is based on the theory of *communication-as-social construction* and the underlying philosophy of *communicative constitution*, which contrasts with the theory of *communication-as-transmission* and the philosophy of *functionalism*. The main point is that communication is so much more than a simple process of transmitting information between senders and receivers; instead communication is a complex process of the ongoing making

Understanding Nonprofit Work: A Communication Perspective, First Edition.
Matthew A. Koschmann and Matthew L. Sanders.

and unmaking of the social realities that constitute our experiences and shape our world. When we limit our understanding of communication to only that of message transmission (the conventional wisdom in much of our society), we paint ourselves into a corner where we can only study message effects, tweak the message content, alternate the channels of communication, and comprehend communication process from economic, psychological, or political perspectives.

Of course, this isn't completely wrong – effective message transmission is essential to every aspect of the nonprofit and indeed our broader society – but it is woefully inadequate to fully account for the complexities of the nonprofit because so much more is happening when we communicate with other people. Conversely, when we see communication as social construction it opens up so many new possibilities for understanding, critique, intervention, improvement, creativity, and progress. That's because communication becomes the fundamental process by which we understand all social phenomena; it directs our attention toward the patterns of interaction that constitute social reality and how those realities subsequently shape successive communication practices. It gives us a better understanding of what things *are* and how they came to *be*, and thus enables a more insightful approach to what we could *do* and who we could *become*. This is what a communication perspective is all about, and it gives us both agency and responsibility for how we envision and create those new possibilities for improving the common good. This is what we mean when we say, "thinking communicatively."

Now admittedly, this alternative way of thinking about communication doesn't lend itself to straightforward prescriptions about how to communicate more effectively in various situations like the transmission models does. In fact, that's one of the advantages of the transmission model and why it is so prevalent in our society – it offers simple explanations of communication behavior (i.e. message exchange between senders and receivers through media channels that are subject to noise and feedback), as well as clear-cut recommendations for improving communication (e.g. be clear, concise, coherent, etc.). But this simplicity comes at a price, namely ignoring a host of other important factors in the communication process (e.g. unintended messages, interpretive differences, and nonverbal behavior), or shoehorning these factors into the rigid components of the transmission model (e.g. treating human emotions as "noise").

In addition, most of those straightforward recommendations often don't even solve the problems we face. They are simply inadequate to explain many of the complexities of nonprofit work that we've described in this book. These simple answers, then, lead to significant frustration, which is why we so often blame our problems on "poor communication" (and of course, it's usually someone else's fault). Our main contention is that we will do better in almost any nonprofit situation if we transcend the simplicity of communication-as-transmission and embrace the complexity of communication-as-social construction. Yes, this will often make things a bit more complicated in the moment and the temptation of simplistic alternatives always looms nearby. But that is exactly the point – going beyond the idea that communication is just a straightforward process of message transmission that we need to manage so we can get on to other things and the "real" work of the nonprofit. However, if you're coming around to the ideas we've developed in this book, hopefully you're starting to see that communication *is* the real work of the nonprofit.

Rather than telling us exactly what to do in various situations, social construction invites us to think about the complexities of human interaction and consider what we are making together in our communication with other people. It doesn't guarantee that we'll get it right every time (or that there's even an objective "right" we could accomplish in most situations), but it does provide a better framework for making sense of what's happening so we can adapt and improve and increase the likelihood of more favorable outcomes more often. That's what we mean when we talk about the *realm of probability* in several places throughout this book. There is no periodic table of communication elements that we can assemble to get predictable outcomes, but rather a landscape of possibilities that can be socially constructed in a variety of ways depending on how we interact with each other, thus requiring a keen awareness of what is emerging in various situations and thinking critically about how we can communicate in response to influence the process of social construction. This is what the ancient Greeks (the first communication scholars) called *phronesis*, practical wisdom or the virtue of good judgment. Therefore, in many ways, this book is not a new approach to communication, but rather a renaissance or a rediscovery of what we have known for millennia, yet lost sight of with the technological and industrial advancements of modern society that moved us toward a mechanistic understanding of communication and human interaction.

A communication perspective has numerous consequences for the nonprofit, most of which involve a fundamental rethinking of how we understand communication and the nonprofit. Therefore, in Chapter 1 we articulated three key implications of communicative thinking to make sense of these possibilities. These include rethinking core concepts of the nonprofit, rethinking nonprofit organizations *as* communication, and rethinking communication as a mode of explanation. Our goal was to provide a framework for thinking communicatively about the nonprofit that could be applied to all sorts of nonprofit issues and topics. Accordingly, we explored the application of a communication perspective across several key aspects of nonprofit work in order to demonstrate the value of this approach.

In the remaining chapters of the book, we looked at five key issues in the nonprofit and demonstrated what a communication perspective enables us to see and understand. We started in Chapter 2 with the related topics of leadership, management, and governance, what we refer to as L-M-G because of their close association in everyday practice and application. Taking a communication perspective helps us expose a number of popular yet unhelpful assumptions that portray leadership, management, and governance as mental, individual, positional, mechanistic, and situational. In contrast, a communication perspective moves us toward a more relational approach we call *communicative L-M-G* that emphasizes social processes over personal cognition, hybrid agency over excessive individualism, a nexus of relations over abstract positionality, living systems over machines, and socially constructed situations over objective circumstances. Communicative L-M-G orients us toward the realm of probability, directing our attention toward how we can increase the likelihood of more favorable outcomes for more people more often through our communication practices. The point is that L-M-G exists in the processes of communication we do *with* other people, not a thing we do *to* them. A communication perspective on leadership, management, and governance – communicative L-M-G – gives us a much better understanding of what is actually happening in these situations, and thus can help us make better decisions throughout the nonprofit.

This communicative approach to L-M-G also provides further insight into what it means to be nonprofit. Despite structures of leadership and the management practices that all types of organizations use that seem directed at control, the nonprofit is primarily relational. Because it cannot force participation and relies on the goodwill of so many to work, volunteer, donate, etc., the nonprofit must govern itself differently as it deals with people on all sides. Doing L-M-G *with* others is the only way that the nonprofit can fully thrive because that is the basis of the kinds of relationships that the sector is built upon. Consequently, communicative L-M-G not only helps us understand how we can practice leadership, management, and governance more effectively and constructively, it also reveals something about the nonprofit itself – that it is deeply relational.

In Chapter 3 we explored how a communication perspective can help us better understand the tensions that nonprofits face as mission-based organizations that function in a market economy. Nonprofits must navigate a complex fiscal and legal environment that is further complicated with social expectations and public pressures that are often unreasonable and uninformed. Many nonprofits respond by pursuing strategies to become more "business-like" as a way to manage the tension of being mission-oriented in a market economy, and thus *marketization* is a significant aspect of today's nonprofit landscape. But is this the best strategy for the nonprofit, or even a good way to conceptualize the issue? A key concern is that market ideology and practice often run counter to civic ideals of justice, fairness, equality, and the common good that – while not unique to nonprofits – are the core tenets that drive the pursuit of a social mission. Taking a communication perspective here helps us see marketization and the notion of being business-like as social constructions; ways of understanding the nonprofit that are created and negotiated in practice though the ongoing interactions of certain people who have the capacity to sustain a particular understanding of nonprofit work, not objective laws of nature. Common terms like "efficiency," "bottom line," or "effectiveness" do not refer to a neutral or natural state of affairs, even if we are tempted to take them for granted. Instead, these terms are used in practice to constitute particular social realities that may favor certain interests and marginalize others. At issue here are the social processes by which certain understandings of nonprofit work come into being and are perpetuated through organizational decisions and policies. Taking a communication perspective makes us more aware of the meanings and interpretations that shape nonprofit work and financial decisions, and gives us the resources to think more critically about when and where the logic of the market is appropriate for the nonprofit.

Furthermore, exploring what it means to be nonprofit and pursue a social mission in a market economy also reveals something about being nonprofit. The nonprofit is an inherently contradictory enterprise that must embrace and manage the tension between mission and market concerns. This contradictory, tension-filled reality of the nonprofit isn't a problem to resolve or a deficiency in the nonprofit sector. Instead, the mission–market tension is a constitutive feature of the nonprofit, and nonprofit organizing requires attention to both ends of this tension. When nonprofits attempt to resolve this tension by choosing one over the other, it compromises the integrity of nonprofit work. To *be* nonprofit means addressing and embracing both mission and market at all times. And it is through everyday communication practices that nonprofits keep this tension alive.

Then in Chapter 4, we looked at how a communication perspective can inform our understanding of nonprofit collaboration. Organizational partnerships are an essential part of the nonprofit landscape, and thus collaborative work is something everyone involved with the nonprofit needs to understand better. It's tempting to see collaboration as a separate organizational form that just "exists" and communication then happens within the collaboration. But a communication perspective helps us see that communication is the mode of being for collaboration; collaborations exist *as* communication and communication constitutes the organizational form of collaboration. Accordingly, we employ the term *collabrocation* to represent this inseparability of collaboration and communication, and to signal the importance of thinking communicatively anytime we engage in collaboration. We want to reinforce the idea that organizational form and communication practice should always be understood together, as mutually constitutive. Collaboration means interacting in certain ways, and that certain patterns of interaction shape specific organizational forms, both of which feed back upon each other for a continual cycle of reciprocal existence. Furthermore, collaboration presents many difficult challenges for the nonprofit, especially in terms of exercising authority, developing a shared identity, taking meaningful action, and achieving a sufficient level of effectiveness. But we can think communicatively about these challenges with a collaboration framework that explains that effective collaboration (value) is the ability to exert influence among members and stakeholders (authority) in such a way that leads to the existence of a social entity (identity) that has the capacity to act and make a difference (agency) in a specific realm of nonprofit work. Thus, to think "collabrocatively" means focusing on the communicative constitution of distinct organizational forms that have the capacity to take meaningful action, and communicating in ways that are characterized by emergence, exploration, and engagement (in contrast to aggregation, representation, and expression).

Again, this also points to an important insight into what it means to be nonprofit. The nonprofit is often driven by partnership rather than other mechanisms of organizing. Perhaps this seems a bit obvious, but this is a profound difference in practice. Businesses organize primarily in terms of commerce and competition. Governments organize mainly through mandates and laws. Partnerships are essential to the nonprofit because those other mechanisms are generally not available for nonprofit organizing. Therefore, nonprofits have to work with constituents who have to manage their own organizations and missions while being collectively focused on others. They often need cooperation to flourish. Recognizing this leads to a focus on communication practices that can foster the collaboration required to form valuable partnerships that enable those in the nonprofit to address complex social issues.

In Chapter 5, we applied a communication perspective to the meaning of nonprofit work itself. Nonprofits operate in resource-scarce environments, they usually cannot incentivize work with market-rate compensation, and they rely on an extensive amount of voluntary labor. Therefore, nonprofits need to encourage participation through mission and purpose – there has to be a greater sense of meaning that motivates nonprofit work. In contrast to economic, managerial, and psychological perspectives that dominate our conventional wisdom about the meaning of work, a communication perspective demonstrates that meaning is not "in" nonprofit work as an objective feature of the work itself, nor is it merely a psychological state of personal perception. Instead, we explained how meaningful work is a *discourse*, a way of talking about work that creates deep structures of meaning that shape how we make sense of our experiences. Meaningful work isn't the work itself; it is the means (i.e. communication processes and practices) by which people imbue their work with meaning. This key distinction has important implications for how we talk about nonprofit work, how we frame our interactions with other people, and how we legitimate and compensate work that people are doing across the nonprofit sector. In particular, a communication perspective foregrounds practices that create memorable messages, connect organizational and personal identities, and link work practices to organizational mission in order to help sustain a discourse of meaningful nonprofit work, while also calling attention to the ethical implications of how the meaning of work is constructed in some nonprofit contexts.

Additionally, the idea of meaningful work shows us that nonprofit work (both paid and volunteer) is driven by the meaning of work instead of other rewards like financial compensation. The focus on meaning is connected to the values that underlie nonprofit endeavors and shows us that how we talk, interact with, and frame both relationships and work matters a great deal. This knowledge should help us organize nonprofit work around the mission and connection that each individual gives to their work, rather than assuming that there is meaning in the work itself or rather than trying to make it look or feel like work in other sectors. Thus, the meaning of work is a core feature of the nonprofit and we must enable those doing the work to interact in ways that allow them imbue their work with the meaningfulness they are seeking so that they will come and stay.

Finally, in Chapter 6 we applied a communication perspective to the notion of international nonprofit work. Of course, a fair amount of nonprofit work is similar across geographic locations: fundraising, volunteer work, civic engagement, and helping vulnerable populations – to name just a few – are prevalent everywhere. But when we look at nonprofit work in other developing countries, we also see a number of features that are either unique or magnified in these international contexts. Things like language and terminology, knowledge and knowing, religion, and financial arrangements. Each of these draws our attention to processes of social construction and meaning negotiation, and thus magnifies the significance of communication. The big idea running through all these themes is that each has a substantial impact on how people communicate while simultaneously being shaped and changed through those same communication processes, and each sets the stage for how nonprofit work is organized and practiced in other countries. International nonprofit organizational communication always involves ongoing negotiations to develop shared meanings about the key concepts that define the work, conflicts over what counts as knowledge in various situations, managing tensions and paradoxes that inevitably arise between religion and modern life, and meeting the financial demands of serving multiple masters with different interests. We'll never know exactly what to expect with international nonprofit work, but we'll do better work if we have the right mindset on a number of key issues, and that's exactly what a communication perspective has to offer.

Once again, international nonprofit work also shows us something about what it means to be nonprofit. At the heart of most nonprofit work is a deep-seated desire to help others in need, and this level of empathy knows no national borders. To be nonprofit means looking beyond ourselves to improve the state of humanity and build civil society, even beyond our own shores. Of course, not everyone involved in the nonprofit will participate in international work, but the same spirit that motivates us to help those in our local communities also inspires us to help others across the globe. International nonprofit work magnifies issues of meaning, knowledge, religious faith, and donor relations, all of which require a level of humility, patience, and a willingness to learn that are at the core of what it means to be nonprofit.

Finally, if we step back from the specific topics we explored in these chapters, we can gain additional, broader insights on what it means to be nonprofit. From a communication perspective, this is one of the most needful things for those of us trying to understand and work in the nonprofit sector. The nonprofit faces a constant struggle to define what it is and explain how it works best because it is always seen as "not" something, or "like" something else. Scholars and policymakers tend to think of the nonprofit as picking up the pieces of what other sectors fail to do rather that addressing needs that are uniquely suited for the nonprofit endeavor.[1] But the nonprofit is a unique sector with distinct goals, needs, and values that fill a necessary space in democratic society that businesses and governments simply cannot fill. The nonprofit has affirmative value in-and-of-itself, not only as a derivative of the failures of other sectors. The nonprofit is what gives life to the development and flourishing of civil society. We need to understand the nonprofit on its own terms; we need to know how nonprofits can be more nonprofit-like, not more like some other kind of organization. A communication perspective gives us important insights to this issue because the notion of "creation" is central to both communication and the nonprofit – both are about what we make together and how we create a better future.

The nonprofit has always been focused on creating a better present and future for those without voice, resources, representation, or societal connections. Therefore, thinking communicatively about the nonprofit gives us a keen insight into what it means to do this work. Rather than being reactive to conditions and structures, a communication perspective shows us that nonprofits can be proactive in shaping the world in the way they want it to be. Sure, the nonprofit has always reacted to problems it sees, but from a communication perspective, those doing the important work of the nonprofit can also create and shape a better world through interactions with other people. Thus, the nonprofit isn't just about fixing problems; it's also about molding a better future through human connection. This, we believe, gives the nonprofit a better way of seeing itself and its role in society. Yes, the term "nonprofit" is fairly entrenched in our vocabulary and we

---

1 See Anheier, H.K. and Ben-Ner, A. (eds.) (2003). *The Study of Nonprofit Enterprise: Theories and Approaches*. Springer Science & Business Media, especially the chapters on "voluntary failure theory."

may be stuck with it for a while. Nevertheless, thinking communicatively can help us see more of what the nonprofit *is*, not just what it *isn't*. Just like communication, the nonprofit is primarily about what it makes, what it creates, not simply what it reacts to. And just like communication, the nonprofit has positive value on its own terms; it's not merely an instrument to be used by supposedly more important entities and interests.

This leads to another important implication of communicative thinking and our understanding of what it means to be nonprofit. Being nonprofit requires a keen appreciation of difference, specifically in how we understand and give meaning to the world around us. A communication perspective enables us to see that difference in practices, policies, culture, etc. are constructions that give meaning to the world. As such, we can seek to understand and respect them. This moves us away from judgments of good and bad, because we recognize that our own ways of doing things are social constructions as well. This lets us take positions of respect, humility, inclusion, and patience as we work with and through those differences. This is the work of the nonprofit. And since all nonprofit work is done in partnership with people from differing conditions and circumstances, a focus on differences in language and meaning is essential for any lasting success to be achieved.

***

So there you have it, the meaning and significance of a communication perspective and its application for five key aspects of the nonprofit: leadership, management, and governance; marketization; organizational partnerships; the nature and meaning of labor; and international work. Each chapter in this book offers a distinct way of understanding the nonprofit and engaging in its important work. These communicative explanations allow us to see key nonprofit issues more carefully, do the hard work of improving the common good more effectively, and better influence the outcomes we are trying to achieve. Of course, there are many other important topics not included here, but this book is not supposed to be an encyclopedia of nonprofit issues. Instead, the five subjects we covered are intended to demonstrate the value and utility of a communication perspective on the nonprofit, and thus provide a novel approach to nonprofit organizational communication. Our hope is that you, the reader, can now incorporate this communication perspective into a host of other topics and issues that are relevant for your specific nonprofit endeavors – that you will "think communicatively" as you approach various decisions and situations that make up the important work of nonprofit organizational communication.

Index

Notes are indicated by the letter 'n' and note number following the page number

Understanding Nonprofit Work: A Communication Perspective, First Edition.
Matthew A. Koschmann and Matthew L. Sanders.